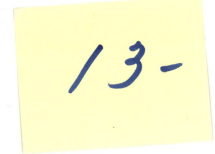

13-

KILIAN HEALY, O. CARM.

Prophet
of
Fire

EDIZIONI CARMELITANE
ROMA

Cover design by Riccardo Palazzi, O.Carm.
Painting by David Herskovitz

This publication was made possible by a grant from the American-Canadian-Peruvian Carmelite Province of the Most Pure Heart of Mary.

First Printing: 1990
Second Printing: 2004

ISBN 88-7288-015-7
ISSN 0394-7750

© Edizioni Carmelitane
Via Sforza Pallavicini, 10
00193 Roma - Italia

Finito di stampare nel maggio 2004
dalla Tipografia Città Nuova della P.A.M.O.M.
via San Romano in Garfagnana, 23 - 00148 Roma
Telefono & fax 06.65.30.467
e-mail: segr.tipografia@cittanuova.it

*To all members
of the
Carmelite family
especially the novices
and Lay Carmelites*

Acknowledgements

The Cloistered Carmelite Nuns
Monastery of the Sacred Heart
Hudson, Wisconsin
who typed the original

Fr Redemptus Valabek, O. Carm.
who got me started on this project

Fr Louis Rogge, O.Carm.
who has encouraged me and
seen the work through
to completion

Contents

Contents

In Appreciation

THE gentle breeze announcing the presence of God again refreshes our spirit in this book on Elijah. Kilian Healy, our brother, is a man alive with the power of Elijah, and a poet of the human spirit. We, Kilian's Carmelite Brothers of the Province of the Most Pure Heart of Mary, cherish this very personable and intense man whose prayerfulness, spirituality and dedication have made the living God present among us.

Kilian Healy is a giant in our midst. He has served the Order of Carmel faithfully as director of formation at Whitefriars Hall within our province. As Assistant General and then as Prior General, he helped lead the Order through the turbulent times of renewal in a gentle, respectful, simple and effective way. Reared in a time of severe and rigid spirituality, Kilian showed us how to be open to new movements of God's Spirit in our times. He taught us flexibility, because we were in God's hands and presence. We trusted Kilian's journey and insights because his convictions come from his lived experience. His credibility comes from his instinctive and Spirit-filled knowledge of spiritual realities. Kilian, your truth resonates in our hearts.

His nickname "Tacky" came from "Tacker," a football hero. It stuck, because Kilian is a tenacious man and a champion athlete in the marathon to God. A man of mortification and self-discipline, Kilian nevertheless loves sweets. It has been our blessing that Kilian Healy sweetens our Carmelite heritage and made the diet of spirituality deliciously more attractive. Charity is his signature. Strong convictions are always modified by respect and reverence for others. Kilian did not force his views on us. He trusts God. And he trusts his brothers. He lives what he believes, and our horizons were raised higher. A private man, he took the risk of sharing his journey, because he is a prophet who speaks of the faithful God!

Kilian is a zealous man of God, who makes us all proud to be Carmelites. Kilian is a saintly man who gently inspires all of us to be the men of prayer we know we are called to be. To our Brother, our Prophet, our Poet and our Friend, we say "Thank you." The gentle breeze which God breathes among us in you, Kilian, has indeed been refreshment for our spirit. Because you share your spiritual journey and insights with us, we are more able to answer the powerful question of God: "Why are you here?" Thank you!

Your Carmelite Brothers
Province of the Most Pure Heart
of Mary

Preface

NEARLY twenty-five years ago Carmelite Prior General Kilian Healy wrote to express his approval of an unsigned article I had published in *La Orden de Nuestra Señora del Carmen*. It was a gesture typical of a great and humble man: to take time from his busy schedule to encourage a young Carmelite teaching high school in Lima, Peru. Father Kilian has changed very little over the years. He is a great and humble man.

Although *Prophet of Fire* was initially intended as a series of presentations for Carmelite novices and tertiaries, it has developed over years of prayerful study into an incisive reflection on the life of the prophet Elijah as presented in the Bible. Fr Kilian's words faithfully reflect the inspired Word and they help us to see our own reality in its light.

Consequently its message is significant for all Christians, and for Jews and Muslims as well.

All three of the world's great monotheistic religions—Judaism, Christianity and Islam—venerate the *Prophet of Fire*. For Jews, Elijah is the forerunner of the Messiah, a messenger between heaven and earth, the rebuilder of God's chosen people. In the Gospels Elijah appears along with

Moses during the transfiguration and bears witness to the Lordship of Jesus. For Muslims, we live because Elijah is alive. For all he is the paragon of fidelity to God.

Elijah is best known, perhaps, as the Prophet of Mount Carmel who defeated the false prophets of Baal. He fought long and hard, usually alone, against idolatry.

An idol is a symbol—a symbol of something that a community or an individual considers of supreme importance. Thus an idol is something created by a community, or by an individual, to be a visible expression—and a self-justification—of what it wants for itself. In worshiping an idol, the community or individual feels itself justified.

A piece of wood or stone, a personal ambition or aim, is unimportant; what is important is that one worships the work of his own hands. Indeed he is worshiping himself. In the course of history certain groups have insisted on the supreme importance of food or sex or national glory, and they have made images for themselves that became the expression or focal point of their self-centeredness. Among the world's cultures idol-worship has frequently involved prostitution, orgies, torture, even human sacrifice.

Clearly the worship of idols is dehumanizing and produces no good fruit; thus, for example, the Elijah-texts in Scripture depict Baal-worship as involving self-mutilation.

In *Prophet of Fire* Father Kilian Healy faces up to the perennial challenge of Elijah: If the LORD is God, follow him; if Baal, follow him.

Like many ancient cultures, today's society often prefers to straddle the issues of good and evil, of right and wrong. We moderns do not want to commit ourselves to God too deeply: we proclaim the principle of peace and justice but promote indiscriminate consumption; we proclaim the principle of fundamental equality for all but insist on personal and national privilege; we proclaim the primacy of the spirit but reject discipline.

All too frequently our consciences are guided by feelings rather than reason: if it feels good do it. We submit our judgment to a false concept of democracy: if the majority thinks it is good, then it cannot be evil. We have become worshipers of our own constructs, and in the process both individuals and societies have begun to self-destruct.

Elijah still calls on the servants of the Most High to throw down our idols and to return to the worship of the One God. The Baals of consumerism and reckless self-interest may be less recognizable than the old idols, but they are even more insidious in misleading the People of God.

Prophet of Fire challenges us to stand up and be counted. If the LORD is God, then we must follow him.

Louis P. Rogge, O.Carm.

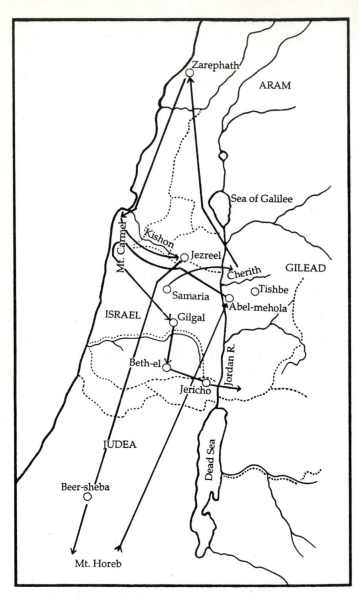

Elijah's Journeys

Introduction

WHY do we single out Elijah for special attention during these final years of the twentieth century?

There are two principal reasons. First, he has an important place in salvation history. His mission to Israel has a message that is valid for people of all times. Second—and this is our main interest here—he is the spiritual leader and model of the members of the Carmelite Order: ignorance of Elijah, his mission, his influence in history is ignorance of the spiritual life of Carmel.

Believers today as in the past can learn from the prophet of Carmel. Chosen by God to be his emissary, Elijah—with a display of remarkable courage and zeal—showed himself to be a true servant of the Lord. Time and again he proclaimed the lordship of the God of Israel by opposing the idolatry and injustice of the formidable King Ahab. To the embarassment of the royal family he exposed the prophets of Baal as frauds. Although his intervention did not succeed in exterminating the cult of Baal, nevertheless he did help to sustain the cult of the one true God in Israel. Elijah, the man of

God, the zealous servant, has left his mark on salvation history. He is venerated by Christians, Jews and Moslems.

If Elijah has left his mark on salvation history, he has also left it on the Carmelite Order. From its origin on Mount Carmel at the dawn of the thirteenth century the Order of Carmel has venerated Elijah as its leader and model. The prophet of Carmel belongs to the roots of the Order. So much so, that if in the future Carmel were to forget its relationship to Elijah, it would soon pass out of existence. For any society, and this is true of a religious society, once separated from its roots slowly fragments. A society without roots is like a flower pulled loose from its bed that blossoms for a while and then withers and dies. Carmel, then, must never be separated from its spiritual father.

To preserve a lively awareness of this Carmel-Elijah relationship, to strengthen and encourage others to find inspiration in it, we propose the following presentations based on the biblical stories of Elijah. Before we do this it will be helpful to indicate the principal biblical sources for our reflections, and to follow this with a brief introduction to Elijah and his times.

1. Scriptural sources

In the Books of Kings we find a number of Elijah stories that form the nucleus from which we draw our thoughts and applications (1 Kgs 17-19; 21; 2 Kgs 1-2:17). Other useful references to the prophet are found in Malachy 3:23-24 and Sirach 48:1-12. In the time of Christ Elijah enjoyed great popularity among the believing Jews, and so he is also mentioned in the New Testament several times. (Mt 11:14; 17:1-13; Mk 9:2-13; Lk 1:17; 9:28-36; Jas 5:17-18). We shall refer to these passages as the occasion warrants.

The Books of Kings are the basic and principal source of our meditations. Compiled over a period of time the final edition was written perhaps in the exilic period, sometime after 561 B.C.E. The unknown author writes to the Jews in the Babylonian exile to convince them that they, and not God, have been unfaithful. He writes as a theologian, but uses history to serve his purpose. While he recalls the infidelity of kings and people to Yahweh, his main intention is not to recall the sins of Israel, but rather to encourage the people lest they despair. God has not abandoned Israel. He has not annulled his covenant. No. God is rich in mercy and love. Israel must trust in him and continue to hope for deliverance. Elijah is one of the prophets chosen by God to bring this message to the people.

2. Elijah and his times

What do we know about Elijah? He is a prophet and a priest. He speaks in the name of the Lord, he offers sacrifice to him on Carmel. His name means "my God is Yahweh." He is a Thesbite from Gilead, a territory east of the Jordan and west of Ammon; a rolling plateau watered by many streams, and part of the northern kingdom of Israel. It was colonized by the Israelites, and remained strictly Yahwist—not an easy prey to the zealots of Baal, the pagan god of fertility.

Unlike some of the prophets, Nathan, for example, who remains unknown, Elijah appears as a clearly drawn historical figure. This is not to say that we have in the sacred writings a detailed life of this man of God. We know nothing of his parents or early family life. Rather, he is a mysterious character, unpredictable in his movements, who makes eagle-like appearances, sudden and dramatic, during the reigns of Ahab, king of the northern kingdom of Israel (874-853), and of his son, Ahaziah (853-852). His historical career is difficult to reconstruct, and what we have in the Bible seems to be based on stories from an older biography of Elijah.

From the Bible we learn that God called Elijah to be his messenger during a most difficult time for Yahwism. The worship of Baal, the god of the Canaanites, had filtered into Israel from the time of the conquests of King David. Matters grew worse when King Ahab, for political and economic motives, entered into marriage with Jezebel, daughter of the Phoenician king, Ittobaal of Sidon. A woman known for her wickedness, Jezebel was deeply devoted to her pagan gods and brought with her 450 prophets of Baal and 400 prophets of Astarte and fed them at her table. So great was her influence that her vacillating husband succumbed to the worship of Baal, followed by the courtiers and the upper classes in the city. Meanwhile, the less educated country people seemed to remain devoted to Yahweh, but even they were not sure of the God they worshiped.

In this environment of religious confusion and syncretism when Israel seemed on the verge of breaking its covenant with Jahweh, Elijah was summoned by God to restore the people to the one true faith. His dramatic appearance and fiery intervention is one of the more interesting episodes in the history of Israel. Long after his departure, when he was suddenly taken up into heaven in a fiery chariot, he would continue to live in the minds and hearts of faithful Israelites.

In the following pages we will keep before us three questions: 1) What is the message that Elijah brought to Israel so many years ago? 2) How have the Carmelites interpreted this message in their tradition? 3) What does the message of ELijah say to us today?

In each presentation there will be four steps: 1) a text from the Books of Kings; 2) a brief commentary; 3) an interpretation of the text in Carmelite tradition; 4) an application of the text for today.

I

Elijah, the Tishbite, from Tishbe in Gilead, said to Ahab: "As the LORD, the God of Israel, lives, whom I serve, during these years there shall be no dew or rain except at my word."

I Kings 17:1

Elijah
confronts King Ahab

O UR translation[1] follows the basic Hebrew meaning, and it is the one to be preferred. The Vulgate offers a different translation that was followed in the Latin Church, and therefore by the Carmelites. The Vulgate version of this text had great influence on the whole Carmelite tradition because of its emphasis on Elijah in God's presence. We shall also use it here and, when the occasion arises, comment on it. The *Revised Standard Version* (1957) reads: "Now Elijah the Tishbite of Tishbe in Gilead, said to Ahab, 'as the Lord the God of Israel lives, *before whom I stand*, there shall be neither dew nor rain these years, except by my word.'"

The event described in this text took place in the ninth century before Christ, in the reign of King Ahab (874-853). At that time Israel was divided into the northern and southern kingdoms. Ahab began his rule in the northern kingdom in the thirty-eighth year of the reign of Asa, King of Judah. Samaria, the capital city of the north, had been founded by Omri, the father of Ahab. The king lived sumptuously in a gorgeous ivory palace: he also enjoyed the comfort of a summer residence in Jezreel. Samaria had no temple dedicated to Jahweh, but

Ahab had built a temple there to Baal. No remains of this temple have been found, but it probably was situated east of the magnificent royal palace.

God was greatly angered when Ahab set up an altar to Baal in the temple (1 Kgs 16:32). To punish him God sent Elijah, the prophet, to foretell the drought that would afflict the country.

Without any previous warning Elijah suddenly appears on the scene to rebuke Ahab. Perhaps the encounter took place in a sanctuary or in some public gathering. Elijah speaks with authority in the name of the one true God. He calls himself "servant of the Lord." It is the living God whom he serves, and not an image sculptured by human hands. Because he is a servant he stands always in the presence of the Almighty, ready to fulfill his commands.

Sirach refers to him as the fiery prophet whose words burn like a fiery furnace (Sir 48:1). All through his life fire will be associated with this man. For he is not an ordinary servant, but God's chosen messenger filled with zeal for the Holy One. Standing before Ahab he sounds this dire prediction: "during these years there shall be no dew or rain except at my word." From secular sources we know the drought actually took place. It lasted three and one half years, and affected not only Israel but neighboring countries. The historian, Josephus, reported that it was recorded by Menander of Ephesus in his account of the reign of Ittobaal of Tyre.[2]

From this scriptural episode we construct the picture of Elijah as the servant of God. He not only astounds the king with his abrupt appearance, but he also insults and humiliates him. Worse still, he predicts a severe punishment for the sin of idolatry, a punishment that will be felt by all the people.

We turn now to ask what effect did this episode have upon Carmelite tradition? And in the first place, how did Elijah enter into Carmelite tradition?

I. Carmelite tradition

Although throughout its history the Order of Carmel has venerated Elijah as its founder and model, there is no reference to Elijah in the original Rule of St Albert written about 1209. The earliest indication of a relationship between the prophet and the Order comes from an eye-witness to the lives of the hermits on Carmel. Jacques Vitry, the Bishop of Acre, writing in 1226 makes this observation. The hermits "lived in solitude after the example and imitation of the saintly and solitary Prophet Elijah, near the fountain on Mount Carmel, called the fountain of Elijah."[3]

It was not the good fortune of the hermits to enjoy for long the peaceful solitude of the mountain. Harassed by the invading Saracens they began to leave Carmel as early as 1238. They migrated to Europe and brought with them the consciousness of their relationship to Elijah. We know this from the fact that once they were constrained to explain their origin and way of life to skeptical Europeans, they identified themselves as successors of the prophets Elijah and Elisha.[4]

In succeeding centuries the Carmelites would continue to profess their relationship to Elijah their model and leader. In one of the most important literary documents of the Order in the 14th century, *The Book of the Institution of the First Monks,* there are many references to Elijah and his link with Carmelites. He is called the chief of the monks, the solitary prophet, the supreme founder of the Order and of its first foundation. But what is of greater interest to us is its commentary on the words of Elijah to King Ahab on the occasion of their first confrontation:

> He [Elijah] deserved by right to stand before the loftiness of the divine majesty because he had set the path of his soul to such great perfection that none born of women was ever of greater fullness of holiness. For, although the Saviour said: "Among those born of women there has risen no one greater than John the Baptist" (Mt 11:11), Elijah is equal to John as the angel Gabriel evidently testified when speaking to Zachary; he asserted that John would go before Christ "in the spirit and power of Elijah" (Lk 1:17).[5]

It should be noticed that the writer, commonly believed to be Philip Ribot, the Provincial of the Province of Catalonia, used the Vulgate translation of the Bible. And in the text under consideration Elijah is not called "the servant of God," but rather "the one who stands in God's presence." This latter version brings out the prayerfulness of Elijah, and Ribot uses this to hold up Elijah "standing in God's presence" as the model of the contemplative life to which Carmelites are called. *The Institution* was the spiritual reading book of the Order for centuries. It influenced St Teresa of Avila and St John of the Cross. And the image of Elijah "standing in God's presence" is the model that was handed down in the Order for young religious to follow.

For example, we find this model present in the 17th century in the *Directory for Novices* in the Reform of Touraine.

> The first and principal obligation of our Institute is to attend and stand with God in solitude, silence and continual prayer, following the wish of our first father and founder St. Elias, the prophet.[6]

Later in the same century Daniel of the Virgin Mary, a highly respected historian of the Order and a member of the reformed Province of Belgium, offers the same instruction:

> To live the reformed Carmelite life it is necessary to return to the principal end of our Institute. What do we find in our leader and founder Elias? Solitude, silence, prayer, and conversation with God in whose presence he always stood.[7]

As we draw closer to our own time we find that one exemplary Carmelite, Bl Titus Brandsma, summed up this long, uninterrupted tradition in these words:

> This living in the presence of God, this placing himself before the face of God, is a characteristic which the children of Carmel have inherited from the great prophet: *Conversatio nostra in coelis est*, 'Our conversation is in heaven.' Elias was not taken up to heaven, but here on earth he lived in heaven and stood with a pious heart before God's throne: 'God lives, I am standing before His face.'[8]

A directory of the spiritual life composed in 1940 for the instruction of novices made every effort to be faithful to the Carmelite tradition of living in God's presence. It had this to say about the Elijan tradition:

> Since this exercise [the practice of living in God's presence] bestows so many great advantages and since it was on that account so close to the hearts of our Carmelite predecessors, it is certainly just that we also earnestly embrace it and become so familiar with it that we will make it, as it were, part of our nature... For this is the spirit of our Order according to the example of our holy Father Elias, who drew his wonderful strength and fervent zeal from his constant remembrance of the presence of the Lord in Whose sight he habitually stood.[9]

This filial relationship to Elijah still lives in the Order. But it is well to observe that Carmelites

29

today do not speak of an historical succession from the prophet as was so often emphasized in the past. It is the spiritual relationship with Elijah that matters. Of what value is an historical succession if the spiritual heritage is weak or dead? Today Carmel does not consider Elijah as the founder of Carmel in a juridical sense, as Benedict is the founder of the Benedictines or Francis of the Franciscans. In Carmel Elijah, standing in God's presence, is the spiritual father of Carmel, the model, the exemplar of contemplative life. The most recent Constitutions of the Order state: "From the prophet we derive a burning desire for the living and true God and the ready spirit to steadfastly witness to His presence and operation in a secularized world."[10]

Finally, the Liturgy proper to Carmel continues the tradition. One of the entrance antiphons for the feast of the prophet, July 20, proclaims: "The prophet Elijah cried out: 'The Lord God of Israel lives, in whose presence I stand.'" It will be noticed that the Liturgy preserves the Vulgate version.

The Opening Prayer of the feast is equally traditional, but combines the meaning of the Vulgate with the basic Hebrew meaning, so that Elijah is presented not only as living in God's presence, but as the witness who serves. "Almighty ever living God, your prophet Elijah, our Father, lived always in your presence and was zealous for honour due to your name. May we, your servants always seek your face, and bear witness to your love."

II. The meaning of the text today

It is obvious that the tradition we have just reviewed was inspired not wholly but substantially by the Vulgate version of the text. But suppose in the future we prefer to follow the basic Hebrew meaning that presents Elijah as the servant of the Lord, does this mean that we must depart from the tradition? No. The more basic and literal meaning of the text is not in conflict with the Vulgate; there is no real discrepancy. There is only a difference of emphasis. The literal meaning of the text presents Elijah not as a contemplative but rather as a man of action. He is not a solitary in a cave, but a servant in the marketplace. Yet the prayerful dimension of Elijah, emphasized in the Carmelite tradition, should not be underestimated. Elijah serves the Lord precisely because he stands constantly in the divine presence, always ready to fulfill his will: "As the eyes of a maid are on the hands of her mistress, so are our eyes on the LORD, our God" (Ps 123:2).

In subsequent chapters we will have ample opportunity to concentrate on Elijah "standing in God's presence," but here we prefer to reflect on the basic Hebrew meaning of the text, and therefore we fix our eyes on Elijah "the servant." What do we see? We see Elijah standing boldly before King Ahab and predicting the long drought that will dry up the land. His words are like a fiery furnace, the zeal of his father's house consumes him (cf Ps 69:10). But what does this mean to us today?

Elijah comes across to us as a man of living faith and indomitable courage. It is this faith and courage that speak to us today.

1. Faith

Consider, first, his faith. Scripture does not make an explicit reference to it. But how else can we explain his confrontation with Ahab? He had to believe intensely in God, surrender to him, and be ready to trust him no matter what trial or suffering faced him. When he foretold the drought he did not foresee the result. He had to believe. And what would he his own fate? He did not know. He could only trust the Lord. In this sense he was truly a man of faith. But where did such faith come from? It was a gift of God. God chooses his servants. He sends his Spirit into the minds and hearts of his disciples and draws them gently. He did this with Abraham and Moses; he does it now with Elijah. Faith always begins with a call from God. Years later Jesus would offer us an explanation in these words: "It was not you who chose me, it was I who chose you to go forth and bear fruit" (Jn 15:16).

The faith of Elijah recalls the faith of Abraham, who believed God when he was told that he and his wife Sarah would have a child in their old age ... that he would be the father of many nations. Though this seemed impossible, Abraham believed and was blessed by God. Faith is a leap into an unknown future; it is a risk that demands trust. God came to Elijah, called him to be his witness in Israel; to prophesy that there would be a drought in the land. God gave him no sign, no guarantee that the prophecy would be fulfilled. He asked only that Elijah trust his word, and Elijah freely and promptly said yes. And because Elijah trusted, the religious and political life of Israel would never be the same.

As we contemplate the faith of the prophet what does it mean for us? Does God require the same faith that he demanded of Elijah? Are we called to believe in him, to surrender to him, to trust him in all our trials? Yes. This is his way, and he makes it known to us through his Son Jesus.

During his ministry, whenever anyone approached Jesus of Nazareth to be healed, he demanded faith before he acted. The leper is cleansed because he comes to Jesus with faith in his healing power: "If you will to do so, you can cure me" (Mk 1:40). And the woman suffering from a hemorrhage of many years and who reached out to touch his garment is healed because of her confidence in him: "It is your faith that has cured you" (Mk 5:34). The faith of Bartimaeus, the blind man, is rewarded with the restoration of sight: "Your faith has healed you" (Mk 10:52). And Jesus is amazed and rewards the faith of the gentile centurion: "I tell you, I have never found so much faith among the Israelites" (Lk 7:9). Again, he cures the daughter of the Canaanite woman: "You have great faith! Your wish will come to pass" (Mt 15:28).

Where there is no faith Jesus does not cure. He "could work no miracle there [Nazareth], so much did their lack of faith distress him" (Mk 6:5). Jesus never worked miracles to force people to believe in him. At times he even seemed reluctant to perform them. People who sought help had to believe first, and then he responded to their needs. To all, the message of Jesus is basically the same: "Your faith has been your salvation" (Lk 7:50).

Today God challenges us to respond to his call with the same faith as Elijah, with the faith that Jesus demanded of those who sought his aid. There is no other way to approach or please the Lord.

St Therese of Lisieux who, in the spirit of Elijah, always lived in the presence of God, sums it all up by saying that her vocation was to love, and the road that leads to love is faith. We must believe and trust God as a child trusts a loving father. For what God asks of us is "the *surrender* of the little child who sleeps without fear in the Father's arms."[11]

A house built on rock is not easily dislodged. The unexpected winds and floods do not sweep it away. So also our spiritual life when built on a strong faith in God is not easily disturbed by hostile forces. Nevertheless, even a person of strong faith must be continually on guard against the hidden powers of darkness. We can never be too alert; our Christian faith is being constantly assaulted by powers beyond our control. To give one example: in America the national news networks—the news media elite—have enormous influence on the political and social life of the nation. In many ways, mostly indirectly, they affect our religious thinking. Our outlook on life, whether we know it or not, is often colored by the news media. Yet the newspeople who inform us are not, with but few exceptions, motivated by Christian principles: "A predominant characteristic of the media elite is its secular outlook. Exactly fifty percent eschew any religious affiliation. Very few are regular churchgoers." On social issues they are very liberal and "strong supporters of ... sexual freedom in general."[12] In a word, we cannot look to newspeople for encouragement in the practice of Christian faith. On the contrary, we must take care that they do not weaken or destroy it. What we need to confront the religious confusion and secularism of our times is the strong, unwavering faith that Elijah manifested in Israel. Our faith is our protection against the enemies of our spiritual life. In the words of St Paul that are found in the Rule of Carmel: "In all things take up the shield of faith by which you can extinguish every flaming dart from the evil one."[13]

2. Courage

But faith is not enough. It is one thing to believe; it is another to proclaim belief under great stress. For this courage is needed, a courage that flows from faith rooted in love. Elijah had such courage.

When he stood before Ahab he did not know what kind of reception he would receive. He knew he was risking his life. Would the king accept him as a messenger of the Lord? Would he listen to him? Or, blinded by his own self-importance, would his majesty look upon Elijah as a troublemaker, a fool to be banished? Surely these thoughts ran through the mind of the prophet. But no matter, he had a mission to fulfill. His own safety and well-being must not stand in the way. Only one thing was necessary: God's dominion over all creation must no longer be challenged. Yahweh is God, and there is no other. And so we see Elijah unarmed, poorly clad, a voice in the wilderness, standing before a haughty ruler. But he is fearless, he is undaunted. He places his life in God's hands and surrenders to his will.

What lesson do we draw from the action of Elijah? Like the prophet we are called to serve the Lord. Each one of us has his mission—to live according to the Rule of St Albert in allegiance to Jesus Christ. But how shall we serve? The Rule says that we should fix our eyes on the prayerful Jesus. There is no explicit command in the Rule to follow Jesus the preacher, or Jesus the healer, or Jesus the teacher. The only specific work commanded in the Rule is: "Let each one remain in his cell … *meditating day and night on the law of the Lord* and *keeping vigil in prayer.*"[14] In other words we are called to follow Jesus in the desert, Jesus contemplating on the mountain, Jesus in the garden of Gethsemane. The Constitutions of the Order add other ministries, but the mission to an apostolate of prayer will never be mitigated.

But is a life dedicated solely to prayer and sacrifice a service? Indeed it is a distinguished service for the church. Those who take part in it "offer God a choice sacrifice of praise. They brighten

God's people with the richest splendor of sanctity. By their example they motivate this people; by imparting a hidden apostolic fruitfulness, they make this people grow. Thus they are the glory of the church and an overflowing fountain of heavenly graces."[15]

But does this hidden life far from the anxieties and sufferings of the people demand courage? Is it not rather a cowardly withdrawal from the lives of the poor and oppressed? On the contrary, one who commits himself or herself to the contemplative life with sincerity chooses not only to be poor and chaste, but for the love of God and others chooses to put to death all that is selfish. The contemplative leaves the world for the good of the world. That this demands courage is clearly apparent from the life story of St Therese of Lisieux.

In 1910 when Celine, the blood sister of St Therese, was asked to testify to the holiness of her saintly sister, she did not hesitate to respond that courage characterized her whole life.

> She showed exceptional courage in the way she bore a lifetime of aridity and internal trials without any diminution of fervour, and in this connection one remembers, particularly, the extremely distressing temptation against the faith which troubled her towards the end of her life.[16]

In reference to this same trial of faith St Therese herself writes:

> I believe I have made more acts of faith in this past year [the last year of her life] than all through my whole life. At each new occasion of combat, when my enemy provokes me, I conduct myself bravely. Knowing it is cowardly to enter into a duel, I turn my back on my adversary without deigning to look him in the face; but I run towards my Jesus. I tell Him I am ready to shed my blood to the last drop to profess my faith in the existence of *heaven*.[17]

St Therese did not have to face an arrogant King Ahab, but she had to face something worse: the powers of unrelenting darkness that plagued her until death.

III. Conclusion

All Carmelites, however, did not and do not lead a purely contemplative life. Most are called to various ministries. Like Elijah they bear witness in the marketplace to the existence of the one true God. Some are called to be preachers, teachers, pastors, missionaries. Like Elijah they can truly say: "The Lord lives, whom I serve." It is true that they do not have to put their lives on the line as Elijah did; but their call to be courageous is nonetheless real. Many live in circumstances that are alien and often hostile to Christian life. For example, some Carmelites live in countries where atheistic communism suppresses religious freedom and the rights of the individual. Others live in societies dominated by capitalistic consumerism that fosters self-indulgence, encourages wealth and greed and therefore makes the following of Christ most difficult. Still others find themselves in countries in a state of development in which the poor and the illiterate are oppressed by totalitarian governments.

In these unfavorable conditions, hostile to Christian life and human dignity, they are called to live out their vocation with great courage. Some are even called upon to risk their very lives. Here we cannot but recall the heroic life of Father Titus Brandsma, a man of our own times. The spirit of Elijah was alive in him. Although his first preference was to be alone with the Lord in prayer, at the outbreak of World War II he went forth when called to be a witness to the Lord. As Elijah confronted Ahab so Titus stood up and defended the rights of religion and freedom of conscience. As the Ecclesiastical Consultant for Catholic journalists he represented the Hierarchy of the Netherlands in fighting for the just freedom of the Catholic press against the unreasonable demands of National Socialism (Nazism). It was this defense of the church's right to teach freely that brought about his arrest and imprisonment. Throughout his internment his courage was an inspiration to his fellow prisoners. Finally on July 26, 1942, sick and exhausted he was put to death in the concentration camp of Dachau. His whole religious life until his death can be summed up in the words of Elijah: "the Lord God of Israel lives, whom I serve."

May the spirit of Elijah continue to burn brightly in the hearts of all Christians. Whether we serve as St Therese the hidden life of the cloister, or as Bl Titus in the marketplace, we need the living faith, the indomitable courage of our father, Elijah. Lord, hear our prayer. May we always stand in your presence. May we always serve with courage.

II

The LORD then said to Elijah: "Leave here, go east and hide in the Wadi Cherith, east of the Jordan. You shall drink of the stream, and I have commanded ravens to feed you there." So he left and did as the LORD had commanded. He went and remained by the Wadi Cherith, east of the Jordan. Ravens brought him bread and meat in the morning, and bread and meat in the evening, and he drank from the stream.

1 Kings 17:2-6

Elijah
hides in the Wadi Cherith

A FTER Elijah had rebuked Ahab, perhaps in Samaria, and had foretold the drought, he went and hid in the Wadi Cherith. Where is Cherith? It is not easily identified. Perhaps it is the Wadi Yabis, that lies east of the Jordan. Since the fourteenth century this Wadi has been called the Wadi of Elijah.[1] In any case Cherith was a place of safety, far from the jurisdiction and clutches of Ahab.

During his sojourn Elijah was fed miraculously by ravens, an event that calls to mind the feeding of the Israelites in the desert during the time of the Exodus (Ex 16:8,12). We do not know how long this man of God remained at Cherith. Scripture says until the stream went dry, and Wadis in Palestine usually go dry after the rainy season. We are curious to know how Elijah occupied himself. The Book of Kings says only that he was in hiding, but since he was God's faithful servant, frequently in communion with him, we are led to believe that he was a true contemplative living in familiar conversation with God. At least this is the way Christians have understood his stay in Cherith, and they have revered him as the model and founder of monastic life. In the Western church Carmelites in particular have fostered and enriched this image.

I. Carmelite tradition

In Christian iconography Elijah is portrayed at the entrance of a cave along the Wadi Cherith awaiting the ravens who bring food in their beaks. The scene awakens in us the vision of a contemplative, alone with God, and providentially fed by him. Time and again artists have recreated this scene, and worthy of mention are the paintings that adorn the refectories of the convents on Mount Athos. Nor can we pass over in silence the many icons in the Middle East, in Eastern Europe, and especially in Russia. Some of these are reproduced even today. In the West, Rubens (d. 1640) has left us a striking painting of the Prophet at Cherith that hangs in the Louvre. Carmelites, too, have contributed to the spread of this iconography: of special interest is the woodcut reproduced in the *Speculum Carmelitanum*, 1680.[2]

Every Carmelite who knows the tradition of the Order finds in these artistic representations a symbol of the Carmelite vocation. The call to Carmel is primarily an invitation to go aside, as Elijah did at Cherith, to be alone with God, communing with him in prayer, completely dependent on his providence.

From earliest times Carmel has tried to keep this vocation clearly before the eyes of its religious. For example, in *The Institution of the First Monks* of the fourteenth century, Elijah in the cave at Cherith is the model and inspiration that is set before the young Carmelite. This book, faithful to the original spirit of Carmel, has influenced the whole spiritual tradition of the Order: to understand the spirit of Carmel thoroughly one must know and understand this work. For this reason we offer a brief summary of its teaching, followed by some observations that will help us understand and trace its singular influence in every century of the Order's existence.

1. The Institution

The *Institution is* the first of *The Ten Books of the Foundation of, and Matters Peculiar to, the Carmelites.* This collection was compiled by Philip Ribot, Provincial of Catalonia, and published in 1370. It contains the history of the Order from Elijah to the migration to Europe under the guise of editing and commenting on four alleged ancient works. Today it is believed that this collection does not antedate the fourteenth century.

The first of these four works, the *Institution of the First Monks,* specifically chapters one to nine, is the one that interests us here. It is the most important of all and owes its popularity partly to the belief long held in the Order, that it was the original Rule of Carmelites, composed in Greek by John XLIV, Bishop of Jerusalem. Actually, like the other three works, it was written in Latin and is a commentary on the Rule of St Albert; it was probably composed in its complete form by Ribot himself. It is of paramount interest to us for two reasons. First, it is a systematic, doctrinal presentation of Carmelite spiritual life. Second, and what is important for our immediate task, it presents this doctrine as a commentary on the life of Elijah during his seclusion in the Wadi Cherith. It invites us to visualize Elijah in the cave of Cherith as the first monk, the ideal contemplative, whose ascetic and prayerful life Carmelites are called to imitate.[3]

According to the *Institution,* after Elijah denounced the idolatry of King Ahab, God gave him two commands: 1) Go and hide in the Wadi Cherith; 2) Drink from the stream. The writer accepts the literal meaning of these words, but then goes on to give them a "mystical" interpretation. "Go and hide" means cleanse yourself of everything that is sinful, and offer God a holy and pure heart. In other words, strive to be perfect. On the other hand, "Drink from the stream" is an invitation to taste and experience the Lord's presence, that is, the joy of contemplation. In these two commands we find the two goals of the Carmelite vocation. The immediate goal is to offer God a holy and pure heart, and this is ordained to a further goal in this world, namely, the enjoyment of the gift of contemplation, if God wills to grant it. The latter is a normal but not necessary effect of the former. But let the *Institution* speak for itself:

> The goal of this life is twofold. One part we acquire, with the help of divine grace, through our efforts and virtuous works. This is to offer God a holy heart, free from all stain of actual sin. We do this when we are perfect and in Cherith, that is hidden in that charity of which the wise man says: "Charity covers all offences" (Prov 10: 12). God desired Elijah to advance thus far, when He said to him: "Hide yourself by the brook Cherith."

> The other part of the goal of this life is granted us as the free gift of God: namely, to taste somewhat in the heart and to experience in the soul, not only after death but even in this mortal life, the intensity of the divine presence and the sweetness of the glory of heaven. This is to drink of the torrent of the love of God. God promised it to Elijah in the words: "You shall drink from the brook."[4]

It is important to realize that the first and immediate goal is something we can attain with the aid of God's ordinary grace. The second goal, however, cannot be earned or demanded by right. It is a pure gift of God. At the same time it is transitory, for our faith is dark, and the weakness of the human condition cannot bear a prolonged experience of God. This gift is not granted to all; at most we can dispose ourselves for it.

Having presented the twofold goal of the eremitical life, the *Institution* then describes the four steps of the journey that was first taken by Elijah. 1) The beginner must go and hide: that is, flee the world, family, friends, riches, and embrace poverty. 2) Once he has withdrawn, he must strive to discipline his body and soul, overcome all temptations, take up his cross, and submit his will to a superior. 3) In silence and solitude he will avoid anger, greed and lust, and willingly embrace chastity. 4) Finally, he will strive to avoid all sins and practice charity. In regard to this latter point the writer offers a long eloquent explanation of Christian charity, quoting the Scriptures profusely, insisting on love of God and neighbor. For him to dwell in Cherith means to have charity, which is the fulfillment of the law.

Fidelity to these four ascetical practices—poverty, chastity, obedience and charity—will lead to purity of heart, the proper disposition for the gift of contemplation. Although the *Institution* does not define the term 'purity of heart,' it is safe to say that the word 'heart' refers to the core of our being from which come all our emotions, thoughts, desires and loves. This is the common meaning in Scripture and in the early traditions of the church.

After this brief sketch of the doctrine, we are ready to examine it more profoundly. Specifically, we shall consider: 1) the doctrine of the *Institution* in relation to Christian perfection and 2) to higher contemplation; 3) to the practice of prayer for the young religious and 4) to ministry; 5) finally, we shall show how this treatise has influenced some of the more important spiritual reforms and movements in the Carmelite Order.

a. PURITY OF HEART AND CHRISTIAN PERFECTION

Purity of heart is not the special preserve of Carmelites. It is the immediate goal, the common purpose, of everyone who sincerely seeks the Lord. In the Old Testament we read: "You shall love the Lord, your God, with all your heart, and with all your soul, and with all your strength" (Dt 6:5). The Psalmist exclaims: "Who can ascend the mountain of the Lord? or who may stand in his holy place? He whose hands are sinless, whose heart is clean" (Ps 24:3-4). In the New Testament Jesus proclaims the same teaching: "Blest are the single-hearted [the pure of heart] for they shall see God" (Mt 5: 8). St Paul, warning Timothy to avoid myths and false teaching and to adhere to sound doctrine, cries out: "What we are aiming at in this warning is the love that springs from a pure heart, a good conscience, and sincere faith" (1 Tim 1:5). The fathers of the early church and in particular the desert fathers were faithful to this teaching. Listen to the Abbot Moses as he counsels a young hermit:

> The ultimate goal of our profession is, indeed as you say, the Kingdom of God. But the immediate goal is purity of heart without which the final end cannot be attained. Let us, then, give our full attention to acquiring purity of heart. Should our thoughts ever wander from it, let us quickly bring back our gaze to it.[5]

The conclusion here is quite obvious. All Christians are called to offer God a pure heart, to be holy as he is holy. The Carmelite tradition first proclaimed in the Rule and clearly explained in the *Institution* is in perfect conformity with Christian teaching.

b. Purity of heart ordained to contemplation

However, what is proper to the teaching of the *Institution* is that it proposes purity of heart not only as the preparation for entering the kingdom of heaven, as is commonly done, but as the proximate preparation for the reception of the gift of contemplation in this world. Purity of heart is ordained to contemplation. Carmel's goal is to experience the divine presence in this world, a prelude to the beatific vision. Contemplation, sometimes called mystical prayer, is the normal although not necessary goal of the Carmelite vocation. In the words of the eminent Carmelite, Bl Titus Brandsma:

> Carmel, unlike the children of our day, is not afraid of the mystical life. The spirit of the Order does not regard it as doing violence to nature but knows that nature in the last analysis is destined for such perfection. Nor is the mystical way the only way. Great sanctity may be achieved without mystical graces and favours. This is apparent from the lives of many saints. It is enough for those on Carmel to live in God's presence, in loving humility, content with what the good God may send.[6]

c. The practice of prayer

It will strike the observant reader strange that in the chapters on the four steps to purity of heart there is no reference to the practice of prayer. One would expect a description of the various ways to pray on the way to contemplation. However, the writer was not of this mind; he was intent on teaching how to cleanse the heart of the obstacles that stand in the way of being completely receptive to the Spirit of God; prayer is not a hindrance but rather a necessary aid. On the other hand, there are a number of references to prayer in other parts of the treatise. For example, in chapter two we are exhorted to meditate word for word on God's command to Elijah to go and hide in the Wadi Cherith, and to drink of the stream; in these words we will discover the true meaning of our prophetic vocation. Prayer is also understood when we are told in chapter six to love God with our whole mind, heart and soul. Again, in chapter eight, on the need to persevere in eremitical life, we are told to be devout in prayer and humble in the confession of our sins. Finally, in chapter nine, we learn that it was through his meditations that Elijah came to dwell in the torrent of divine love. The inference is that through our meditations we too can hope to come to the same end.

In succeeding centuries, beginning with Blessed John Soreth, all the reformers—including St Teresa—influenced to some extent by the *Institution*, would offer various methods of prayer to facilitate the way to contemplation.

d. ADAPTING THE FOUR STEPS

Although all are called to purity of heart not all will follow the same path. The four steps described in the *Institution* would hardly be a suitable path for Christians living in family life. They would be ideal, however, for those who are hermits or pure contemplatives. Would they be practical for Carmelites who have left the hermitages and cloister for the cities? With some adaptation we believe they are. The *Institution* was written for those who had entered into the cities and exercised an active apostolate in the church. It was published after the Order had become mendicant. Toward the end of the 14th century the Carmelites had some three hundred houses and most of them were in the cities. There were still some hermitages, but they were more the exception that the rule. The Order was contemplative and active, and the signs of the time can be seen clearly in the leadership of the Order. The Priors General were no longer hermits but chosen from among the doctors of theology. When they retired from office they did not return to hermitages as so many former Priors General had done, but often became bishops as Father Smet tells us in his book *The Carmelites*.[7]

If this is true, why then was the *Institution* directed to the eremitical life? Was it written in opposition to the active life, with the hope that there would be a return to the former way of life? There is no reason to believe this. Rather, it was written to teach the young Carmelite that the primary purpose of his vocation is to cultivate the eremitical spirit. His first call is to imitate the hermits of Carmel, whose model was Elijah. Priority must be given to prayer and contemplation. A Carmelite might find himself engaged in studies at a university or involved in an apostolic ministry, but he must always have the heart of a hermit. Elijah in the cave at Cherith, communing with the Lord, must always be kept before his gaze. He must cultivate an I-Thou relationship with God, the source of his spiritual relationship with others.

That the *Institution* was aware of an active ministry in Carmel is clearly apparent in book three, chapter seven, wherein it recounts the history of Carmel, a history that is, however, imaginative rather than factual. There we find Elijah, his successor Elisha, and the sons of the prophets leaving the desert at the command of the Lord to go into the cities and towns to preach. Consequently, Elijah is presented not only as the model of the eremitical life, but also as a model for ministry among the people. But it is ministry that flows from a heart on fire with the love of God.

e. INFLUENCE OF THE *INSTITUTION*

One of the chief values of the *Institution* is the important place it has had in all major reforms within in the Order. While it is true that its popularity was partially due to the mistaken belief that it antedated the Rule of St Albert, its real value consists in its clear presentation of Carmelite spirituality. It is for this reason that it became time and again the guiding light and inspiration for those engaged in the reform and renewal of Carmelite life.

One of the more important reforms of Carmel took place in the fifteenth century. In 1451 Bl John Soreth, a Frenchman, was elected Prior General and remained in office until his death in 1471. He is one of the outstanding generals in the history of Carmel, and was beatified by Pius IX in 1866.

Soreth began immediately to restore common life within the Order and to bring it back to its original eremitical spirit as the source for its ministry. He had hardly begun his work when in 1452 he received spiritual support from certain women. Papal authorization was granted to receive women into Carmel, and this gave rise to the canonical status of the Carmelite sisterhood.[8] In various countries Soreth welcomed women into Carmel and was successful in interesting the Duchess of Amboise to open convents in France. After the death of her husband the Duchess herself entered Carmel and today is venerated as Bl Frances of Amboise.

Soreth was indefatigable in his work of reform. He aided and abetted the Mantuan Congregation, a reform movement already in progress in Italy. For his efforts he merited to be called its promotor, father and enthusiastic supporter. But there were more pressing needs in other countries that had been ravaged by the Black Death, the Hundred Years' War (1337-1453) and the Western Schism. There was a need to return to the common life and to a new spirit. He began by visiting many provinces, enacting the resolutions of chapters, preparing new constitutions, enforcing pontifical decrees, and even writing a commentary on the Rule of St Albert. In this latter document he writes that Carmelites must return to their original contemplative spirit realized by Elijah at Cherith. In the preface to his commentary he recalls the dwelling of Elijah near the stream of Cherith, and in doing this we see how deeply he is influenced by the *Institution.*

He states that Elijah is the first monk, the father, the founder and model of Carmel. To strengthen his argument he appeals to scripture and specifically to the story of Elijah dwelling in solitude in the Wadi Cherith. He comments on the text "go and hide by the Wadi Cherith." His spiritual interpretation is substantially that of the four steps of the *Institution:* namely, Elijah fled the world, his father's house and family; he embraced poverty, chastity and obedience. Filled with charity (Cherith) he arrived at the state of perfection. At this point Soreth exclaims: "Do you not see, brothers, that the Rule of our profession was first given by God to Elijah [at Cherith] in a shortened form?"[9] It is obvious then, that Soreth, following the tradition clearly expressed in the *Institution,* calls the Carmelites of his day to return to their source, namely to the imitation of Elijah living in God's presence in the cave of Cherith.

But let it be noted that the reformer general wishes to return to the eremitical spirit of Elijah, not to the eremitical life. His Carmelites are friars, not hermits, but he feels that the friars, to be true to their profession, must adapt their life in such a way that the eremitical or contemplative spirit will always prevail. He also reminds them that Elijah and the school of prophets that followed him left the desert on occasion. He recalls the long stay of Elijah in the house of the widow of Zarephath. Consequently, although they should not expect to enjoy the silence and solitude of the desert living in the cities, still some form of solitude must be preserved for a life of prayer. Therefore, he calls for silence and solitude in the monasteries, in the cell and in the heart.[10]

> For him the cell of the Carmelite is 'holy land,' a meeting place with God, to be dwelt in as much as possible, but he distinguishes the exterior and interior cell, the heart which must be kept free for God, for the Carmelite, involved in the world and in the service of his neighbor, is no longer a hermit.[11]

How successful was Bl John Soreth in renewing the eremitical spirit of Carmel? Father Smet believes his greatest accomplishments took place in the Lower German Province, but we do not have a complete record of his reform.[12] However, one thing is certain. He believed that Elijah, dwelling near the Wadi Cherith, was the first Carmelite. All Carmelites must imitate his life of silence, solitude and prayer. It was this life that inspired the *Institution* and the Rule of St Albert. And it is a desire to return to the spirit of this life that prompted the writing of his Commentary on the Rule.

In the sixteenth century another great spiritual reform took place in Carmel, the most profound and successful of all its reforms. It was the Teresian reform begun by St Teresa of Avila with the support of St John of the Cross. In their writings neither makes reference to the *Institution*, but both were acquainted with it since there was in Teresa's time a Spanish translation in the convent of the Incarnation. That she profited from it can be seen in the following statement:

> So I say now that all of us who wear this holy habit of Carmel are called to prayer and contemplation. This call explains our origin; we are descendants of men who felt this call, of those holy fathers on Mount Carmel who in such great solitude and contempt for the world sought this treasure, this precious pearl of contemplation that we are speaking about. Yet few of us dispose ourselves that the Lord may communicate it to us.[13]

St Teresa did not expect all her sisters to enjoy the gift of contemplative prayer. But she places the blame often on our human weakness: we do not dispose ourselves as we should. What she demands of her sisters is what the *Institution* asked of young religious. Let us be generous and offer God a pure and holy heart that he may deign to grant us his joyful presence in this world.

Commenting on the influence of the *Institution* in the writings of St Teresa and St John of the Cross a Teresian scholar declared:

> In orienting Carmelites towards the heights of the contemplative life, Teresa of Jesus and John of the Cross have been singularly faithful to the traditional ideal of the Order as explained in the ancient *Institution of the First Monks*.[14]

Following the deaths of these two outstanding witnesses of the Carmelite prophetic vocation, the *Institution* enjoyed new popularity. It was edited in 1599 and again in 1617 by Father Thomas of Jesus, the most outstanding discalced friar of the seventeenth century, and it was published among his collected works in 1684. There is no doubt that his appreciation of this Carmelite classic influenced him in his plan to build a desert monastery in every province of the Order. There the friars could go from time to time, to live in silence, solitude and prayer, undisturbed by any active ministry.

In the century that followed St Teresa, a religious revival took place in France that was so successful that the seventeenth century is often referred to as the golden age of French spirituality. In this revival the Carmelite order had its modest part with the Reform of Touraine that remained within the parent branch of the Order. In this reform the *Institution* had an influential role. Father Daniel of the Blessed Virgin Mary, in his commentary on Elijah, presents the prophet hiding in the Wadi Cherith as the model of contemplative life. He exhorts his fellow Carmelites to follow the example of the prophet. They will find his way of life at Cherith explained in the *Institution*.

The soul of the Reform of Touraine was the blind lay brother, John of St Samson. His life and his teaching breathes the spirit of the *Institution*. Bl Titus Brandsma describes his teaching in these words:

> Those who have entered the Order of Mount Carmel should keep in mind that God calls them to the enjoyment of his presence even in this life; that He wills us to contemplate Him, to lose ourselves in Him; that we should regard this as the highest obligation and never allow either study, work, or pastoral duties to push it into the background.[15]

The popularity of the *Institution* and its abiding influence is noticeable even in the twentieth century. Before World War II, when the Order was undergoing spiritual and numerical growth, it was felt that a directory of formation for young religious was imperative. Novice masters throughout the Order requested this and the result was *The Carmelite Directory* (1940). It is inspired by the Reform of Touraine, but more fundamentally by the spirit of Carmel that finds its exemplar in Elijah communing with God in the cave of Cherith. In the preface of the Directory we read: "We are ... of the opinion that nothing would be of greater advantage in our explanation of the Carmelite life, than following the Rule of John 44 [the *Institution*], as it is called." True to this principle the *Directory* outlines Carmelite life in two parts: 1) A Holy Heart (part III); and 2) The Contemplative Life (part IV). In these two sections the *Directory* explains the twofold goal of Carmel enunciated first in the *Institution*, as the twofold goal of Elijah in the cave at the Wadi Cherith.

It will be observed that all these references to the twofold goal of Carmel antedate the Second Vatican Council (1962-1965), which in many ways has changed the direction of the church and religious orders. Following the spirit of the Council, Carmel too has sought to renew itself and adapt to the changing times. The Order, like the church, is still in a period of transition. As we look to the future does the *Institution* with its contemplative ideal still have a preferred place in the spiritual life of the Order? It certainly does, and this is true not only for the cloistered Carmelite nuns who retain their purely contemplative way of life, but it is also true for Carmelite friars and all lay Carmelites who in the spirit of Vatican II are immersed in the redemption of the world. In the most recent Constitutions (1971) the friars are reminded that they should perform their ministry in the church "while still preserving their special characteristic prayer life." And should there be any doubt about its nature, the twofold goal of Carmel expressed in the *Institution* and kept alive in the long tradition of the Order is repeated verbatim. To this eremitical spirit the Carmelite is told to add the ministerial dimension of his vocation.[16]

2. Elijah as model

We began this section by recalling the iconography that presents Elijah being fed by the ravens in the Wadi Cherith. We have demonstrated that this scene has had a special attraction for Carmelites beginning with the *Institution* in the fourteenth century. Elijah dwelling in his cave near the stream of Cherith, communing with God, a fiery furnace of love, is the model who incorporates the solitary contemplative spirit of Carmel. Every successful reformation or renewal of the Order has been founded on a return to the *Institution*'s eremitical spirit of prayer. As the Order takes up renewal today its problem is how to be faithful to this eremitical spirit in a world in which people are torn from one another by gross injustice. The new Baal of Greed, incarnate in money and power, is merciless to the weak and the poor. What is Carmel's response ?

II. The flight to Cherith: is it relevant

If Carmel intends to be a vital, effective community in the new age of history that is slowly but inevitably opening up, it must realize that its mission takes place within the church and for the church, the sacrament of salvation for all. And the church realizes that to fulfill its purpose it must make God the Father and his Incarnate Son present and in a sense visible to the world. In this service Carmel has a small but distinct function. What precisely will it be? In its long history Carmel's great contribution to the church is found especially in its reform movements. Each time that Carmel returned to its eremitical spirit, and gave itself more generously to its contemplative dimension, the Order was blessed with holiness that gave new life to the church. Therefore experience is teaching us once again that the only safe route to follow is to renew the eremitical ideal of the Order. We must return in spirit to Elijah living in silence, solitude and prayer at Cherith. The prophet is still a relevant model.

Carmelites who still observe a purely contemplative life, and this is especially true of the cloistered nuns, should have no difficulty in renewing their spirit and in adapting to the needs of the times. They should be convinced that their vocation places them in the heart of the church, that the church itself considers them her glory and the source of heavenly grace for the people. They need to realize that by their prayerfulness they make God present in the world and call forth his mercy for the poor and needy. Their apostolate is hidden, but none the less real. Therefore, their mission should never give way to other forms of service and evangelization. The People of God need them, where they are.

1. Contemplatives in action

On the other hand, other members of the Carmelite family, especially the friars who labor in active ministries, are often tempted to abandon an intensely contemplative way of life. Confronted by the enormous needs of the poor and the flagrant abuse of justice, they are inclined to throw themselves into the marketplace to share the needs of the afflicted. Their love for the poor is commendable; but if they were to abandon or weaken their prayer life and begin to work for the Lord without the Lord, in the long run they and their apostolate would suffer. For the contemplative dimension of their vocation is the only secure foundation for any form of ministry. Activity without interiority leads to frustration and perhaps in the end to a loss of faith. Psychologists call it "burn out." The fire in the furnace that is not regularly fuelled dies out and gives off no warmth; so also the soul that is not nourished by constant prayer grows weak in love and loses its zeal for others.

Hence, we are not surprised that modern spiritual writers are quick to remind us that the only fruitful ministry is that which flows from a life committed to discipline, and from a prayerful spirit that turns frequently to commune with the Lord. Without this interior life of prayer, they tell us, we cannot know and love God, and therefore we will not be able to make him known and loved by others. They base their teaching on the rich tradition of the church, and especially on the desert fathers for whom purity of heart is the immediate goal of the eremitical life. We can read with profit the books of Henri Nouwen, especially *The Way of the Heart*, and the writings of George Maloney, S.J., *The Prayer of the Heart*. They describe the practices of self-denial, silence and solitude that lead to a prayerful heart. This is also, as we have seen, the tradition that we have received in Carmel.

But one of the strongest supports for the importance of the eremitical spirit of Carmel is found in the authoritative declaration of the Holy See addressed to all religious on the necessity of cultivating the contemplative dimension of religious life. The document states:

> The contemplative dimension is the real secret of renewal for every religious life. It vitally renews the following of Christ because it leads to an experiential knowledge of him. This knowledge is needed for the authentic witness to him by those who have heard him, have seen him with their own eyes, have con-

templated him and touched him with their own hands (cf. 1 Jn 1:1; Philip 3:8).

The more open religious are to the contemplative dimension, the more attentive they will be to the demands of the Kingdom, intensely developing their theological depth, because they will look on events with the eyes of faith. This will help them to discover the Divine Will everywhere.[17]

Encouraged by the support of spiritual writers and the authoritative voice of the church, we should not only feel secure in the nature of our vocation but should be encouraged and inspired to be ever more faithful. Indeed, we must be convinced that fidelity to purity of heart and living constantly in the presence of God is the special contribution that Carmel can make to the life of the church and to a better world. We want to proclaim the gospel, but let us first bear witness in our own lives that God dwells within us.

It has been said that every Christian owes something to Carmel. Certainly its saints have contributed to the rich prayer life of the church. In the future we can offer no better service than to live in complete dedication to our prayerful charism. In the spirit of St John of the Cross we must dig down deep in Christ by denying ourselves and fixing our eyes on Jesus, going aside and being absorbed in prayer as he was. Only in this way will we be ready to lay down our lives for others.

But in this battle against selfishness we must adapt to the times. In the choice of ascetical practices change is necessary. Modern spiritual writers warn us that we need to "'demythologize" the writings of the desert fathers. We must sift the essential truths that are valid for all times from the cultural elements in which they are couched. The demons of the desert are not our demons; the boredom of the desert is replaced by the noise of the city.

We know, for example, that the Carmelites of the past were advised to flee from the din and squalor of the cities. We recall the passionate plea of the Prior General Nicholas of Narbonne, who saw the return to hermitages as the only hope of the Order:

> In the city, you are seeking God in the midst of filth. Do you really think you are likely to find the one you are looking for in surroundings so completely opposed to him?[18]

2. The urban desert

There is no doubt that hermits then and now do find the Lord in the desert. But is that the only place to find him? St Teresa did not think so. When she began her reform, inspired by the eremitical spirit of the fathers on Carmel, she did not build her monasteries in country places but rather in the cities. And although she appreciated the solitude of a hermitage from time to time, she chose the eremitical community form of life for her sisters. She believed that in a small community, "Christ's little flock," the sisters, could be faithful to the stock from which they had sprung: the holy prophets.

Today Carmelite friars go a step farther. We do not even find the enclosure relevant. We are drawn to the cities, and we do not see the world as evil in itself but as in need of redemption. In the spirit of the Second Vatican Council we believe "the whole human race must be brought into the unity of the family of God.[19] We wish to share the lives of the hungry millions and of those who suffer discrimination because of race, color or creed. Can we retain a contemplative spirit while immersed in battle to help the poor and needy in their struggle for justice? In our minds there should be no doubt that we can; first, however, we must convince ourselves that only fidelity to a life of intense prayer can prepare us to be witnesses of God's mercy to others. This commitment to prayer, to the contemplative dimension of our life, is the only security we have for a fruitful ministry. Without it there is the danger of working for the Lord but forgetting the Lord of all work.

3. *Fruits of contemplation*

In our struggle to foster a contemplative spirit we can take courage from the holy men and women who have gone before us. Whether in the cloister or in active ministry they show us how to live the Carmelite charism. They teach us how to pray always; how to rest peacefully in the presence of a loving God, and so to be a leaven to the world in which we live.

We think immediately of St Therese of Lisieux who lived constantly in God's presence. Even in her last days, weighed down by weakness and sickness, she continued to pray. How did she pray? Her prayer was often silent, wordless, but still active and unceasing, because her whole being was turned to the Lord and rested in him who breathed in her. In her final illness she could say: "I ask Jesus to draw me into the fullness of His love, to unite me so closely to Him that He live and act in me."[20]

One day her sister Celine (Sister Genevieve) visited her in the infirmary and found her with hands joined and eyes raised to heaven. She said:

"What are you doing? You should try to sleep."

"I cant sleep, I'm suffering too much, so I am praying."

"And what are you saying to Jesus?"

"I say nothing to Him, I love Him!"[21]

But let us take an example from one in active ministry. In 1946 Father John Brenninger, Carmelite, died in Rome. In his younger years he had longed for the life of Cherith, but he found himself called by obedience from his native Germany to live in a large monastery in the Eternal City amidst crowded apartment buildings and noisy, traffic-filled streets. Besides administrative duties as counselor to the Father General and later as rector of St Albert's International College, he was engaged in teaching, writing and pastoral work. On Sundays he was occupied from early morning to midday in hearing the confessions of the faithful.

In spite of his busy schedule his personal life was marked by silence, solitude and prayer. Day in and day out he preached to his community by example that the eremitical spirit of Carmel is the primary spirit of the Order. In his weekly conferences he encouraged renewal. His own dedication to the contemplative life was the secret and the source of his remarkable active ministry. Unable to go to the desert, he created the desert in his own heart where he communed with the Lord Jesus. He was a student and a disciple of the Reform of Touraine.

In his final years, during World War II when food was scarce in Rome, he shared his portion with the poor. Weakened by the lack of sufficient nourishment he came down with tuberculois and, after a long and painful illness, died at the age of fifty-six. In his lifetime he integrated the contemplative and ministerial dimension of Carmel: the latter received its dynamic force from the former.

All this is clearly brought out in the *Carmelite Directory of the Spiritual Life,* of which he was the anonymous compiler; into this work he had put the fruit of his years of study, prayer and experience. His great desire was to give novice masters and their charges a guide that would help them live the true spirit of Carmel. For him this involved the Elijan spirit in which we offer God a holy and pure heart while awaiting the gift of contemplation. In the *Directory* he wrote: "The spirit of prayer is the most important part in the make-up of the true Carmelite, even after the Order has passed to the active life and the external apostolate."[22] Companions of Father Brenninger tell us that what he taught, he faithfully practiced.

The true spirit of Carmel is found not only in the cloister and among the friars; it is found as well among Lay Carmelites. Directors can surely testify to the purity of heart, the prayerful life, and the great spirit of charity of many Carmelites living in the world. Unfortunately, the laity do not write much, and so we have no way of sharing the beauty of their interior lives. Would that many might make known to us the gifts they have received from the Lord. One who did this under obedience to her director was Mary Petyt (1623-1677). She lived as a recluse near the Carmelite church in Malines, Belgium, following the Rule of Carmel. She developed a unique devotion to the Blessed Virgin Mary: she contemplated Mary's virtues and found that their source was Mary's intimate union with God. With the help of Mary, whom she recognized as the greatest contemplative, she herself entered into union with God and enjoyed the sweetness of his presence. In the declining years of her life she wrote in her journal:

> The manner of living in God wherein, through His grace, God has set me for some time, is an intimate enjoyment of the Divine Being, in a lofty eminence of

light and peace. This manner of enjoying God and experiencing divine things cannot even be compared with any of the preceding manners. Here, God reveals Himself in a more lofty light. He allows the soul to understand and to experience wonderful things in himself, things which cannot afterwards be remembered or expressed in words.[23]

Whether we are in the cave at Cherith like Elijah, or confined to a bed of suffering like St Therese, or busy in the city like the indefatigable Father Brenninger, or living in the world like Mary Petyt, the message we are given is the same. The real desert where we will find God is in our heart. When we empty the heart of inordinate self-love, the Lord comes and makes his dwelling within. "And since He doesn't force our will, He takes what we give him, but He doesn't give Himself completely until we give ourselves completely."[24]

4. Prayer and contemplation

One final question needs to be answered. In our journey to purity of heart, besides the ascetical practices that cleanse us of sin, is there a way of prayer that will prepare us for the gift of contemplation? The biblical story of Elijah at Cherith and the *Institution* offer none, and perhaps wisely, since there are as many ways to pray as there are people who pray. Some make progress by faithfully practicing oral prayer whether alone or in community. The slow, deliberate recitation of the Our Father, the Hail Mary, the Rosary, or a psalm may be all that a person can do, and yet fidelity to this form of prayer brings about an intimate union with our Lord and the peace that the Lord alone can give. Others find help in some form of methodical prayer that often leads to a simple, contemplative awareness of God's presence. We can still read with great profit *The Way of Perfection* of St Teresa, Doctor of the Church, in which she teaches various ways to pray. Here we offer one form of prayer practiced by contemplatives, active religious and devout laity. Its roots go back to the hermits of the desert in the early centuries of the church, and it was codified in the twelfth century. It is called a ladder for monks that lifts them from earth to heaven.[25]

It is composed of four steps or rungs: reading, meditation, prayer, and contemplation. A more contemporary formula describes these steps as listening (reading and meditation), waiting (prayer), experiencing (contemplation).

We summarize it in the following steps:

Step One: We go aside to a quiet place for about a half hour or an hour. We fix our eyes and heart on Jesus. Taking up the scriptures we read slowly; we re-read if we wish, and even read aloud. Reading may be taken in a wide sense to include listening to another or to a tape, or even fixing our eyes on a painting, a fresco or a crucifix.

Step Two: We ponder the message, spending as much time in reflection as seems useful. Much depends on how well we are able to use our imagination or reasoning power.

Step Three: We respond to the Lord who awakens thoughts and desires within us. Our prayer is unrehearsed, very personal, expressing itself in praise, thanks, sorrow, petition.

Step Four: Our prayer becomes simple, wordless, more passive. It is similar to the communication that goes on between two people who are deeply in love. They enjoy each other's presence, and no words or few words are necessary. This is contemplation. This is similar to the prayer of contemplation that admits many degrees, that the *Institution* calls the second goal of the Carmelite vocation. And St Teresa seems to describe its different levels in the last four mansions of her *Spiritual Castle.*

Is this method effective? It would seem so. It has been practiced in the church for centuries, and highly recommended by spiritual writers and directors. St John of the Cross praises it in these words: "Seek in reading, and you will find in meditation; knock in prayer and it shall be opened to you in contemplation.[26]

Today spiritual writers often reflect on this fourth step, contemplation. They perceive it as a distinct way of prayer, and they recommend its practice to those who have gone beyond discursive or meditative prayer. It is a traditional form of prayer practiced by the desert fathers and made popular again by the anonymous fourteenth century English author of *The Cloud of Unknowing.*[27]

It has been updated in our time and given the name "centering prayer" by Thomas Merton. It is described by many to be a contemplative prayer without thoughts and without images, the prayer of quiet. It is presented in three simple rules.

Rule One: At the beginning of prayer we take a minute or two to quiet down and then turn in faith to God dwelling in our depths; and at the end of the prayer we take several minutes to come out slowly, mentally praying the Our Father.

Rule Two: After resting for a bit at the center in faithful love, we take up a single, simple word that expresses this response and we begin to let it repeat itself within.

Rule Three: Whenever in the course of the prayer we become aware of anything else, we simply and gently return to the prayer word.

If we wish to practice this prayer well, we need first to be faithful to reading, meditation and prayer. If this leads us to more simplified prayer, then "centering prayer" can be helpful, but even here perseverance is necessary. Will it be beneficial? Some who have practiced it assure us that it is. But the safest way to judge its worth is by its fruits. If it makes us more loving, gentle, peaceful, joyful and generous, then surely it is a prayer of the Holy Spirit.

III. Conclusion

Contemplation in its higher forms (experiential awareness of God) may be the normal outgrowth of a devout Christian life, but since it is a special gift of God, not all receive it. But whether we do or not, we should recognize it as the flowering of a prayerful life, mindful that what is of prime importance is that, in season and out of season, we continue to try to offer God a holy and pure heart. Purity of heart, the fullness of charity, union of our heart with God is the goal we must pursue. This is God's will.

In the light of all this is the following suggestion too idealistic? Every Carmelite community should have a painting of Elijah in the Wadi Cherith. It should hang in a prominent place, preferably—as in the monasteries of Mount Athos—in the dining room. Since the fourteenth century, and perhaps even before this, the Carmelites have recognized in this biblical scene a symbol of their prophetic voca-tion. Its message to them has been and still is:

Imitate Elijah.

Go hide.

Live in silence and solitude.

Offer God a pure and holy heart..

Then, be filled with his love, and experience in your heart the delight of his joyful presence.

III

After some time, however, the brook ran dry, because no rain had fallen in the land. So the LORD
said to him: "Move on to Zarephath of Sidon and
stay there. I have designated a widow there to provide
for you." He left and went to Zarephath. As he arrived at the entrance of the city, a widow was gathering sticks there; he called out to her, "Please bring me
a small cupful of water to drink." She left to get it,
and he called out after her, "Please bring along a bit
of bread." "As the LORD your God lives," she
answered, "I have nothing baked; there is only a
handful of flour in my jar and a little oil in my jug.
Just now I was collecting a couple of sticks, to go in
and prepare something for myself and my son; when
we have eaten it, we shall die." "Do not be afraid,"
Elijah said to her. "Go and do as you propose. But
first make me a little cake and bring it to me. Then
you can prepare something for yourself and your son.
For the LORD, the God of Israel, says, 'The jar of flour
shall not go empty, nor the jug of oil run dry, until
the day when the LORD sends rain upon the. earth.'"
She left and did as Elijah had said. She was able to
eat for a year, and he and her son as well. The jar of
flour did not go empty, nor the jug of oil run dry, as
the LORD had foretold through Elijah.

Some time later the son of the mistress of the house fell sick, and his sickness grew more severe until he stopped breathing. So she said to Elijah, "Why have you done this to me, O man of God? Have you come to me to call attention to my guilt and to kill my son?" "Give me your son," Elijah said to her. Taking him from her lap, he carried him to the upper room where he was staying, and laid him on his own bed. He called out to the LORD: "O LORD, my God, will you afflict even the widow with whom I am staying by killing her son?" Then he stretched himself out upon the child three times and called out to the LORD: "O LORD, my God, let the life breath return to the body of this child." The LORD heard the prayer of Elijah; the life breath returned to the child's body and he revived. Taking the child, Elijah brought him down into the house from the upper room and gave him to his mother. "See!" Elijah said to her, "your son is alive." "Now indeed I know that your are a man of God," the woman replied to Elijah. "The word of the LORD comes truly from your mouth."

1 Kings 17:7-24

Elijah
stays with the widow

ELIJAH, threatened by King Ahab, fled from Samaria to Cherith and then to Zarephath. Where is Zarephath? It was located seven miles south of Sidon in the territory of King Ittobaal, the father of Jezebel. The name survives in modern Sarafind. The ancient city was a center for the manufacture of glass, and had a fine harbor of three small bays.

In this new setting one would think that the prophet would escape not only the wrath of Ahab, but also the famine that had devasted Israel. But this was not to be. Even the land of Phoenicia was laid low by the drought.

At Zarephath Elijah met a widow, recognized no doubt by her dress, and asked her for a drink of water. In accordance with Eastern hospitality she acceded to his request even though water was scarce. Reflecting on this kindly gesture we cannot help but observe that this prophet, no longer welcome in his own country, is befriended by a foreigner. However she is embarassed by his plea for food. She had scarcely enough flour and oil for one final meal with her son. But Elijah is quick to reassure her that in feeding him she need not worry. In some miraculous manner he provides that her jar of flour never goes empty and her jug of oil never runs dry. Indeed, the woman, the child and Elijah have enough food throughout the year long famine.

Who is this widow? We know nothing about her except that she is a woman of property. Her dwelling is large enough to have an upper room on the roof of the house where the prophet lodges. It is interesting to compare this description with Elisha's dwelling in similar circumstances (2 Kgs 4:8-11).

The hospitality of the widow to the rejected prophet of Israel would one day be praised by Jesus and offered as an example for Christians to follow: "He who welcomes a prophet ... receives a prophet's reward: he who welcomes a holy man because he is known to be holy receives a holy man's reward. And I promise you that whoever gives a cup of cold water to one of these lowly ones because he is a disciple will not want for his reward" (Mt 10:41-42). It should be noted that Jesus does not expect a prophet to be accepted by his own. He knows that one day he himself will be rejected as Elijah was: "No prophet gains acceptance in his native place. Indeed, let me remind you, there were many widows in Israel in the days of Elijah when the heavens remained closed for three and a half years and a great famine spread over the land. It was to none of these that Elijah was sent, but to a widow of Zarephath near Sidon" (Lk 4:24-26).

During the prophet's sojourn at Zarephath the widow's hospitality is countered by the sudden and unexpected death of her only son. The mother's reaction is typical of the times. She perceives her misfortune as a punishment for her sins, and it is the unheralded presence of the prophet that has brought her guilt to light. "Have you come to me to call attention to my guilt and to kill my son?" (1 Kgs 17:18). The tears of the widow melt the heart of the prophet, a reaction that seems unusual in a man who had brought death through famine to so many. He turns to Yahweh and, by his repeated prayers and prostrations, succeeds in bringing the child back to life. The woman is overwhelmed by what she perceives as divine intervention. She not only recognizes in Elijah a prophet who speaks the truth, but she acknowledges that Yahweh is God.

The death and revival of the widow's son is not without parallel in scripture. Its similarity with the story of the child of the Shunammite woman brought back to life by Elisha is striking (2 Kgs 4:34). So also is the account in the New Testament of the youth Eutychus revived by St Paul (Acts 20: 9-10).

Stories of restoration to life are rare in the scriptures, but they always serve a purpose. Consequently, in the case of Elijah and the widow's son we are tempted to ask: Why did the chronicler narrate this event? Was it to reveal that Yahweh, the God of Israel, is also the God of the pagans? indeed the only God that gives life? that the Baal of the Phoenicians has no power to give life or to send rain, because he is not a living God? Was this event intended to manifest that even gentiles and the poor, like widows, are loved by Yahweh and are often more open to receive a divine messenger? Again, did the writer intend to contrast the compassion of Elijah for this Phoenician woman with his severity toward the other Phoenician woman, Jezebel, wife of King Ahab? Finally, was this story meant to be just one of the many events in the Elijah cycle to reveal that Elijah is one of the great prophets of the Lord, and that those who receive a prophet are rewarded?

All these questions have received an affirmative response in various places in Hebrew and Christian literature. However, what is of great interest to

Christians is the application that Luke in his gospel makes of this story. He uses it to relate the mission of Jesus with that of Elijah. Just as Elijah raised the son of the widow of Zarephath from the dead, so Jesus restored to life the son of the widow of Naim. When the people saw Jesus raise the boy to life and give him back to his mother, their reaction was similar to the cry of the widow of Zarephath: "A great prophet has risen among us; ... God has visited his people" (Lk 7:16). Luke in this scene presents Jesus as the new Elijah, one who comes in the spirit of the prophet. Yet Jesus is greater than Elijah, for the prophet of Israel raises the boy to life only after repeated prayers and prostrations. In contrast Jesus revives the boy with a word. "Young man I bid you get up"(Lk 7: 14).

Luke's gospel is clear evidence that both Jews and Christians in the first century had great veneration for Elijah. Moreover, in the course of time this devotion did not wane but rather continued unabated among Christians in the early centuries. After the Constantinian peace, pilgrims came from Europe to the Holy Land up until the Crusades and visited all the holy places. Even a small place like Zarephath engaged their attention. A chapel had been built there that recalled the miraculous power that the prophet displayed in the home of the Sidonian widow. There Christians prayed to Elijah that he might come to their aid: they revered him not only as a fiery prophet, but as a man of compassion. One account left to us by a Christian pilgrim in the sixth century states:

> [Zarephath] is a tiny Christian town where is located the chamber which had been made for Elias; there also is the bed where he slept, and the stone bowl in which the widow worked her bread. Many relics may be seen there of miracles which have taken place.[1]

I. The Carmelite tradition

The hermits on Mount Carmel in the thirteenth century were surely aware of the places in the Holy Land that had been made sacred by the presence and wonderful deeds of Elijah. Consequently they were acquainted with his visit to the Sidonian widow, and of the subsequent influence that visit had on Christian piety.

Without any attempt to go into a lengthy study of this tradition we wish here to recall only two references that Carmelites made to this visit. One reference is bound up with the historical succession of the Carmelites from Elijah. The other is of a more spiritual nature and attempts to show that Carmelites who migrated to Europe and lived in towns and cities could still be contemplatives. For Elijah their founder and model remained a faithful contemplative even in the home of the Sidonian widow far from the silence and solitude of Cherith.

We shall consider first how the visit to the widow influenced early Carmelite history. When the Carmelites were forced by the Saracens to abandon the mountain of the prophet and to migrate to Europe, they brought with them their Elijan traditions. When asked to explain their origin they declared they were the successors of Elijah and Elisha. To strengthen their claim they resorted to the tradition that was centuries old, namely, that the first disciple of Elijah was Jonah, the son of the widow of Zarephath. The widow had placed him in Elijah's care after the prophet had restored him to life. This Jonah became the celebrated prophet of Nineveh. These assertions may astound us today, but they were not invented by the Carmelites; they can be found in early Christian sources. For example, St Jerome (d. 420) in his *Prologue on Jonah* identifies him as the son of the Sidonian widow. So also does Severus of Antioch, a Monophysite Patriarch (512-518) honored in the Coptic church as a saint and martyr; he states that this tradition had Hebrew sources. That the Jewish people were aware of some relationship between Elijah and Jonah is beyond doubt and is confirmed by the following statement in a recent book. Elie Wiesel, a survivor of the Auschwitz holocaust, in his delightful story about Elijah calls our attention to the legend found in the Talmudic narratives: "One source places Jonah after David and Samuel. We are even asked to believe he was equal to Elijah, who ordained him."[2]

The relationship between Elijah and Jonah found in early Christian literature served the medieval Carmelites well. They made the most of it, as can be seen in *The Institution of the First Monks:*

> Among those prophet-disciples of Elias, the first in the order of time to be called to the monastic life by Elias was Jonas, of the region of Geth, in Affir, the son of the widow whom Elias met in Sarepta of the Sidonians while she was gathering wood and in whose house he hid while King Ahab had a death-search made for him among all his regions and inhabitants.

> This Jonas, as a boy, Elias had raised from the dead while lodging in his mother's house. For this reason, the mother, out of devotion, gave the boy to Elias to be instructed in the prophetic discipline of the monastic life; and, having become a disciple of Elias, the lad ministered unto him. When Elias was praying to God on Mount Carmel for rain, he sent this boy Jonas to look from the mountain to see if anyone appeared at sea. When he looked he said, "There is nothing."[3]

As this legendary account continues, it informs us that after Elijah ascended into heaven, Elisha, his successor, sent Jonah to Remoth-Gilead to anoint Jehu the new king of Israel. Later, at God's command, this same Jonah was to proclaim to the people of Nineveh that unless they repented and turned to God the city would be destroyed. Jonah's reluctance to fulfill this mission and its final outcome is recorded in the Book of Jonah.

It is obvious that the Elijah-Jonah relationship which began in the home of the widow of Zarephath was not the fruit of Carmelite fantasy, but rather an ancient story that was eagerly accepted by the Carmelites, since it strengthened their belief that the Order of Carmel had its origin from Elijah and the school of the prophets. Nevertheless, the Elijah-Jonah relationship, interesting though it is, does not seem to have had any influence on Carmelite spirituality. It does show, however, that the first Carmelites who came to Europe from the East were conscious of a spiritual link with the prophetic spirit of Elijah.

We turn now to the second reference in Carmelite tradition of the visit of Elijah to the widow. It is of greater interest because it refers to the contemplative dimension of the Carmelite life.

In the fifteenth century Blessed John Soreth, Prior General and reformer of Carmel, was determined to renew the contemplative spirit of the Order for friars living in towns and cities far from the solitude of Cherith and Mount Carmel. To prove that city dwellers could be contemplatives, he recalled the year long visit of Elijah in the home of the Sidonian widow. Did the dwelling of Elijah in the home of the widow mean that he ceased to be a man of profound prayer? No, says Soreth. Even in the city Elijah remained a hermit at heart. Deprived of the ideal solitude of Cherith he created a sanctuary in his heart where he communed with the Lord. Therefore, says Soreth, there is no reason why Carmelites drawn to the cities for the sake of

77

ministry cannot be hermits at heart. Exterior solitude is desirable and a blessing, but not always possible or even necessary. But interior solitude admits no substitute; it must be cultivated even in the noise of busy cities. Elijah, dwelling in the house of the widow, is a model for those whose only desert is the heart.[4]

This same counsel was reiterated two hundred years later in the *Directory for Novices* of the Reform of Touraine:

> And although after many centuries we have been transported from the deserts of Palestine to the cities and populated towns of Europe, nevertheless, this obligation of continually being attentive to God in prayer has always remained the same. Our Rule on this point has never been changed.[5]

In 1941 *The Carmelite Directory of the Spiritual Life*, faithful to the tradition of the Order, stated:

> All, however, showed themselves faithful to this axiom, "The primary and chief heritage of Carmelites is to commune with God by prayer and contemplation." There has never been any disagreement among our authors on this point.[6]

Finally, the most recent Constitutions of the Order (1971) affirm that Carmelites share in the active ministry of the church while "preserving their special characteristic prayer life, founded in the precept of the Rule concerning continual meditation on the law of the Lord, vigilance in prayer, and the putting on of spiritual armor."[7]

Today Carmelites will be faithful to their charism if they are constantly attentive to the Lord who dwells within them. Keeping him company they imitate the example of Elijah who stood always in God's presence even when forced by circumstances to dwell far from the solitude of the desert in the home of the Sidonian widow.

II. The meaning of the text today

The advice of Bl John Soreth to city dwelling Carmelites in the fifteenth century, to create a desert in their hearts, is more relevant today than in his time. Life in the latter part of the twentieth century is more active, more nerve-wracking, more mobile. With jet travel we can go not only from city to city but from continent to continent in a matter of hours. Television brings the whole world into our homes. Consequently, the culture of one people intermingles and often becomes confused with that of another. Civilizations too undergo change and even deterioration. Today, for example, we are confronted with the frightening decline in Christian values in the Western world. Just how serious this change is was brought to our attention by Pope John Paul II in his pilgrimage to London on May 29, 1982. Speaking to a vast crowd of people in Wembley Stadium he declared:

> The world has largely lost respect of human life from the moment of conception. It is weak in upholding the indissoluble unity of marriage. It fails to support the stability and holiness of family life. There is a crisis of truth and responsibility in human relationships. Selfishness abounds. Sexual permissiveness and drug addiction ruin the lives of millions of human beings. International relations are fraught with tensions, often because of excessive inequalities and unjust economic, social, cultural and political structures, and because of slowness in applying the needed remedies. Underlying all of this there is often a false concept of man and his unique dignity, and a thirst for power rather than a desire to serve.[8]

That these words of the Holy Father are not mere rhetoric can be shown from actual conditions in the United States. One of two marriages ends in divorce. Twenty percent of homes with children are without a father. Over one and a half million abortions take place each year. In the city of New York one person in forty suffers from drug addiction.

In spite of the moral depravity throughout the world the Holy Father, like the prophets of old, does not leave us without hope. He exhorts us to lift up our hearts, not to be afraid, for the Holy Spirit is with us. We Christians, he tells us, from the time of baptism are called to be prophets; we have a mission to be a light to the world and the salt of the earth. If this is true for all Christians, then it is time for Carmelites to reflect on their specific mission in the church and respond to the appeal of the Vicar of Christ. The Lord speaks through the church, and we need to hear his voice. But how can we be faithful to our mission in a practical way? How can we live a sincere prayer life in a society that has little regard for Christian values and much less for the contemplative life? In the face of worldly opposition a spiritual revival, a conversion if you will, must take place in the Carmelite family and it must begin within the heart of each Carmelite. But how do we begin ?

There is no simple or easy answer. The initiative, of course, is with God. He must first touch our hearts, moving us away from selfishness and turning our hearts to him. But he is always calling us; we need only to answer. Fortunately many do. Conversions to Christ are not unusual. Most remain hidden from public view, but great saints have told us of their experience. St Paul related his encounter with the Lord on the road to Damascus. We know how the Spirit touched the hearts of Cornelius and many others in the primitive church. We are familiar with the change of heart in the lives of St Francis of Assisi, St Teresa of Avila, St Ignatius of Loyola and many others. We recall the conversion of Paul Claudel during Vespers in Notre Dame Cathedral in Paris on Christmas Day. "Lo, You were

Someone all of a sudden," he tells us in his *Magnificat*. In our time Dorothy Day relates her own conversion from radical communism to Christ. And the conversion of Thomas Merton, the Trappist monk, is familiar to many. But do not less spectacular but just as sincere conversions take place every day? The Holy Spirit leads some from sinfulness to repentance, others from mediocrity to fervor, and even the devout to total surrender.

It is our conviction that each one of us sometime or other is drawn by a hidden grace into a profound experience of God's presence within us. In the beginning this grace may be hidden, imperceptible, but gradually leading us to the Lord. Ordinarily the change will not be sudden and dramatic, but it will be compelling, drawing us away from selfishness to greater generosity. The process at times may be painful. We cannot tell when the Spirit will draw us in this manner or how often he will touch us, but always we must be open to his powerful presence.

The Carmelite who has accepted the call to follow Christ according to the spirit of the Order must be aware of the Lord's invitation to a life of intimacy. He or she must be open to the Spirit even in times of great dryness; even in the face of opposition or ridicule. The daily prayer of the Carmelite must be: "Here I am Lord, I have come to do your will." Do we have this attitude? It too is a grace of God, and if we should lack it, we can prepare for it. How can we prepare to be generous with the Lord? For a Carmelite there is a need to ask: What place does prayer play in my daily life? How can I strengthen my life of prayer? We learn to pray by praying, and one exercise that can help us is to practice the exercise of the presence of God. It comes with the highest recommendation from the saints and the spiritual writers. It has enjoyed a long tradition in the Carmelite Order. It has therapeutic as well as spiritual and apostolic value. For it not only brings calm and tranquillity to our frayed nerves, but leads to intimacy with Christ and awakens us to a desire to give ourselves more generously to the service of others. To paraphrase the spiritual writers: Whoever gives himself or herself to this exercise faithfully cannot fail to attain the holiness demanded by one's state in life.

1. The Presence of God

Anyone familiar with this exercise knows that it has nothing to do with "saying many prayers" or spending many hours in church. Rather it is an exercise that invites us first to realize that there is no time, no place, no circumstance in which we cannot be attentive to God. And if we learn to be attentive to him as to a loving, merciful Father, then we can learn to converse with him in a loving, friendly way. But can we be attentive to God constantly? Voices of experience tell us that we can. One such voice is St Therese as one of her sisters, Marie of the Sacred Heart, testified.

> Sister Therese loved God ardently and never ceased to think of him. One day I asked her: "What do you do in order to think of God always?"
> "It is not difficult," she replied; "we naturally think of someone we love."
> "Do you never lose his presence, then?" I asked.
> "Oh, no; I doubt if I have ever been three minutes without thinking of him.[9]

Interesting too is the testimony of St Paul of the Cross, founder of the Passionists.

> One day he said to his director, "If anyone should ask me at any time what I was thinking about, it seems to me that I could reply that I was thinking of God ... It seems to me impossible not to think of God,

since our spirit is wholly filled with God and we are entirely in Him."[10]

The saints may not have had great difficulty in thinking of God constantly, but that is not our experience. We know how frequently our minds wander even into absurd fantasies, but we also know that when our love for someone is very profound then our thoughts easily gravitate toward the beloved. A mother, for example, has no problem thinking of a seriously ill child. Our task then is to grow in the love of God, and we believe that the exercise of the presence of God can help us, for its purpose is to focus our attention on the Lord, so that we come to know him better, and gradually taste and see his goodness. Hence we recommend to all, and especially to Carmelites, this exercise. More specifically we suggest the following two ways to practice it: first, being attentive to God, our Father; second, fixing our eyes on Jesus, our Lord and Savior.

a. THE FIRST WAY

God lives and is present in all things and to all things. He sees and knows all things; nothing escapes his gaze. Therefore, we should walk in his presence as Abraham was told: "Walk in my presence and be blameless" (Gen 17:1). Elijah followed this pattern: "God lives, whom I serve" (1 Kgs 17:1). The Psalmist, filled with the same sentiments, breaks forth in song: "O Lord, you have probed me and you know me, you know when I sit and when I stand; you understand my thoughts from afar ... Where can I go from your spirit? From your presence where can I flee? If I go up to the heavens, you are there; if I sink to the nether world, you are present there. If I take the wings of the dawn, if I settle at the farthest limits of the sea, even there your hand shall guide me, and your right hand hold me fast" (Ps 139: 1-2, 7-10).

Nothing, absolutely nothing escapes the Lord's attention. He knows each one of us by name. "Nothing is concealed from him; all lies bare and exposed to the eyes of him to whom we must render an account" (Heb 4:13).

But this all-powerful and all-knowing God is merciful: "For I am the LORD your God, who grasp your right hand; it is I who say to you, 'Fear not, I will help you'" (Is 41:13). "Because you are precious in my eyes and glorious, and because I love you, I give men in return for you and peoples in exchange for your life. Fear not, for I am with you" (Is 43:4-5).

This merciful love of God is greater than that of a mother for her child. "Can a mother forget her infant, be without tenderness for the child of her womb? Even should she forget, I will never forget you. See, upon the palms of my hands I have written your name" (Is 49:15-16).

From the above we can conclude that scripture presents God as living, as ordaining all things intelligently and wisely, indeed lovingly. But human experience also bears this out. For example, scientists in their study of man and the universe bear eloquent witness to the divine presence in the universe. Einstein once stated: "I believe in [the] God who reveals himself in the orderly harmony of what exists."[11]

Sir John Eccles, a neurobiologist and a Nobel Prize winner, declared his belief in these words:

> There is a fundamental mystery in my existence transcending any biological account of the development of my body (including my brain with its genetic inheritance and its evolutionary origin); I see science as a supremely religious activity but clearly incom-

plete in itself. I also see the absolute necessity for belief in a spiritual world which is interpenetrating with and yet transcending what we see as the material world ... Similarly I believe that anyone who denies the validity of the scientific approach within its sphere is denying the great revelation of God to this day and age. To my mind, then, any rational system of belief involves the conviction that the creative and sustaining spirit of God may be everywhere present and active; indeed I believe that all aspects of the universe, all kinds of experience, may be sacramental in the true meaning of the term.[12]

But one of the most interesting accounts of a scientist's experience of divinity in the universe is the story of Edgar Mitchell, an astronaut, and the sixth man to land on the moon. Recalling this experience he writes:

But there was another aspect to my experience during Apollo 14, and it contradicted the 'pragmatic engineer' attitude. It began with the breathtaking experience of seeing planet Earth floating in the vastness of space. The first thing that came to mind as I looked at Earth was its incredible beauty. Even the spectacular photographs do not do it justice. It was a majestic sight, a splendid blue and white jewel suspended against a velvet black sky. How peacefully, how harmoniously, how marvelously it seemed to fit into the evolutionary pattern by which the universe is maintained. In a peak of experience, the presence of divinity became almost palpable and I knew that life in the universe was not just an accident based on random processes. This knowledge came to me directly, noetically. It was not a matter of discursive reasoning, of logical abstraction. It was an experiential cognition. It was knowledge gained through private subjective awareness, but it was—and still is—every bit as real as the objective data upon which, say, the navigational program or the communications system were based. Clearly, the universe had meaning and direction. It was not perceptible by the sensory organs, but it was there nevertheless—an unseen dimension behind the visible creation that gives it an intelligent design and that gives life purpose.[13]

There can be no doubt that here we find human experience in perfect harmony with scripture.

Whether we listen to the scriptures or to the scientists, the message is the same. God lives; he is all-powerful, all-wise, he "swings the world a trinket at his wrist." But the Maker and the Architect of the universe is not just a Transcendent Being who dazzles the mind, elicits our praise and thanksgiving; he is also rich in mercy and love. He chooses to enter into an intimate personal relationship with each of us. He is "our Father." In Jesus we find this revelation of the Fatherhood of God, the most profound mystery of our faith. Jesus had a unique relationship with God whom he called "Abba," Father. And this relationship runs through the gospels. The first words of Jesus recorded by the gospel were spoken to Our Lady and concerned the Father: "Did you not know that I must be in my Father's house?" (Lk 2:49); and his dying words were: "Father into your hands I commend my spirit" (Lk 23:46). During his ministry he would proclaim: "No one knows the Son but the Father, and no one knows the Father but the Son and anyone to whom the Son wishes to reveal him" (Mt 11: 27). And when asked by the apostles, "Lord, teach us to pray," Jesus responded: "When you pray, say: 'Father.'" (Lk 11:1-2) In the Nicene Creed we have this clear and explicit statement: "We believe in one Lord, Jesus Christ, the only Son of God, eternally begotten of the Father, God from God, Light from Light, true God from true God, begotten, not made, one in Being with the Father."

This unique relationship of the Son with the Father is shared by us in a limited way. Through his death and resurrection Jesus has redeemed us and raised us up to share in the divine life so that we become the adopted children of God: "The proof that you are sons is the fact that God has sent forth into our hearts the spirit of his Son which cries out 'Abba!' ('Father!')" (Gal 4:6; cf Rom 8:15). Because we are God's children we enter into a personal relationship with God and address him as "Abba," "Our Father" who art in heaven.

How many Christians experience this loving relationship to God our Father? How many are aware that he is rich in mercy and love, slow to anger, gentle and always forgiving? Do we really experience this loving presence of our Father in our daily life? If we do, then at any time of the day and in any place, under any circumstance we can turn to him confident that he listens. The slow and deliberate prayer of the "Our Father" that Jesus taught us can keep us in God's presence. For centuries hermits in the desert who could not read found the Our Father to be their daily psalter. Did they experience in their heart the fatherhood of God? If they did they found the pearl of great price, the kingdom of God that begins here on earth.

"To call God my Father and to know myself his child, that is heaven to me," writes St Therese in one of her poems. She was delighted to find confirmation of this personal experience in the scriptures: "Unless you change and become like little children, you will not enter the kingdom of God" (Mt 18:3). Herein lies the secret of holiness, and once she was convinced of this she made it her mission to teach it to others. Her little way is "the way of confidence and total abandon."[14]

If we pray for anything, it should be for the grace to experience our heavenly Father's merciful love so that we can give ourselves in complete surrender to his will. Once we experience our Father's mercy we shall turn to him often in our thoughts and live quietly in his presence. Once we experience this presence we need no rules; without effort we place ourselves in the hands of him whom we know loves us, and in bad times as well as good we trust in his merciful love.

b. THE SECOND WAY

Fix your eyes on Jesus Christ, our Lord and Savior.

We can walk in the presence of God our Father, but we can also turn to the Son of the Father, the Lord Jesus Christ, our Savior. The letter to the Hebrews encourages us to do this. "Since he [Jesus] was himself tested through what he suffered, he is able to help those who are tempted. Therefore, holy brothers who share a heavenly calling, fix your eyes on Jesus, the apostle and high priest whom we acknowledge in faith, who was faithful to him who appointed him" (Heb 2:18 - 3:1-2); "He is always able to save those who approach God through him, since he forever lives to make intercession for them" (Heb. 7:25). The exhortation is clear and compelling: Fix your eyes on Jesus. Why? He has suffered as we do and shows us how to bear suffering and cope with life. Moreover, he still lives and intercedes for us. Therefore at any moment of the day or night we can turn our hearts to him confidently, for he knows our needs. Indeed at any moment we can reach out to him who said "Follow me" to find inspiration, courage, guidance.

But how does one suceed in keeping the presence of Jesus constantly in one's thoughts? To recall the presence of the Lord we have pictures and statues of Jesus; we have crucifixes that we place in our homes, schools, hospitals and churches. These symbols call our attention to the Lord and his work of salvation. "There is no salvation in anyone else, for there is no other name in the whole world given to men by which we are to be saved" (Acts 4:12). Jesus should be before our eyes and in our hearts; his name should be on our lips.

St Teresa of Avila understood the value of images and paintings of the Lord. To her sisters she gave this advice:

> What you can do as a help in this matter [learning to be attentive to Christ] is try to carry about an image or painting of this Lord that is to your liking, not so as to carry it about on your heart and never look at it but so as to speak often with Him; for He will inspire you with what to say.[15]

Just how comforting and powerful an image or painting can be, especially in times of trial, came home to me when I visited the concentration camp of Auschwitz in Poland, where millions had been exterminated. In one of the small cells reserved for prisoners condemned to death by starvation, there before my eyes was the unmistakeable image of the Sacred Heart of Jesus scratched on the wall. The prisoner had used some blunt instrument to draw the figure of the Sacred Heart. Gazing on this image in that small cell that resembled an animal cage, I marvelled at this simple but eloquent profession of faith. Even in this worst of places the walls cried out: Jesus is Lord! I do not know who the prisoner was, nor did I ask. Perhaps his name is unknown, but his message was loud and clear. In loneliness and abandonment Jesus is our hope and comfort. I remembered the words of scripture: "Come to me, all you who are weary and find life burdensome, and I will refresh you" (Mt 11:28).

There is no doubt that the signs and symbols that we meet in daily life touch our hearts and influence our actions. A picture of Jesus can be an instrument of peace in our loneliness, of patience in our suffering, of courage in our fearfulness, of love in our temptation to hatred.

And if we learn to gaze often and fondly on Jesus, an inner transformation can take place that will show itself externally as we become outwardly like Jesus: patient, gentle, courageous and merciful. In other words, living in the presence of Jesus gradually brings us to become like him. We may even receive the special grace to desire to embrace joyfully the cross of Christ, and to live a life of suffering, a victim with Christ for the salvation of others. Did the prisoner of Auschwitz offer himself as a victim in union with Christ? We do not know. But we feel confident that in his solitary confinement, with only an image of the Sacred Heart for company, he experienced the peace that Christ promised his disciples.

If the image of the Sacred Heart can bring growth in faith and hope, so also can a crucifix. A friend once confided that in times of great stress he goes aside and takes the crucifix in hand and quietly gazes on the Lord. He does this for about fifteen minutes. Invariably his experience has been that all resentment toward others passes away; he becomes calm and enters into a more personal relationship with the suffering Christ. In a word, he found this prayer had three effects. First, it was therapeutic. It brought calm and peace to his troubled nature; any rebellious feeling gradually faded away. Second, he felt more in union with Christ, better prepared to carry his cross and to face up to his responsibilities. Third, he felt better prepared to serve Christ in others, even in those who seemed most disagreeable and were often the cause of his anxieties and stress.

Besides using images of Christ and the crucifix there are many other practices that help us to live each day in the presence of Jesus. For example, some make it a practice to pause during their daily work, even hourly, to reflect on the presence of the Lord. They turn their thoughts to him as he dwells within them with the Father and Holy Spirit.

In this they follow a practice pleasing to St Teresa and St John of the Cross. The latter informs us:

> It should be known that the Word, the Son of God, together with the Father and the Holy Ghost, is hidden by His essence and His presence in the innermost being of the soul ...
>
> God, then, is hidden in the soul, and there the good contemplative must seek Him with love, exclaiming: "Where have You hidden ...?"[16]

Very often those who seek to walk with Jesus throughout the day speak to him in short prayers called "aspirations." Such prayers appeal to those engaged in domestic tasks or works of manual labor that do not require intense concentration. They are most suitable for the elderly who find they cannot engage in profound meditation. The sick too find them helpful.

2. The 'Jesus Prayer'

One form of aspirational prayer that has once again found acceptance is the Jesus Prayer. It is an ancient Christian practice that comes down to us especially through the desert fathers. It is expressed in the more or less classical formula, "Lord Jesus Christ, Son of God, have mercy upon me, a sinner." It is a beautiful prayer that acknowledges that Jesus is our Lord and God, that we are sinners and need his healing grace, and that we believe he is truly in us and with us. It can be repeated often throughout the day and night. Not only has it had great success in the Eastern church, but many in the West also claim that it has been helpful in their spiritual growth.

In this way of prayer we center our minds and hearts on Jesus. In the beginning this prayer will be sporadic and more an act of faith than of love. With time it will become more frequent, more heartfelt, especially if at the same time we discipline ourselves, learning to control our thoughts, emotions and affections which incline us toward a worldly and sinful life.

Some spiritual writers speak of three stages in this prayer. First, it is a prayer practiced aloud, a prayer of the lips, and gradually it becomes more frequent and easier. In the second stage the prayer is more inward; it rises within our hearts even without a conscious act of our wills; it becomes more or less part of our daily life. Without effort we find ourselves saying "Lord, Jesus, be with us." In the third stage it enters into the very core of our being, into our heart, as they say, and becomes constant. In this final stage we have the perfection of prayer. The soul no longer strives to pray, for the Spirit of God within does the praying. There are no longer many acts; there is unceasing prayer. As can be seen this final stage is a pure gift of God. It is given to whom God wills to give it, but we can prepare for it by offering a pure and holy heart to God. There can be no unceasing prayer without purity of heart.

III. Conclusion

From the foregoing survey it is clear that there are different ways to walk in God's presence. True, there are others, and we are free to choose the way or ways that appeal to us. One way does not exclude the other. We can, for example, use images to recall the Lord's presence and at the same time employ aspirational prayer. These private exercises can in turn be a fitting preparation for deeper recollection when we enter into liturgical prayer in our community or parish.

One of the great dangers to avoid in this exercise is discouragement. Too often we are tempted to look for immediate success and there is none. We expect to "feel good" and this does not occur. This lack of immediate fruit should not deter or surprise us. Our only task is to believe and trust in God's goodness, awaiting patiently his good pleasure. Discouragement may also bore in on us from the outside; the spirit of secularization that pervades the social and political life of our towns and cities can touch us and slowly erode our faith in a loving Father.

Furthermore, the low level of public morality—which not only exists in our society but is even encouraged—can make us wonder whether our witness to the presence of God in the world is vain and foolish. In the face of such indifference and even hostility we need to meet the challenge: our prophetic witness is necessary. God is a living God; Jesus has risen from the dead, never to die again; and the Spirit has come upon us. We are not called to see the success of our ministry and much less to measure it. Our task, as the letter to the Hebrews tells us, is to fix our eyes on Jesus. But we must be prepared to pay the price of a prophet: we will often be rejected and insulted even by those we love and wish to help.

The lonely and abandoned prisoner of Auschwitz was deprived of the beauty, grace and comfort that comes from participation in the Eucharistic liturgy, yet he found a way to keep the memory of Jesus before him. The image of the Sacred Heart scratched on the wall became for him a means to live in the presence of the Lord. It is the living and merciful Jesus who gave him hope, strength and consolation when the powers of darkness threatened to destroy him.

As we face the powers of darkness, surely not as powerful and evil as in Auschwitz, we need not fear. As we struggle to be witnesses of the living God we need not be concerned whether our modest impact on society will be felt. In calling us God has not asked us to be successful, but only to live in his presence and serve him. Our vocation like that of Elijah is to be a prophetic witness. "God ... lives, whom I serve." Like Elijah we must be content to proclaim the message with our life. Our task, like his, is to sow the seed and to leave the fruit to God's good time. We will do this if we make our heart a garden where we strive to cultivate the presence of the living God.

IV

Long afterward, in the third year, the Lord spoke to Elijah. "Go, present yourself to Ahab," he said, "that I may send rain upon the earth." So Elijah went to present himself to Ahab.

Now the famine in Samaria was bitter, and Ahab had summoned Obadiah, his vizier who was a zealous follower of the Lord. When Jezebel was murdering the prophets of the Lord, Obadiah took a hundred prophets, hid them away fifty each in two caves, and supplied them with food and drink. Ahab said to Obadiah, "Come, let us go through the land to all sources of water and to all the streams. We may find grass and save the horses and mules, so that we shall not have to slaughter any of the beasts." Dividing the land to explore between then, Ahab went one way by himself, Obadiah another way by himself.

As Obadiah was on his way, Elijah met him. Recognizing him, Obadiah fell prostrate and asked, "Is it you, my lord Eljiah?" "Yes," he answered. "Go tell your master, 'Elijah is here!'" But Obadiah said, "What sin have I committed, that you are handing me over to Ahab to have me killed? As the Lord, your God, lives, there is no nation or kingdom where my master has not sent in search of you. When they replied, 'He is not here,' he made each kingdom and nation swear they could not find you. And now you say, 'Go tell your master: Elijah is here!' After I leave you, the spirit of the LORD will carry you to some place I do not know, and when I go to inform Ahab and he does not find you he will kill me. Your servant has revered the LORD from his youth. Have you not been told, my lord, what I did when Jezebel was murdering the prophets of the LORD—that I had a hundred of the prophets of LORD, fifty each in two caves, and supplied them with food and drink? And now you say, 'Go tell your master: Elijah is here!' He will kill me!" Elijah answered "As the LORD of hosts lives, whom I serve, I will present myself to him today."

So Obadiah went to meet Ahab and informed him. Ahab came to meet Elijah, and when he saw Elijah, said to him, "Is it you, you disturber of Israel?" "It is not I who disturb Israel," he answered, "but you and your family, by forsaking the commands of the LORD and following the Baals. Now summon all Israel to me on Mount Carmel, as well as the four hundred and fifty prophets of Baal and the four hundred prophets of Asherah who eat at Jezebel's table." So Ahab sent to all the Israelites and had the prophets assemble on Mount Carmel.

Elijah appealed to all the people and said, "How long will you straddle the issue? If the LORD is God, follow him; if Baal, follow him." The people, however, did not answer him. So Elijah said to the people, "I am the only surviving prophet of the LORD and there are four hundred and fifty prophets of Baal. Give us two young bulls. Let them choose one, cut it into pieces, and place it on the wood, but start no fire. I shall prepare the other and place it on the wood, but shall start no fire. You shall call on your gods, and I will call on the LORD. The God who answers with fire is God." All the people answered, "Agreed!"

Elijah then said to the prophets of Baal, "Choose one young bull and prepare it first, for there are more

of you. Call upon your gods but do not start the fire."
Taking the young bull that was turned over to them,
they prepared it and called on Baal from morning to
noon, saying, "Answer us, Baal!" But there was no
sound, and no one answering. And they hopped
around the altar they had prepared. When it was
noon, Elijah taunted them: "Call louder, for he is a
god and may be meditating, or may have retired, or
may be on a journey. Perhaps he is asleep and must
be awakened." They called out louder and slashed
themselves with swords and spears, as was their custom, until blood gushed over them. Noon passed and
they remained in a prophetic state until time for offering sacrifice. But there was not a sound; no one
answered, and no one was listening.

Then Elijah said to all the people, "Come here to
me." When they had done so, he repaired the altar of
the LORD which had been destroyed. He took twelve
stones, for the number of the tribes of the sons of
Jacob, to whom the LORD had said, "Your name shall
be Israel." He built an altar in honor of the LORD
with the stones, and made a trench around the altar
large enough for two seahs of grain. When he had ar-
ranged the wood, he cut up the young bull and laid it
on the wood. "Fill four jars with water," he said, "and
pour it over the holocaust and over the wood." "Do it
again," he said, and they did it again. "Do it a third
time," he said, and they did it a third time. The water
flowed around the altar, and the trench was filled
with the water.

At the time for offering sacrifice, the prophet
Elijah came forward and said, "LORD, God of
Abraham, Isaac, and Israel, let it be known this day
that you are God in Israel and that I am your servant
and have done all these things by your command.
Answer me, LORD! Answer me, that this people may
know that you, LORD, are God and that you have
brought them back to their senses." The LORD's fire
came down and consumed the holocaust, wood,

stones, and dust, and it lapped up the water in the trench. Seeing this, all the people fell prostrate and said, "The LORD is God! The LORD is God!" Then Elijah said to them, "Seize the prophets of Baal. Let none of them escape!" They were seized, and Elijah had them brought down to the brook Kishon and there he slit their throats.

Elijah then said to Ahab, "Go up, eat and drink, for there is the sound of a heavy rain." So Ahab went up to eat and drink, while Elijah climbed to the top of Carmel, crouched down to the earth, and put his head between his knees. "Climb up and look out to sea," he directed his servant, who went up and looked, but reported, "There is nothing." Seven times he said, "Go look again!" And the seventh time the youth reported, "There is a cloud as small as a man's hand rising from the sea." Elijah said, "Go and say to Ahab, 'Harness up and leave the mountain before the rain stops you.'" In a trice, the sky grew dark with clouds and wind, and a heavy rain fell. Ahab mounted his chariot and made for Jezreel. But the hand of the LORD was on Elijah, who girded up his clothing and ran before Ahab as far as the approaches of Jezreel.

1 Kings 18

Elijah's
victory on Carmel

I N the third year of the drought that had ravaged the land God commanded Elijah to depart from the home of the Sidonian widow and to return to Israel. There the prophet informed King Ahab that the drought was about to end. But the coming of the rain would take place according to God's plan only after Ahab and his people had been brought to their knees, acknowledging that Yahweh alone was God in Israel.

In one of the most dramatic events recorded in the Bible Yahweh's victory is described in three acts: the preparation, the contest, and the consequences.

1. Act one: The preparation

Elijah is sent to meet Obadiah, the vizier of Ahab, who seems to be the first minister of state in the Kingdom of Israel. He is out foraging for food for the horses and mules of the royal stable. Where this meeting took place is not known. From the onset Obadiah, who had always been faithful to Yahweh, is confused and in fact frightened when Elijah asks him to inform Ahab of his presence and of his desire to speak with him. Obadiah seems not to trust the prophet: he is aware of his penchant to appear and disappear mysteriously. But the prophet assures him that he will not deceive him and will meet Ahab that very day. The arrangement is made and a stormy confrontation takes place. The king accuses Elijah of being "the disturber of Israel." The prophet retorts that the king and his family are the real cause of Israel's misery. To prove his case Elijah challenges the king to assemble the people with the prophets of Baal and of Asherah on Mount Carmel. There he will prove that the worship of Baal, permitted by the weak king, is an abomination and the true reason for Israel's woes. The king agrees.

2. Act two: The contest

Ahab assembles the prophets of Baal and the people. (A select group surrounding the royal family seems to be indicated, although Jezebel is absent.) Perhaps some pilgrims visiting the holy mountain were also present. The assembly gathers on Carmel. It is well to recall that this mountain was an abode of prehistoric man, where some 2,000 caves have been counted. It was considered a holy mountain by the pagans, and from time immemorial had been the domain of Baal (Baalism in its various forms involved nature worship). It is not known when the cult of Yahweh began there, but most likely it was sometime after the coming of King David or King Solomon. In the course of time it had become a holy mountain for the Israelites. Elisha, the successor of Elijah, would one day dwell there (2 Kgs 4:25). It also became a popular meeting place for the people where they gathered to celebrate the new moon and the sabbath (2 Kgs 4:23).

However even before this, in the time of Elijah we find on Carmel altars erected both to Baal and to Yahweh. It seems the people wanted to keep one foot in the faith of Baal and the other in the faith of Israel. But Baal seemed to prevail, for the altar of Yahweh had been destroyed, presumably by Jezebel (1 Kgs 18:30). In the eyes of Elijah this was intolerable. He would show the people once and for all that Yahweh is a jealous God. The people must stop vacillating. They must choose Baal or Yahweh. "If the Lord is God, follow him; if Baal follow him" (1 Kgs 18:21). This radical decision was not to the liking of the people: they remained silent. They would wait and follow the winner.

But Elijah went ahead with his plan, which was for him the will of Yahweh. Two sacrifices were to be offered: one on the altar of Baal, the other on the ruined altar of Yahweh rebuilt by Elijah. The contest began. First, the pagan prophets called on Baal to send fire (lightning) from heaven. Throughout the day they sang, they danced, they slashed themselves with swords and spears, but "no one answered, and no one was listening" (1 Kgs 18:29). At dusk they admitted defeat. Then Elijah prepared his sacrifice and called on Yahweh to send fire from above, and the Lord answered. Lightning came and consumed the holocaust, and the people cried out: "The Lord is God, the Lord is God" (1 Kgs 18:39).

This contest has always fascinated readers of the Bible; pilgrims and tourists visiting Carmel usually ask to see the place of sacrifice. They are guided to el-Muhraqa (Arabic for "place of burning") on the eastern slope of Carmel. It is here they are told that, according to a long-standing tradition, the sacrifice of Elijah took place.

The victory of Elijah over the prophets of Baal was the work of Yahweh. It was he who sent the lightning from heaven. Following the divine intervention Elijah ordered all the prophets, four hundred and fifty of them, to be slaughtered in the nearby river of Kishon. This bloody event may seem to us an act of brutal vengeance, a sheer gesture of fanaticism, but examined in its proper perspective it was not. For Elijah was complying with the law that imposed the death penalty on any act of apostasy. "Whoever sacrifices to any god, except to the LORD alone, shall be doomed" (Ex 22:19). And the book of Deuteronomy retains this provision; it even invokes the "ban," the total destruction of every living thing in a city that worshipped other gods (Dt 13:13-17).

3. Act three: The consequences

The victory of Yahweh was not complete with the sacrifice of Elijah and the slaughter of the pagan prophets. He who had closed the heavens had also forewarned that he would open them. True to his word, and in answer to the prayer of Elijah, a small cloud, the size of a man's hand (not foot as the Vulgate states), appeared in the sky rising above the sea. The promised rain was about to descend and Elijah, aware of this, warned Ahab (who perhaps had had a change of heart) to head for home without delay lest he be caught up in the torrent of rain. As a fitting conclusion to the victory Elijah himself ran triumphantly (perhaps ecstatically) before the chariot of the king and escorted him to his summer residence in Jezreel (this is now modern Zerin, about fifteen miles from el-Muhraqa).

I. Carmelite tradition

What message from the sacrifice of Elijah on Carmel does our tradition hand on to us? Strange as it may seem, Carmelite writers, unlike Jewish and early Christian writers, did not focus their attention on the contest between Elijah and the false prophets, but rather on the consequences of the victory, that is, on the cloud that appeared in the heavens. The reason for this is not difficult to find: in the Middle Ages the Carmelites were not challenged as Elijah was to defend the rights of the one true God, rather they were hard-pressed to defend their right to exist as a religious order. They were asked, often with hostility: Who are you? Where do you come from? Who is your founder? With their backs to the wall they had recourse to the Bible. They believed that both their identity and origin could be found in the raincloud rising above the sea and perceived by Elijah on Carmel. Since the biblical passage that recounts this incident has influenced the history and spirituality of Carmel more than any other Elijan biblical story, we shall repeat it here and then offer our reflections:

> [After the sacrifice on Carmel and the slaughter of the prophets of Baal] Elijah then said to Ahab. "Go up, eat and drink, for there is the sound of a heavy rain." So Ahab went up to eat and drink, while Elijah climbed to the top of Carmel, crouched down to the earth, and put his head between his knees. "Climb up and look out to sea," he directed his servant, who went up and looked, but reported, "There is nothing." Seven times he said, "Go look again!" And the seventh time the youth reported, "There is a cloud as small as a man's hand rising from the sea." Elijah said, "Go and say to Ahab, 'Harness up and leave the mountain before the rain stops you.'" In a trice, the sky grew dark with clouds and wind, and a heavy rain fell." (1 Kgs 18: 41-45a).

1. The Cloud, a symbol of Our Lady

The literal sense of this passage offers no problem. The cloud was a sign that the heavens were about to open and send a torrent of rain to end the dryness that had ravaged the parched land of Israel for three years. In this way God fulfilled his promise. But Christian commentators have gone beyond the literal sense and have come up with various spiritual interpretations. For example, some have seen the cloud as a symbol of the Lord Jesus, who would bring to the world a torrent of saving grace. Others perceive the cloud as a symbol of the cleansing waters of baptism. Carmelites adopted another interpretation: for them the cloud seen by Elijah contained the figure of a woman, the Virgin Mary. Thus the cloud became the key that opened the door to the understanding of Carmel's identity.

We do not know with certainty the author of this interpretation, found for the first time among Carmelites in the fourteenth century. However, the most complete version of the story is found in the *Institution of the First Monks*, the venerable document, so often cited in these pages, which binds us to our origins and helps us see from within the ideal of Carmel.[1]

Subsequent writers following the lead of the *Institution* repeated the story adding only cosmetic changes. The great fifteenth century exponent of the Carmelite point of view on Mary, Arnold Bostius (died 1499), wrote:

> Just as the cloud rose light and sweet from the bitter waters of the sea, so Mary came of our human race, yet was free of all sin, even from her origin.[2]

2. The legend of Elijah's vision

By the seventeenth century we have an accepted tradition in the Order, and the common version of the legend that influenced the whole Order thereafter is this: Elijah gazing at the rain cloud rising above the sea saw in it the figure of the Immaculate Virgin conceived without sin, who one day would be the mother of the Savior. Overwhelmed by the vision of this Virgin, he was inspired to make a vow of perpetual virginity. Later he recounted his mystical experience to his disciples secretly (there is no mention of this in scripture) and urged them to follow his example. Until then Elijah and his disciples had lived solitary lives of poverty and obedience, but from that time on they would add a vow of virginity. In this way monastic life came into being and was continued by the followers of Elijah and his successor Elisha down through the Old Testament. At the dawn of the Christian era, indeed at Pentecost, the hermits of Carmel, followers of Elijah, were converted to Christianity. They recalled the vision of the Virgin in the cloud granted to their father, and they recognized in Mary, the Mother of Jesus, the woman whom he had foreseen. Whereupon they chose Mary as their patroness, and they looked upon her as the ideal model of the purity of life to which they were called. This inspired them to cultivate devotion to the mysteries of her Immaculate Conception and virginal motherhood, and to call themselves the "Brothers of the Virgin Mary of Mount Carmel."[3]

Although this beautiful legend of the Middle Ages (a time in which legends abound) has no historical value, it would lose its true meaning if we saw in it only a charming story, the fruit of a fertile imagination. For its value is found in the spiritual message it contains, namely, that Carmelites in the

Middle Ages acknowledged Elijah as their spiritual father, one who had given them a way of life, and Mary was their patroness and perfect model of the way of life that consists in purity of heart.

II. Elijan-Marian devotion

The cloud rising above the sea and seen by Elijah on Mount Carmel remains as a symbol of devotion to Elijah and Mary even to this day. It is supported by a rich literature, many works of art, and the official acts of the Order. Writers who enjoy prestige in the Order vigorously and lavishly explained the mystery of Mary in the cloud. Paintings, frescoes and engravings appeared in many Carmelite churches and houses. And the official escutcheon of the Order *(Vexillum Carmelitanum)* witnessed to this tradition.

This official approval of the tradition deserves special consideration. The oldest known escutcheon of the Order was published in the Constitutions of 1499. It presents the mountain of Carmel surmounted by the Virgin Mary with the Child Jesus in her arms. She is clothed with the sun, the moon beneath her feet and a crown of stars upon her head (cf. Rv 12:1). Two texts surrounding the emblem of the Order inform us that Mary is the "Mother and Splendor of Carmel," and that Elijah and Elisha, are "the leaders of Carmel." The meaning is clear: Elijah and Elisha are the spiritual guides and the Virgin Mary is the ideal model who draws us to imitate her purity of heart that we may like her be worthy to enter intimacy with God. It is obvious that the artist was inspired by the story of Elijah's vision of Mary in the cloud.

Many other escutcheons have appeared with slight variations in other official documents of the

Order. However, with the passing of time the shield was radically changed[4] and the figures of the prophets and Mary appeared only symbolically, represented by three stars on brown and white fields, symbols of the mountain and the cloud; this emblem with some variations is still current in the Order today. However, we can only lament that many Carmelites today are not aware of the legend of Elijah's vision of Mary in the cloud. Indeed, they would be surprised to hear that their ancestors in the Middle Ages believed that the Order had its origin in the cloud rising above the sea.[5]

1. Our Lady of the Brown Scapular

Toward the end of the sixteenth century, during the Counter-Reformation, the iconography of Carmel underwent another change, and this was occasioned by the rise of the devotion to Our Lady of the Brown Scapular. As a result of this devotion, preached throughout Europe and South America, paintings and statues of Our Lady holding in her hand the brown scapular which she offers to St Simon Stock took the place of the images of Mary appearing to Elijah in the cloud. And in some places the feast of Our Lady of Mount Carmel was celebrated as the feast of Our Lady of the Brown Scapular. Gradually Carmelites too gave more attention to Mary, Mother of Carmel (bestower of gifts) than to Mary, Splendor of Carmel (model of purity). This is apparent to anyone who examines the contemporary writing and art of Carmel. For example, there are countless books and pamphlets in many languages in this century that promote the scapular devotion, whereas the vision of Elijah is noted only in passing. And while we have many paintings and statues of Our Lady of the Scapular in our churches, chapels and houses, there are few paintings of Elijah looking up at Mary wrapped in the cloud. Still she is for all Carmelites not only our mother, but the Splendor of Carmel, the Virgin Most Pure, who inspires our imitation. May our Carmelite nuns, devoted to a purely contemplative life, restore to us devotion to Our Lady Most Pure.

However, we cannot leave this subject without making reference to one successful and gratifying attempt to unite both aspects of this Carmelite tradition, Mary our Mother, and Mary, Splendor of Carmel. We refer to the 1948 painting by John Keating in the chapel of the Carmelite Spiritual Centre, Gort Muire, Dublin. In this painting we see Our Lady with the Child Jesus in her arms; she is standing on a cloud that rises above the sea near Mount Carmel. On the left of the mountain is Elijah looking up at Our Lady. On the opposite side is St Simon Stock receiving from her right hand the Brown Scapular, the sign of salvation. In this one picture two aspects of Marian devotion are brought together: Mary, the Splendor of Carmel, model of purity, and Mary, Mother of Carmel, bestower of gifts. But on closer inspection we perceive a summary of all the characteristic elements of Carmel. In the first place, we see Mount Carmel itself, the place of our origin, then the Virgin Mary, Mother and Patroness, Elijah the spiritual father, and finally St Simon Stock, the representative of all Carmelites, who are recipients of Mary's gifts and Elijah's spirit.

2. Origin of the Elijan-Marian tradition

At this point someone may ask: Does our Elijan-Marian tradition depend on the spiritual interpretation of the cloud seen by Elijah? In other words, if the legend of the vision of the Virgin had not been propagated in the Order, would we have had the Elijan-Marian devotion? The answer is yes. Our devotion and tradition are not founded on the legend. On the contrary, the latter grows out of the former. Long before the legend existed, the hermits of Carmel venerated Elijah and Mary; in the course of time the legend was created as a literary device to explain the devotion.

All this is made clear to us by a competent, contemporary historian. Writing on the origin of the Order he states:

> The site chosen for the hermitage, the fountain of Elijah [on Carmel], is worthy of note, for it was to have a profound influence on the subsequent history of the Order ... The hermits of Carmel must certainly have been aware of the peculiar appropriateness of the place they chose. They must also have been conscious of continuing the life Elijah had inaugurated in that very place.[6]

Migrating to Europe not many years after their foundation, the hermits brought with them this consciousness of their origin. This is clearly apparent from the *Constitutions* of London (1281), the oldest we possess. There we read that the Carmelites considered themselves to be the followers of Elijah through an uninterrupted succession. This understanding of their origin is the "seed from which issued over the centuries the luxuriant growth of the Elijan legend."[7]

Commenting on the origin of the Marian dimension of Carmel the same historian declares:

> From the account of a French pilgrim written about 1231 we know that the oratory in the midst of the cells [on Mount Carmel] was dedicated to the Blessed Virgin: ... In time the hermits of Mount Carmel became known as the "Brothers of Our Lady of Mount Carmel." As early as 1252 the term occurs in

papal documents, so it probably already enjoyed popular usage ... From these tiny seeds grew the wide-spreading tree of the Marian devotion of the Order.[8]

Based on this reliable testimony we conclude that the Elijan-Marian devotion has its historical roots not in the legend of the cloud but in the consciousness of the hermits on Carmel living near the fountain of Elijah at the beginning of the thirteenth century. There they were influenced by the life of the prophet to live in continual prayer. There they dedicated their little chapel to the Virgin Mary and placed themselves under her protection. In the course of time they brought their twofold devotion to Europe, and there it gave rise to many stories and legends. And as we have seen one of the more influential legends was that the Blessed Virgin had appeared to Elijah in the cloud. This story was handed down from generation to generation, and was commonly accepted as an historical fact. Because of this many believed that the Order of Carmel really began with the vision of the cloud, for it was then, they thought, that Elijah was inspired by the vision of Mary to begin monastic life.

Today we are told by our competent historians that the history of the Order began not with Elijah on Carmel, but with the hermits on Carmel organized under the Rule of St Albert. Still the legend of the cloud is a real treasure. It is a beautiful symbol of Carmel's devotion to Mary as the patroness and splendor of Carmel. It was most influential in the spread and enrichment of Marian devotion in Carmel. It inspired young religious to give themselves to a prayerful life after the example of Elijah, truly a spiritual father, and to a life of purity after the example of Mary. And even today we must admit that anyone who reflects on Elijah looking up at the Virgin in the cloud is reminded of his or her vocation to contemplation and purity of heart—a vocation symbolized in the raincloud, but not dependent on it. That is why we said earlier that of all the Elijan stories, the one that has had the greatest influence on the spirit of Carmel is the story of the cloud rising above the sea after Elijah's victory on Carmel. And this is one reason why in the revised liturgy of the Solemnity of Our Lady of Mount Carmel (July 16) the first reading in the Mass is taken from the story of the cloud found in the First Book of Kings.

One final thought: it is important to keep this Elijan-Marian devotion in proper perspective. It is not an end in itself. It is only a means, a way of life, not the goal to be attained. For the goal of our life is the same as that of all Christians. We are called to holiness, to purity of heart, to union and intimacy with Christ. Elijah's battle cry was "My God is Yahweh," and ours is "Our God is Jesus." Therefore, it is Jesus on whom we must fix our eyes. He is the summit of the mountain toward which we climb. But on our journey Elijah and Mary are our model companions and guides. With their assistance, the prayer and support of the faithful and our own cooperation, we hope to correspond to God's grace and attain that purity of heart which will dispose us to experience even in this life the consoling intimacy of the divine presence. God lives and we are conscious of his presence.

III. The meaning of the legend

From their beginning Carmelites looked to Elijah as a model of prayer. "Elijah was only a man like us, yet he prayed earnestly that it would not rain and no rain fell on the land for three years and six months. When he prayed again, the sky burst forth with rain and the land produced its crop" (James 5:17-18).

And they turned to the Virgin Mary as a model of purity of heart. "Rejoice, O highly favored daughter! The Lord is with you. Blessed are you among women" (Lk 1:28). "Mary said: I am the servant of the Lord. Let it be done to me as you say" (Lk 1:37).

This Elijan and Marian devotion which had its roots on Mount Carmel and developed down through the centuries was greatly enriched, as we have seen, by the legend that flourished in Carmel, namely that Elijah had a vision of the Virgin Mary in the raincloud over Carmel. For many centuries down to our own time Carmelites meditated on this story. They fixed their gaze on the Virgin Most Pure, the model they must imitate. They wore their white cloak, a symbol of her purity, as a sign of their own vocation to become pure in heart. Today as we reflect on this legend we ask: Does it have anything to say to us ? We think it does.

At this moment we have before us a beautiful engraving, the design of a Dutch artist, Abraham van Diepenbeke, who died in 1675. It depicts the scene from the legend of Elijah on Mount Carmel in which the prophet is clothed in a white cloak looking up ecstatically at the Immaculate Virgin Mary enveloped in a cloud that rises up from the Mediterranean Sea. Our Lady, Splendor of Carmel, is clothed with the sun, the moon beneath her feet and over her head a crown of stars (cf Rv 12:1).

What does the legend that inspired this engraving say to us? It is educational and inspirational: educational because it throws light on the Marian spirit that characterized the life of our ancestors from the Middle Ages. It informs us that they believed in the Immaculate Conception long before it was declared a dogma; that they honored Mary as the Virgin Most Pure; and, in particular, that they venerated her perpetual virginity which inspired them to a life of perfect continency.

But the legend is more than a lesson in the history of Marian devotion in Carmel. It is also even for us today, inspirational. For it challenges us to carry on this Marian tradition, to place ourselves under Mary's patronage; to imitate her complete dedication to the service of the will of God. To put it another way, the legend speaks out and proclaims: fix your eyes on the Virgin of Virgins; contemplate her purity of heart, her faith, hope, love, obedience, humility, chastity; imitate her total surrender to God's will; invoke her aid, for she intercedes for you at the right hand of her Son in heaven.

If we turn now to the prophet Elijah the legend is equally educational and inspirational. It teaches us that Carmelites in the fourteenth century recognized Elijah as their founder, and as a man dedicated to a life of perfect chastity. It recalls the words of the *Institution*: Elijah "gladly bound himself by perpetual virginity for God's sake and was the first man to do so."[9]

Today we may smile at this statement; but it is not without foundation, and it does have a message for us. Long before the Order of Carmel was established by the Albertine Rule, there was an ancient Jewish tradition that Elijah was a celibate. The scriptures do not clearly state this, but they do seem to imply it. For Elijah in the Bible is anything but a homebody: he has no wife, no children, no vineyard or farm to cultivate. He is very mobile; he comes and goes mysteriously. He is always in the service of the Lord, or running away to a deserted place. If he had a wife she was the most neglected of women! Relying on biblical and talmudic sources Elie Wiesel says of Elijah: "He has no particular profession; in fact, he is unemployed, homeless, and a bachelor."[10]

Early Christian writers adopted this Jewish tradition: St Ambrose bears witness to the celibacy of Elijah.[11] St Jerome states that not only Elijah, but his successor Elisha and many of the brotherhood of the prophets were celibates;[12] he also calls Elijah the "monk" of the Old Testament.

It should come as no surprise, then, that enriched with this knowledge of Jewish and Christian tradition, the Carmelites on Mount Carmel and their European successors came to see in Elijah the ideal celibate who had bound himself to a life of perfect continency.

Even today Carmelites can take inspiration from the life-style of Elijah. It matters little whether he was vowed to celibacy. What does influence us is that he lived the life of a celibate: he was heartloose and footloose; a man who stood constantly in God's presence ready to serve. In his solitary life he is a model that shows us how to bear up under fatigue, failure, discouragement. In every crisis he served the Lord with unswerving loyalty until at last he was taken up into heaven in a fiery chariot.

From these considerations it should be clear that Carmelites today as in the past can take inspiration and hope from the legend of Elijah's vision of the Virgin Mary in the cloud. In a word, the legend challenges us as it did our ancestors to fix our eyes on the Virgin Mary. Her life is not a legend. It is a reality. We are asked to contemplate the purity of Mary, her surrender to the will of God, and to be ready to give ourselves completely as she did to the service of the Lord.

Such a vocation makes many demands: we are asked to leave all to serve the Lord, and that includes a willingness to embrace a life of perfect chastity or, if living among the laity, to live chastely according to our state in life.

These thoughts lead us to the final lesson we would like to draw from the legend of the cloud. In doing this it is important to distinguish between the world of Elijah and ours. In his time Elijah had to confront the Israelites who were torn between faith in Yahweh and in false gods. Some were unwilling to choose; they were content with a sort of syncretism. Our world is different. There are some believers, but there are others who deny God's existence, or doubt his existence. Still others feel no religious stirrings and are indifferent. Again there are those who claim there is no need of God since the positive sciences explain all things. In this confused theological atmosphere there has arisen a substantial increase in social problems among young people in almost every category: suicide, crime, alcoholism, drug abuse, venereal disease, pregnancy outside of marriage. In such a world a life of chastity for the love of God has little or no meaning. Yet in our hearts we feel called to challenge this secular humanism, much as Elijah challenged the idolatry of his day. But do we have the faith and the courage to embrace a life of chastity? When the world around us sneers at chastity and tells us that the church imposes upon her people an inhuman sexual ethic, what place are we willing to give to a life of chastity in Carmel? What answer do we have for the public and social attitude that prevails among us, namely, that any form of sexual expression is all right as long as it is done with consent?

In the reflections that follow we shall have perfect chastity in mind, that is, chastity until death, but much that will be said can be applied to those who have no vow, but strive to live chastely according to their state in life.

1. Chastity

In the first place, let it be said that by chastity we mean the virtue that regulates the sexual appetite in all human beings, both the married and the single. It would seem that all societies admit the need for some sexual moderation. Among Christians, however, there is an added motive to be chaste. From the moment of baptism they become temples of the Holy Spirit. By this fact they are sacred, and should therefore be pure in body and mind. "You are not your own. You have ben purchased, and at a price! So glorify God in your body" (1 Cor 6:19-20).

Some have freely chosen perfect chastity—that renounces all genital pleasure—as a state of life.

> Innumerable is the multitude of those who from the beginning of the Church until our time have offered their chastity to God. Some have preserved their virginity unspoiled, others after the death of their spouse, have consecrated to God their remaining years in the unmarried state, and still others, after repenting their sins, have chosen to lead a life of perfect chastity; all of them at one in this common oblation, that is, for love of God to abstain for the rest of their lives from sexual pleasure.[13]

2. Love: motive of chastity

Obviously such an offering is primarily an act of love: a turning of the whole person to God to please him in everything. Nothing but love is a worthy motive for such a total surrender of self. But this love has its roots in faith by which one believes in Jesus as Lord, and surrenders in faith and trust to him. It is founded also on hope, that the God of mercy who has given one this desire for chastity will in his merciful love grant also all the graces necessary to preserve it. This free, total offering of self is only a beginning. A constant struggle ensues to grow more firm in one's commitment. It is a lifelong process in which one grows in intimacy and fidelity to Christ, determined to share with him one's total self.

We insist on love for God, love for Christ—who is God incarnate—as the motive for a dedicated life of perfect chastity. Any other motive is insufficient. This is not to say that celibacy chosen in order to be free to dedicate one's whole life to apostolic work for Christ is not praiseworthy. Indeed it is. But apostolic ministry in itself does not demand a celibate life, although it may greatly facilitate one's ministry; there are many married couples who are engaged in effective ministry. In fact, it is in and through their married status that they have found a strong love for God that motivates them to serve others unselfishly. What we wish to say is that celibate life is not necessary for ministry. Ministry, therefore, is not the primary motive for the choice of perfect chastity; the love for God is. We choose celibacy primarily to please God, to offer ourselves to him as an act of adoration and love. And we do this in response to the call we experience within us. It is this love for God that fills our hearts and overflows in love for others: to love Christ totally means to love as he loved, and he so loved us that he laid down his life for us. Having given ourselves to the Lord, we are then free to serve him wherever we are called and in whatever ministry that is given us.

3. Renunciation

Although the resolve to be chaste is a positive giving of self, it demands the renunciation of the threefold satisfaction of the married state: the use of

117

genital sex, marital companionship, and physical parenthood. All these satisfactions are good, and the fact that they are cherished by most people—and highly esteemed in the scriptures—brings out not only how costly this self-denial is, but how generous must be the love that motivates it. Such love freely given is not common. Indeed it cannot be acquired; it is a gift of the Holy Spirit, and the response to it must be free. Speaking of this gift Jesus declared: "Some there are who have freely renounced sex for the sake of God's reign. Let him accept this teaching who can" (Mt 19:12). In other words, it is because of Jesus that we choose celibacy: to be one with him in whom the reign of God exists. We wish to share more intimately in his way of life; to follow the way he lived on earth.

4. No half-hearted love

From the above it follows that anyone who wishes to promise or vow perfect chastity has no business entering this state if the offering is half-hearted. Just as anyone who enters marriage half-heartedly is doomed to travel a rocky road that more than likely will end in divorce, so also one who vows perfect chastity half-heartedly will experience trials, frustrations and sadness that eventually may lead to a request for a dispensation. Half-way devotion in married or vowed celibate life is a contradiction in terms. The Carmelite, therefore, should embrace his or her celibate life freely, whole-heartedly, or not at all. How wrong, how selfish, then, the Carmelite who would justify his or her sacrifice of married life by indulging in good living, expensive vacations, private pleasures, under the pretext that he or she deserves some compensation. Worse still is the Carmelite who finds no joy in the gift of self. A joyless giver has no place in religious life. St Teresa was fond of saying: from sour-faced saints deliver us, O Lord.

This is not to say that to choose this state is to choose a bed of roses. On the contrary, it means to accept the reality of hardship, to be ready to live a somewhat austere life. It means to embrace the cross, and Pope Pius XII did not hesitate to call lifelong celibacy a form of martyrdom.[14] Even so, if joy, the sign of vitality, is missing from the lives of Carmelites they will not only live a life unworthy of human beings, they will also repel rather than attract those who need to hear the good news of Jesus Christ.

5. Celibacy and friendship

At this point someone might interject that a joyful life demands human friendship. But is there any place for friendship in celibate life? The true celibate will have no difficulty entering into friendship. Celibacy even fosters friendship. Indeed, one of the legitimate compensations of religious life is the true friendship that exists among the members of a community; members of a community offer moral support to one another. They create family. When St Teresa founded her first convent of St Joseph in Avila, one of the conditions laid down was that the sisters join in friendship. The sisters understood this to mean that they were to love one another and be loved; that there were to be no cliques among them, no exclusive groups, but only genuine affection fostered toward all. For this reason St Teresa insisted on founding small communities, for in large communities friendship would not be possible. Listen to her own words:

... in this [community] where there are no more than thirteen—nor must there be any more [the number was to be increased to twenty-one]—all must be friends, all must be loved, all must be held dear, all must be helped.[15]

And in her letters St Teresa does not make a secret of her love for others. Here is one example from a letter to Sister María de San José:

It was a great comfort to me to get your letter, not that it is anything new, for your letters rest me as much as other people's letters weary me. I assure you that, if you love me dearly, I for my part return your love and like you to tell me of yours. How unmistakable a trait of our nature is this wish for our love to be returned! Yet it cannot be wrong, for Our Lord wishes it too ...[16]

In letter to Ana de Jesús, Prioress of Beas, writing about St John of the Cross, she states: "He is indeed the Father of my soul and one of those with whom it does me most good to have converse."[17]

It is friendship fostered in religious communities that is the great support of chastity. The Second Vatican Council understood and encouraged this when it stated:

Above all everyone should remember—superiors especially—that chastity has stronger safeguards in a community when true fraternal love thrives among its members.[18]

From the above one should not conclude that friendship should be confined to members of one's own community. Ordinarily friendship will begin there, but will go beyond to those with whom we collaborate in work, or with whom we serve in ministry, or even with some whose paths we cross at chance meetings. As is obvious these friendships will have various degrees of intensity, not excluding—with one or another—a warm, intimate relationship that can enhance our prayer, community living, ministry, and our union with God.

6. *The voice of experience*

Those of us who have lived in various Carmelite communities have experienced the value of true friendship. Looking back we can truthfully say that not only has God given us the gift of perfect chastity but he has given us the gift of community life to support it. The friends we have known and have cherished, especially those within our Carmelite community, have been a steadying influence and a source of joy in our service in the church. Consequently, the consecrated chastity that we have experienced in Carmel and that we believe is the shared experience in other religious communities, is a clear and eloquent witness to the Western world that there is no genuine psychological or biological need for genital pleasure. This testimony is an answer to those who say perfect chastity is impossible. It is impossible for those who rely on their own efforts, or who instead of recognizing the need of self-denial seek every form of pleasure, influenced as they are only by the social, public attitude of a secular society. But for those who are given the gift of celibacy and who respond freely to it, it is not only possible but joyful, and, as we shall see, fruitful.

7. *Chastity is productive*

There is nothing sterile about perfect chastity. On the contrary it is fruitful, because it is not only a gift of grace that inspires us to offer our lives to

Christ, and thus grow in holiness through intimacy with him, but it is also a charism for the good of the church. Through this gift we are moved to love others and to serve all our brothers and sisters as Christ did. Free from the cares of married life we are free to serve wherever God calls. We may be drawn to an apostolate of prayer and sacrifice, that is, to the purely contemplative life, a life of faith in which we do not see the fruit of our labor. Again, we may be called to one of the many forms of active ministry. Indeed it is a fact that works of charity are often the field of consecrated persons. They labor among men, women and children of every age and condition. They labor lovingly and therefore unselfishly, to alleviate poverty and suffering, but above all to bring the poor to a knowledge and love of Christ. In this way they help to lead them to share in the life of the church through the sacrament of baptism in which they become new creatures, children of God and the heirs of heaven. In a word, consecrated chastity is not only a sign of holiness in the church, it is productive of holiness in others; it is life-giving and knows no limits.

IV. Conclusion

In exhorting Christians to live a chaste life after the example of Christ, the church has recommended prayer to the Blessed Virgin Mary. She was the first and most faithful disciple of Christ. It is to her intercession and protection that all Christians are asked to hasten, for in the experience of the church "never was it known that anyone who sought her aid and protection was left unaided."

As we have just seen, Carmelites have always been faithful to this tradition. From their first days on Carmel they cultivated devotion to Mary as their patroness. And in the course of time they profited from the legend of Elijah's vision of the Virgin in the cloud. It strengthened their love for her. Today we acknowledge that the Elijan vision of the Virgin is a legend, but we readily accept the message that this legend teaches: namely, the truth, founded in the Bible, that Mary is the model for all Christians. She is the Virgin Most Pure whose heart belongs completely to God. Consequently, we too fix our eyes on Mary as our ancestors did. We learn from her. She is the Splendor of Carmel, the Virgin Most Pure.

Today as in the past we Carmelites are Elijan and Marian. We follow the example of the solitary, celibate Elijah who stood always in God's presence ready to serve, and we place ourselves under the patronage of Mary, the model of purity of heart and, in a special way, of consecrated chastity.

As we strive each day to be faithful to this vocation we ask our heavenly Mother and Patroness to intercede for us that we may truly be witnesses of God's presence in the world as Elijah was, and an example for all God's people. May our life be for them a sign to look beyond the horizon of this world to the kingdom of love, peace and justice that awaits those who live and die in God's friendship.

V

*Ahab told Jezebel all that Elijah had done—that he
had put all the prophets to the sword. Jezebel then
sent a messenger to Elijah and said, "May the gods
do thus and so to me if by this time tomorrow I have
not done with your life what was done to each of
them." Elijah was afraid and fled for his life, going to
Beer-sheba of Judah. He left his servant there and
went a day's journey into the desert, until he came to
a broom tree and sat beneath it. He prayed for death:
"This is enough, O LORD! Take my life, for I am no
better than my fathers." He lay down and fell asleep
under the broom tree, but then an angel touched him
and ordered him to get up and eat. He looked and
there at his head was a hearth cake and a jug of
water. After he ate and drank, he lay down again, but
the angel of the LORD came back a second time,
touched him, and ordered, "Get up and eat, else the
journey will be too long for you!" He got up, ate and
drank; then strengthened by that food, he walked
forty days and forty nights to the mountain of God,
Horeb.*

1 Kings 19:1-8

Elijah's flight to Horeb

As we have seen in the previous chapter not "all Israel" was present on Carmel to witness the contest between Elijah and the prophets of Baal. It was rather a select group that in the name of Israel proclaimed that Yahweh is God. That this select group did not represent all the people, Elijah was to learn on returning to the king's palace at Jezreel. For Queen Jezebel, the patroness of the Baals, was furious when Ahab told her of the slaughter of the prophets on Carmel. She vowed that Elijah would meet the same fate. Baalism, as far as she was concerned, would continue in Israel. That she succeeded can be clearly seen from the gathering of worshipers of Baal in Samaria some years later during the reign of Jehu, former commander of the army of Ahab. Jehu was an enemy of Baalism and trough trickery brought together all the devotees of Baal in the temple at Samaria. While they were at worship he had them all massacred. "Thus Jehu [not Elijah] rooted out the worship of Baal from Israel" (2 Kgs 10:28).

But to return to Elijah, flushed with his victory on Carmel, we find that, having been informed in Jezreel of Jezebel's threat to kill him, he fled the city. His flight took him south though Judah to Beersheba, a distance of some one hundred and twenty miles. Beersheba was a city and oasis of the Negeb, today called Bir-es-seba. It has a memorable history. Among other things it was there that God had renewed his promise to Abraham and Isaac (Gn 26:23-24). Throughout the history of Israel until the exile, Beersheba was the southern limit of Israelite territory and indeed of its territorial ambitions (2 Sm 17:11 ff). It was in this city that Elijah left his servant and, discouraged, threw himself down under a tree—a broom tree that is common in the desert and is more like a large shrub, never growing more than ten feet tall, with long branches, small leaves and yellow and white flowers. It still flourishes in the desert and offers shade to the nomads.

As we contemplate the pitiful state of Elijah lying under the broom tree we notice that his flight is motivated by fear and not by the command of the Lord. This is in sharp contrast with his first flight from the anger of Ahab, whom he had denounced for his idolatry and to whom he had foretold that in punishment for his wickedness Israel would suffer from a long drought. At that time it was the Lord who command him to "go east and hide in the Wadi Cherith." Later it was the Lord who told him "to move on to Zarephath," and again when the time came for the contest on Carmel and the end of the drought it was the Lord who said: "Go show yourself to Ahab." But now when he flees from Jezebel there is no command of the Lord. The prophet seems to be motivated by despair: "Elijah was afraid and fled for his life" (1 Kgs 19:3).

Arriving in the desert he is a broken man, physically, emotionally, perhaps spiritually. He has no will to live. Is this the same man who defied King Ahab, who miraculously supplied food for the widow of Zarephath, who prayed to God and restored her son to life, and who brought fire down from heaven on Carmel? How the mighty one has fallen! From the heights of his stupendous victory over the prophets of Baal he has tumbled into the valley of darkness. Did fear rob him of his power of discernment? Scripture doesn't say, and the commentators do not agree.

In the desert Elijah pleads with the Lord to take his life. It seems he had lost hope, because he had failed to convert Israel to Yahwism. But why had he lost hope? According to one commentator, the reason for his despair was that he was convinced that the pure faith of Yahwism was doomed to extinction in Israel.[1] For Elijah to live in Israel where Yahweh was no longer the one living God was intolerable. It was better to be dead.

But Elijah was shortsighted. In God's plan Israel would not be lost to the worship of idols. Indeed, the mission of Elijah must continue. He was to have a hand in preserving the true faith, but he did not know this as he fell asleep under the broom tree, hoping that he would never again see the light of day.

God's ways are not our ways and in the course of time the prophet was awakened by an angel who offered him a jug of water and a hearth cake. After he ate and drank he fell back to sleep, only to be aroused again by the angel who gave him food and drink with the command to get up "else the journey will be too long for you." Refreshed by the repast Elijah arose and walked forty days and forty nights to the mountain of God, Horeb. We understand the forty days and nights as symbolic, since he could easily have walked the distance of some two hundred miles in less than forty days.

What was the reason for the journey? The Bible does not say, but we know that Horeb is another name for Sinai, and that it was on this mountain that the Lord had revealed himself to Moses. Could it be that Elijah sought the Lord on the mountain to pour out his troubles? It would seem so, for this is exactly what he did once he arrived there.

As we look back and reflect on Elijah lying under the tree we ask: what kind of man was he? He was a poor, weak human being. He was filled with fear of the woman Jezebel, and his escape to the desert left him exhausted. Moreover, he appears overwhelmed by the darkness of despair: he had failed in his mission. Again, he suffered from disillusionment at the hands of his own people who had continued to waver in their worship of the one true God. Finally, he saw no hope for the future of Yahwism in Israel. Overwhelmed by so much adversity he cried out: "This is enough, O LORD. Take my life, for I am no better than my fathers" (1 Kgs 19:4).

However in this his darkest hour the Lord did not forsake him. He sent an angel to feed, comfort and strengthen him for his journey to the holy mountain. Once again Elijah enjoyed the comforting experience that Yahweh lives, and will not be daunted.

By way of summary two things stand out in this story of Elijah: the sense of failure that gripped the prophet, and the subsequent revelation that the Lord was still at his side. In his own eyes Elijah felt that Israel was lost to Yawheh. In Yahweh's eyes this was not so. To give courage to the fallen prophet an angel of light visited him, fed him, and then sent him on his way to meet the Lord himself on Horeb. There the prophet would receive his new mission for Israel.

I. Carmelite Tradition

In the four previous chapters we have shown that well-defined traditions have been handed down in Carmel, and in all these Elijah stands out as the model, that is, the ideal contemplative and the faithful servant of the Lord.

Now, as we contemplate Elijah's flight into the desert the whole picture changes. No longer do we recognize the fiery prophet standing radiantly in God's presence and ready to serve. Rather we come face to face with a tired, discouraged, broken old man who longs to die as he falls asleep under a broom tree. Surely in this forlorn state Elijah is no longer the model for the Carmelite.

But let us not be too hasty in our judgment. For this crisis in Elijah's life, so important for his own prophetic development, teaches us a most salutary lesson. It forewarns that the life of the disciple will be no better than that of the master. The journey of the Carmelite, like that of his spiritual father, will be rough and rocky. Trials, afflictions, stress, failure will dog the life of the Carmelite. The desert experience of Elijah will be shared by the disciple. There is no escape from suffering.

Yet all his not lost. Suffering—as in the case of Elijah—can be purifying. Under the broom three he underwent a conversion. He died to all that was selfish in himself and rose transformed by the grace of God. In his hour of deep distress the Lord sent him a comforting angel. Replenished by food and drink and guided by the command of his heavenly consoler, he went forth to meet the Lord. In the desert God was not absent, he was only hidden, and Elijah learned that self-reliance is self-defeating. By himself he was incapable of serving the Lord, but with divine grace he was a new man with a renewed mission.

From this desert experience of the father of Carmel we too learn that in our trials the Lord is always present; that he never abandons us. By ourselves we are useless servants, but with his grace we can serve faithfully. And so the desert experience of the prophet of Carmel encourages us to place our trust and confidence in the Lord and not in ourselves.

Did Carmelites understand this? Does tradition tell us that they found in the flight of Elijah a lesson for their own lives? We believe it does. A brief survey of the literature, the art and the liturgy of Carmel will help to confirm this.

1. Literature

One would expect that the logical place to find a meditation on the trial of Elijah in the desert would be in the *Institution of the First Monks*, that splendid spiritual reading book that inspired Carmelites especially from the fifteeth century. It presents, as we have seen, Elijah as the ideal model of the Carmelite. While it does point out the obstacles that the young Carmelite will encounter on his journey to purity of heart, and strongy encourages perseverance, it makes no mention of the crisis that afflicted Elijah in the Sinai desert; it centers only an his experience at the Wadi Cherith.

Nevertheless, the silence of the *Institution is* compensated by later Carmelite writers. Two of the better known, John Baptist de Lezana, a Spaniard (d. 1659), and Daniel of the Virgin Mary, a Belgian (d. 1687), wrote "lives" of Elijah. The former relates Elijah's flight to the desert and his journey to Horeb without any special comment. The latter, although not a professional historian and lacking in critical sense,[2] offers a more detailed explanation substantiated by various authorities. For example, he points out that certain Fathers (Saints Ambrose and Basil) interpret the flight of Elijah not so much as fear of Jezebel but as fear that death at her hands would be the end of the true faith in Israel, since he believed he alone remained of the prophets. In this he was mistaken. For Obadiah had claimed to have hidden true prophets of Yahweh in caves (1 Kgs 18:13), and among the people there were thousands "who had not knelt to Baal or kissed him" (1 Kgs 19:18).

Daniel also refers to the commentary of Cornelius de Lapide (d. 1637), a highly esteemed Jesuit who for forty years enlightened and delighted his students first at Louvain and then at Rome with his lively lectures on scripture. Cornelius sees the spiritual dereliction of Elijah in the desert as foreshadowing the agony of Christ in Gethsemani. He also refers to the food and drink given by the angel to Elijah as a figure and symbol of the Eucharistic banquet. The writings of Daniel contained in his *Speculum Carmelitanum*,[3] widely diffused in the Order, certainly helped the Carmelites to grow in a knowledge of their father Elijah. They would also take comfort in the fact that as Elijah was strengthened by the food of the angel, so Christians are strengthened by the body and blood of Christ in the Eucharist.

Coming closer to our own time we have the story of the prophet retold to us in the book on Elijah written by the former Prior General of the Order, Elias Peter Magennis (d. 1938).[4] The author tells the story in a lively fashion, offering his own insights as well as those of commentators, often unnamed. He discusses the flight of Elijah diffusively in two chapters[5] and informs us that the reason for Elijah's flight was the conviction that he had failed in his mission to exterminate Baalism from Israel.

For this reason he left his servant in Beer-sheba and went alone into the desert. "His pilgrimage into the desert to find out the reason of his failure was to be made in the company of no mortal."[6] His utter desolation in which he asked to die, says Magennis, is "a prefiguring of the loneliness and the abandonment of the God-man in the days that preceded and accompainied His agony."[7]

Commenting on the repast offered by the angel the same writer tells us that Elijah saw in this divine gesture a sign that he was still the messenger of the Lord. Without further hesitation he set out for Horeb to fulfill his new mission whatever it might be. Magennis also reminds us that commentators saw in the bread offered by the angel a figure of the Holy Eucharist. While he does not mention his sources one feels he is faithful to the Carmelite tradition found in the writings of Daniel of the Virgin Mary.

In his delightful book on the prophets, *The Road to Freedom*,[8] Carlos Mesters, O. Carm., a competent contemporary scripture scholar whose books and pamphlets have been widely used in the pastoral renewal programs in Brazil since the 1970's, has a charming chapter on Elijah under the juniper tree as

> the image of the man who still believes in God. He has not lost his faith. But he does not know how to stand up to this new crushing reality and still hold on to faith. It seemed an unreal and alienating faith which was without a true answer to the problems of the day. On account of this he abandoned the battlefield, not so much from cowardice but from incapacity, not knowing what to do.[9]

In other words, Elijah felt he had failed: he could only hope to die, for he was a useless servant.

But his prayer to die was not answered, for God had other plans. As Mesters tells us, God gave Elijah what everyone needs in a time of great discouragement and confusion: his enlightening and comforting grace. "Divine assistance showed itself in the form of an angel coming to comfort and advise him."[10] Strengthened by the food of the angel, Elijah set out for Sinai-Horeb, where he sought God whom he knew had once spoken on the same mountain to Moses. Writers like Mesters help Carmelites and others to find in Elijah's trial in the desert reason for hope in times of crisis. God may be hidden from us, but he is never absent.

2. Art

The familiar stories of Elijah were expressed in paintings, frescoes and engravings as we have mentioned. The scene of the flight into the desert is no exception. We recall the frescoes of Gaspard Dughet, a Frenchman, that adorn the Carmelite church of San Martino ai Monti in Rome.[11] His unusual landscapes of the life of Elijah are said to be unique in church decorations. He has given us in painting what others have expressed in writing. Nor can we overlook the drawings of Abraham van Diepenbeke in the *Speculum Carmelitanum* of Daniel of the Virgin Mary: among this series of remarkable drawings we find Elijah being comforted by the angel in the desert. This drawing, no doubt, has been the object of many meditations in Carmel.

However, even when the whole series of Elijah events was not depicted, the desert scene was often singled out for special attention in paintings and frescoes, especially in European Carmelite churches. Some of these are brought to our notice by Joachim Smet especially in his excellent chapters on "The Fine Arts in Italy and Spain" and "The Fine Arts in the Ultramontane Provinces."[12] Louis Réau in his article "L'Iconographie du Prophète Élie"[13] mentions that the Belgian Carmelites in the eighteenth century decorated the pulpits and communion rails of their churches with the angel bringing food to Elijah in the desert. Although many of these fine works of art have disappeared, still to this day one can see in many Carmelite churches and chapels (and in other churches as well) the scene of Elijah and the angel in the desert. This scene, so rich in symbolism, is a constant reminder in a secularized world that God in his own way will always make his presence felt.

3. Liturgy

Perhaps the liturgy more than the literature and the art in Carmel kept before the religious the spiritual meaning of Elijah's desert flight. For example, the feast of Corpus Christi celebrated before the revised liturgy of the Second Vatican Council, saw in the feeding of Elijah by the angel a figure of the Eucharistic banquet that strengthens us, and especially the dying, on the journey to God. The response for the third lesson of Matins on the feast itself, and on the Sunday, Monday and Thursday within the Octave, read: "He [Elijah] looked and there at his head was a hearth cake and a jug of water—he got up, ate and drank; and then strengthened by that food he walked to the mountain of God" (1 Kgs 19:6,8).

But it is on the feast of St Elijah that the desert scene is portrayed with solemnity. A Mass in honor of St Elijah appears in the Carmelite missal for the first time in 1551. The introit recalls the flight of Elijah to the desert. A later edition of the missal (1587), after the Council of Trent, places the scene of the angel feeding Elijah in the postcommunion prayer as a symbol of the Eucharistic banquet. In this the prayer follows the Council of Trent in its decree on Holy Communion, in which it refers to Elijah being fed by the angel as a symbol of the Eucharist: "We travel our pilgrimage to the heavenly kingdom strengthened by the Eucharist.[14] The missal of 1935 contains the same postcommunion prayer.

Finally, the revised liturgy of Carmel[15] celebrates the feast of St Elijah as a Solemnity and retains many references to his flight. The three antiphons for the Office of the Readings recall his distress in the desert and the comforting angel. And the fourth intercession of the Morning Prayer reads: "As he walked to Mount Horeb, you filled Elijah with strength; may we who are strengthened by the Body and Blood of Christ press on unwearied in our journey to you."[16]

Again, the communion antiphon for the mass of St Elijah declares: "Elijah ate and drank, and, strengthened by that food, walked all the way to the mountain of God" (1 Kgs 19:8). Interesting too is the Solemn Blessing over the people: "God provided for Elijah in the desert food and drink that endowed him with miraculous strength. May the eucharistic banquet he has furnished for all who follow in the footsteps of his Son strengthen you for life's journey. Amen."[17]

To sum up: literature, art and liturgy in Carmel have never allowed us to forget God's merciful assistance to Elijah in the desert when he was overcome with exhaustion and discouragement. The lesson for us is loud and clear: the disciple is no better than the master. We must be ready, therefore, to face trials, afflictions, rejection and even failure. Yet we should never despair, for the Lord who sent a comforting angel to his prophet will know how to comfort us.

One sign among many that his divine assistance is always with us is the Holy Eucharist, the sacrament of the body and blood of Christ, which we receive daily and which gives strength for the journey to the Kingdom.

II. Elijah's flight to the desert

What does Elijah's flight say to us today? Enlightened by our psychologists we would say that Elijah was the victim of stress and in need of outside help. Fortunately for him God sent a comforting angel. As we contemplate the afflicted prophet do we have anything in common with him? Indeed we do. Stress is a common pheomenon of the twentieth century, the source of much physical and mental illness that not only saps one's vitality but shortens one's life.

However let us add that not all stress or tension is bad. For example, when it follows from some successful venture or archievement it can be heathy.

> For mental health is based on a certain degree of tension between what one has already achieved and what one still ought to accomplish, of the gap between what one is and what one should become.[18]

In this sense we think of the ecstatic, exuberant Elijah running victoriously all the way to Jezreel before the chariot of Ahab.

1. Under the broom tree: Stress

But not all stress is good. When it comes from disappointment, failure, or the loss of a loved one, it has a negative effect and is called distress. It afflicts the loser. It is stress in this latter sense that Elijah experienced under the broom tree, and that concerns us here. Some would go so far as to say that this kind of stress is their daily bread. Most, however, would be more temperate and admit that there are certain times when they are vulnerable to stress, and perhaps even experience it. This should not be surprising since the changing situations in history have made the present time one of fear, despair and loss of hope. One need think only of the anger and frustration of both the young and the old who have taken to the streets in major cities marching in protest against the very existence of nuclear weapons. But even without the threat of a nuclear holocaust, society spawns many sources of stress, and this in turn triggers much illness. "Two thirds of office visits to family doctors are prompted by stress-related symptoms."[19] Headaches, ulcers, heart trouble, chronic backaches and strokes are commonly held to be stress-related.

After reading this report a friend vounteered the information that a few days later, within the space of twenty-four hours, three people had come to him with a tale of depression. The first was a lawyer who complained that the daily demands of clients had worn him to a frazzle. Another was a government worker engaged in foreign affairs who felt exhausted by the continual demand to come up with answers to international complications. The third was a secretary who felt depressed by the hostile environment generated by insecure, restless office managers. Such stories are repeated time and time again in every walk of life.

So common is the danger of stress that its evil effects have become a cause of alarm for the American Catholic clergy. Worried by the early death of many priests, and the precarious health of others, the bishops declare: "In recent years much research has been carried out showing that stress is one of the truly major health problems facing Americans and expecially American males." They point out that priests are no exception. Consequently, they found it necessary to inform them of the nature, the sources and the responses to stress.[20]

Turning to the Carmelite family, we ask how vulnerable are we to stress? Each one will have to answer that for himself. But there is no denying that besides our personal weaknesses, our very vocation to lead an intensely prayerful life in a secularized and materialistic society, for which God practically does not exist, can be the source of anxiety that constantly tests our fidelity. We are daily confronted with the accusation that our life is meaningless. Who has not heard the taunt: Of what value is prayer and penance? Where are the fruits of your labor?

2. Stress: Its causes

In the light of this negativism it is important that we become familiar with the four general sources of stress in order to cope wisely with them. At the same time we must be aware that what may be a source of great stress for one, may be for another only a minor worry.

Environment is the first source of stress for many. Our living or working situation can become an almost intolerable burden. Then, too, there is the lack of support from family, friends, and co-workers that can contribute to a state of great anxiety. Poor health, whether physical or mental, is another factor that tends to bring on severe tension and even depression. Finally, a weak, superficial spiritual life can leave us without hope, enthusiasm and joy, and so dispose us to boredom, laziness and unhappiness.

We have no intention of responding to these four sources of stress. This would take us too far afield. However we would like to focus attention on environment, to indicate how it can play havoc with daily living: when Elijah was confronted by the angry Jezebel and he realized that he had not erased Baalism from Israel, he ran away in fear and discouragement. As he lay prostrate in the desert we can apply to him the words of the Psalmist:

> *I am like water poured out;*
>   *all my bones are racked.*
> *My heart has become like wax*
>   *melting away within my bosom.*
> *My throat is dried up like baked clay,*
>   *my tongue cleaves to my jaws;*
>   *to the dust of death you have*
>   *brought me down.*
>
> Ps 22:15-16

Could not the distress of Elijah or something similar happen to us? Are we better than our father? I think of Titus Brandsma, Edith Stein, our Polish Carmelites and others arrested and confined to concentration camps during World War II. Were they not candidates for stress?

Granted, we are not challenged with the worship of Baal as Elijah was; nevertheless we are faced with something worse. The whole world, not just one nation, faces the menace of atheism. Time and again we have been told that the only thing worthy of man's worship is man himself. Some believe this; others may not, but often act as if God did not exist. They have forgotten God. Listen to the Russian exile, Alexander Solzhenitsyn, as he laments:

And if I were called upon to identify briefly the principal trait of the *entire* 20th century, here too, I would be unable to find anything more precise and pithy than to repeat once again: "Men have forgotten God."[21]

The Russian exile sounds like a prophet of doom, but he is not. He is a realist who points out the evironment that we have created, and then calls on us to reach for "the warm hand of God that we have so rashly put away." He simply tells us that the future depends on mankind's response to God's loving goodness.

If it is true that we of the twentieth century are being sucked into the vortex of atheism and self-destruction, how shall we respond? Shall we allow ourselves to be overcome by stress and give in to fear, frustration, and despair? How do we cope with stress? There is no simple answer.

Everyone who feels stretched out needs appropriate help for a specific problem. Hence, it does no good to say "Take up your cross" to someone who needs medical aid or counselling or who is involved in an impossible working situation where personalities continually clash, and where dialogue or even a change of occupation could help. To ask people in these situations to carry their cross when the common sense of the behavioral sciences could help would be unconscionable. But even when we take ordinary human precautions to confront a stressful situation, we are not always out of the woods. Without a sound spiritual foundation we are still vulnerable to stress.

3. Stress: Spiritual attitude

With this in mind what we would propose here is the cultivation of a basic spiritual attitude that will serve as the foundation of a well-balanced life. The attitude we refer to is a response to God's loving gift of faith whereby we place all our trust and confidence in his merciful love. We need to cultivate confidence in the God of mercy, and realize that our worst enemy is self-reliance. We cannot confront life's problems with our own strength alone; we are fundamentally dependent on a transcendent power. Not to recognize this dependence on the sustaining power of God is to live inhumanly.

That we are helpless without the sustaining power of the Almighty is exemplified in the story of Elijah. In the desert he prayed for death because he believed he had failed. God did not grant his request; he came to him in the form of an angel and strengthened him for the journey ahead. Without angelic help Elijah would never have reached Horeb. The food and drink proffered by the angel refreshed his body and spirit, and God's grace lifted up his soul and gave him courage to walk to the mountain.

The plight of Elijah calls to mind the agony of Jesus, the new Elijah, in the garden of Gethsemani. Threatened by the stress of the crucifixion that faced him, he cried out to his Father to take the chalice from him. It was not taken; instead the Father sent him a comforting angel who consoled him as he prepared for his journey to Calvary.

St Paul, the apostle to the Gentiles, tells us that at times he was vulnerable to stress. He openly confesses to the Corinthians that in moments of desperation God comforted him: "When I arrived in Macedonia I was restless and exhausted. I was under all kinds of stress—quarrels with others and fears within myself. But God, who gives heart to those who are low in spirit, gave me strength with the arrival of Titus" (2 Cor 7:5-6).

143

From where does our strength come when we are low in spirit? Where is our comforting angel? One answer is that the Lord himself comes to us in the Holy Eucharist. How often do we have a real experience of his presence? "God provided for Elijah in the desert food and drink that endowed him with miraculous strength. May the eucharistic banquet he has furnished for all who follow in the footsteps of his Son strengthen you for life's journey. Amen."[22] Surely, all of us can recall moments when the Eucharist gave us hope, courage and consolation.

A friend who spent five years in the concentration camp of Dachau told me that on several occasions he was able to celebrate the Eucharist secretly with fellow priest-prisoners. These where precious moments of hope and peace. It was in Dachau, he said, that he experienced the Eucharist as the loving, comforting presence of the Lord.

Others have told us that the Word of God has been the bread of life for them in time of stress. Soldiers under fire, prisoners in the loneliness of their cells, have borne witness to the comfort the scriptures have given them. St Therese tells us how the Word of God consoled her in a time of depression. Living in spiritual darkness without the joy of faith that she had experienced during her lifetime she recalls taking up the Holy Book and reading these words:

As one whom a mother caresses, so will I comfort you (Is 66:13). Ah never did words more tender and more melodious come to give joy to my soul. The elevator which must raise me to heaven is Your arms, O Jesus.[23]

4. St Therese's experience

Influenced by this passage from the life of St Therese we turn to her for greater enlightenment. It seems to us that she offers the key to a well-balanced, integrated life that will help us to ward off the dangers of stress. That key is the cultivation of a personal relationship with God, and specifically with God as a loving, merciful Father. In a word, she teaches us how to live with ourselves and with others.

From early childhood St Therese began to experience the fatherhood of God. She was God's child, he was her Father. This loving relationship began in the family home. It was heped along by the goodness of her father, Louis Martin, in whom she saw a reflection of the loveableness of God. Later she would acknowledge this in her writings: "When I think of you, dear little Father, I naturally think of God, for it seems to me that it is impossible to see anyone more holy than you on the earth."[24]

The merciful love of her heavenly Father would become the focal point of many meditations. One day one of the sisters in the convent wished to speak with Therese and entering her cell found her sewing with a radiant expression on her face. Taken aback the sister said: "'What are you thinking of?" Therese responded: "I was meditating on the Our Father. It is so wonderful to be able to call God our Father." As she said it tears came into her eyes."[25]

It is interesting that the saint of Lisieux attributed to Jesus all the qualities of a loving father. Her relationship to Jesus was to one who loved her as a father. When she was asked to teach the novices the felt totally unprepared. She was only a

145

young religious herself, without experience, and the thought of leading others distressed her. But she faced up to the challenge and never flinched. She showed the depth of her spirit, her integrated personality, a knowledge of her own limitations, and understanding of God's goodness. Let us listen as she tells her story:

> I saw immediately that the task was beyond my strength. I threw myself into the arms of God as a little child and, hiding my face in His hair, I said: "I'm too little to nourish Your children; if You wish to give through me what is suitable for each, fill my little head and without leaving Your arms or turning my head, I shall give your treasures to the soul who will come and ask for nourishment ... happily for my Sisters, since the time I took my place in the arms of Jesus, I am like the watchman observing the enemy from the highest turret of a strong castle.[26]

In this passage, if we study it carefully, we will find a way to cope with difficult situations in life. The way, Therese's way, is simply to surrender oneself completely into the merciful arms of the Lord. Such a spiritual disposition will not remove the sources of stress, but it will help to prepare us to meet them.

A few months before her death Therese was asked by her sister, Mother Agnes, about the way she wanted to teach souls after her death. She answered,

> Mother, it is the way of spiritual childhood [she never used this expression in her own writings]; it's the way of confidence and total abandon. I want to teach them the little means that have so perfectly succeeded with me, to tell them there is only one thing to do here on earth: to cast at Jesus the flowers of little sacrifices, to take Him by caresses; that is the way I have taken Him, and it's for this that I shall be so well received.[27]

This little way of the saint of Lisieux is the fruit of the personal experience that upheld her in her journey of faith. And as she grew in her loving trust in God, she was delighted to find her way spelled out by Jesus in the gospel. This convinced her she was on the right track: "Unless you change and become like little children, you will not enter the kingdom of God" (Mt 18:3). This was the teaching that sustained her in the physical, mental and spiritual sufferings that began with the death of her mother when she was only four and half years old, and continued until her death at the age of twenty-four. Because of what we know about her suffering, we can say that all her life she was vulnerable to stress. Yet she managed to live an extraordinary life of gentle peace. She was truly a well-balanced person. As her sister Celine said of her after her death, she did ordinary things extraordinarily well.

In this she has set an example for her brothers and sisters in Carmel.

III. Conclusion

She shows us how to live with ourselves and others; how to embrace suffering and, in so doing, how to cope with impossible situations. For us and for all others who wish to listen to her, she has an answer: Place yourself in the hands of your Father, in the hands of merciful love. Trust him. Cultures and civilizations come and go; our culture is surely different from that of Therese, yet she declares to us that our heavenly Father is changeless. All we need to do is trust him. Seek only his will. Do we really believe this? God is waiting for us to answer. The only adequate response is that of Therese, who reflects what the Psalmist had said centuries earlier:

But you, O Lord, are a God merciful and gracious,
slow to anger, abounding in kindness and fidelity.

Turn toward me, and have pity on me;
give your strength to your servant,
and save the son of your handmaid.

Grant me a proof of your favor,
that my enemies may see, to their confusion,
that you, O Lord, have helped and comforted me.

Psalm 86:15-17

VI

There he came to a cave, where he took shelter. But the word of the LORD came to him, "Why are you here, Elijah?" He answered: "I have been zealous for the LORD, the God of hosts, but the Israelites have forsaken your covenant, torn down your altars, and put your prophets to the sword. I alone am left, and they seek to take my life." Then the LORD said, "Go outside and stand on the mountain before the LORD; the LORD will be passing by." A strong and heavy wind was rending the mountains and crushing rocks before the LORD—but the LORD was not in the wind. After the wind there was an earthquake—but the LORD was not in the earthquake. After the earthquake there was fire—but the LORD was not in the fire. After the fire there was a tiny whispering sound. When he heard this, Elijah hid his face in his cloak and went and stood at the entrance of the cave.

A voice said to him, "Elijah, why are you here?" He replied, "I have been most zealous for the LORD, the God of hosts. But the Israelites have forsaken your covenant, torn down your altars, and put your prophets to the sword. I alone am left, and they seek to take my life." "Go, take the road back to the desert near Damascus," the LORD said to him. "When you arrive, you shall anoint Hazael as king of Aram. Then you shall anoint Jehu, son of Nimshi, as king of Israel, and Elisha, son of Shaphat of Abel-meholah, as prophet to succeed you. If anyone escapes the sword of Hazael, Jehu will kill him. If he escapes the sword of Jehu, Elisha will kill him. Yet I will leave seven thousand men in Israel—all those who have not knelt to Baal or kissed him."

1 Kings 19: 9-18

The zeal of Elijah

S TRENGTHENED by the food of the angel Elijah travelled "forty days and forty nights" until he came to Horeb-Sinai. The text indicates a long journey and recalls the long wandering, "forty years," of Israel in the desert.

Here on this mountain of mystery the Lord spoke to Elijah. The text that follows is not without its problems: twice the Lord asks the prophet what he is doing on the holy mountain, and twice the prophet makes the same response. This is an obvious duplication. Some reliable commentators think the text would read more smoothly if verses 9b-11a were omitted; they believe these verses were inserted unnecessarily or accidentally by a later editor. In any case the sense of the passage is not changed and appears to be the following:

On coming to Horeb Elijah entered a cave; while he was there the Lord—whom no one can see and live—"passed by." Aware of the divine visitation Elijah covered his face with his cloak and went to the entrance of the cave. There the message of the Lord came to him: "Elijah, why are you here?" (1 Kgs 19:13).

The Lord's question and Elijah's response are open to various interpretations. Some see the Lord's words as a severe rebuke to the prophet for excessive zeal in putting to death the prophets of Baal on Carmel. However there is no foundation for this opinion, for Elijah had not been unjust. He had only followed the law that decreed severe punishment for idolaters (Ex 22:19). Moreover, the Lord himself was about to declare that those who continued to worship Baal would be put to the sword (1 Kgs 19:17).

Another interpretation holds that Elijah is indeed rebuked, but for another reason: namely, because he had deserted the battlefield of Israel for the quiet retreat of Horeb. This, it is said, was unworthy of a prophet; he should have stood his ground and confronted Jezebel and her followers. Hence, God is saying: What right have you to be standing on holy ground, Elijah ? To this accusation the prophet offers his apology for a seemingly cowardly action. But this position is also unsatisfactory: Elijah had not been unfaithful. He fled because he alone among the prophets was left to defend the cause of Yahweh. He had to survive to keep the faith alive in Israel: "I alone am left, and they seek to take my life" (1 Kgs 19:14).

A third and more likely interpretation finds in Elijah's encounter with the Lord a friendly, intimate, and comforting meeting. It is the encounter of the loyal servant with his heavenly father, a meeting in which the prophet expresses his bitter sorrow for the defection of Israel and his own failure. Still, in a personal, moving expression of faith he declares his undying loyalty to Yahweh. In response the Lord informs him that all is not lost. There is nothing to fear. Indeed, he will prove this by sending Elijah on a new mission that in the end will strengthen the faith of Israel. There will indeed be much bloodshed, but Israel will see that Yahweh alone is God.

It should be noticed that Yahweh does not answer Elijah directly, but instead orders him to return to Israel. There he will have a new and difficult task. It will foment political revolution. What is the mission? Elijah's prophetic office is about to come to an end, so he must first appoint a successor, Elisha, the son of Shaphat. Furthermore, he must anoint Hazael, the future King of Aram, and Jehu, the new King of Israel. These two kings will eventually "crush Israel to pieces." Idolaters will not be spared. Yet,. not all Israel will be punished for there was still to remain in Israel a faithful remnant: "Yet, I will leave seven thousand men in Israel, all those who have not knelt to Baal or kissed him" (1 Kgs 19:18).

Yahweh's answer to Elijah is the key to the understanding of the passage. It shows that the prophet was mistaken in believing he alone in Israel was faithful to the Lord. It also points out that faith in Yahweh was not about to be exterminated. Israel surely will be chastised from within by Jehu and from without by Hazael, but in the end an Israel faithful to Yahweh will survive. Yahweh is in command, not Elijah.

As subsequent events will show, Elijah personally sought out and found his successor, Elisha: but as to the two kings, he did not personally anoint them. In the case of Hazael, it was Elisha, not Elijah, who designated him King of Aram. And as for Jehu, it was one of Elisha's disciples who anointed him King of Israel after the destruction of the dynasty of Omri (2 Kgs 9:1-13). In his time Hazael would ravage Israel (2 Kgs 8:12-15), and as for Jehu he, not Elijah, would exterminate Baalism from Israel (2 Kgs 10: 28).

If we turn our attention once again to the encounter of Elijah with Yahweh on Horeb-Sinai, we will notice the similarity of this meeting with that *i* Moses on Sinai. The narrator of the Elijan story seems to have in mind the cleft of the rock in which Moses was sheltered when Yahweh "passed by" in all his glory (Ex 33:18-23) .

Given the similarity of events it is clear that Yahweh who once appeared to Moses to make known his covenant with his people is the same jealous God who now reveals himself to Elijah. The covenant he had established with Moses is reconfirmed and reestablished with Elijah. Israel was and remains his people. It is only fitting then, that both events took place on Horeb-Sinai, the mountain of the Lord. Moses proclaimed the law; Elijah sustained it in Israel.

Yet, we cannot help but notice the glaring contrast between the two meetings. When Moses went up the mountain the wind blew, the earth trembled, and lightning came down and made manifest God's presence. But when Elijah stood before the cave on the same mountain, and the wind blew, the mountain trembled and lightning came down, God was not in them. Rather a moment of quiet settled on the mountain side. Then, a gentle, comforting breeze announced the presence of the Lord. Hence we are led to believe that the Lord came to Elijah in silence, that he entered into the depths of his soul, filled him with his Spirit. One senses that there is a great intimacy between God and the prophet, similar to the gentle, friendly intimacy between God and Adam and Eve as he walked with them in Paradise. As the Lord spoke to Adam and Eve so now he speaks with Elijah. And in answer to his paternal demand Elijah, ever the faithful servant, reassures the Lord that his heart is still on fire, still beats with loving zeal: "I am most zealous for the LORD, God of hosts." In answer to this profession of faith the Lord informs Elijah that all is not lost: there is still a faithful remnant in Israel. His covenant with the people still stands. Elijah's mission has not been in vain.

I. Carmelite tradition

The encounter of Elijah with God on Mount Horeb has had a profound influence in the spiritual life of Carmel. Time and again this mountain scene has been a favorite subject of literature, art and liturgy in the Order.

There are various interpretations which Carmelites have given to this scene, but one interpretation that has come down to us and is generally accepted is this: When the Lord of Israel asked Elijah what he was doing on the holy mountain, the prophet defended himself admirably. Although worn out from travel, trials and even failure, he could nevertheless cry out bravely and truthfully from the depths of his heart that he had always been and still was the faithful servant of Yahweh. "I have been most zealous for the LORD, the God of hosts" (1 Kgs 19:10).

For Carmelites the cry of the prophet is the testimony of a man whose heart burns with love for the LORD. So impressed have they been by this *cri de coeur* that they have made it their own. For centuries the words "I have been most zealous for the Lord, the God of hosts" have echoed and reechoed in the monasteries and churches of Carmel. Indeed, with time they became the motto of the Order and were blazoned around the shield of the Order in its coat of arms.

The Order could have easily chosen other words of the prophet to identify its spirit. One thinks immediately of the Vulgate text, so often used in Carmel's liturgy, that refers to Elijah's confrontation with King Ahab: "God lives in whose presence I stand." Time and again these words crop up in the Order's tradition to remind its members of their vocation to live always in the presence of the Lord. Yet, when it came to selecting a motto, Carmelites preferred Elijah's profession of faith on Horeb. With their spiritual father, Carmelites are determined not only to stand always in God's presence, but to do so with hearts burning with love.

The question naturally arises: when did the Carmelites first choose this motto, and under what circumstances? To the best of the writer's knowledge the oldest shield or coat of arms that the Order possesses is found in the frontispiece of the Constitutions of Carmel of 1499, and in the frontispiece of a *Life of St Albert* published the same year. It is reproduced in the Missals of 1500, 1504 and 1509.[1]

The description of this 1499 coat of arms[2] gives us a better understanding of the spirit of the Order. It is in the shape of an oval upheld on either side by an angel. The oval is divided in the center by a horizontal line, and the lower level is in the form of a triangle and resembles a mountain; it is without decoration. The upper level shows the Virgin Mary, seated on a stool-like chair and holding the Child Jesus in her lap with her hand. The Child holds a globe in his right hand and a sword in his left. On the Virgin's head is a crown with flowered points, and her head is surrounded by twelve stars. Beneath her feet is the crescent of the moon with the words *Luna sub pedibus eius* (the moon beneath her feet).

Various interpretations have been given to this emblem. The writer is impressed with the following: in the lower level of the oval the triangle is a symbol of Mount Carmel; the upper level or field is itself a symbol of a cloud, the cloud seen by Elijah

Carmelite *Vexillum* or coat of arms
from the Constitutions of 1499

rising above the sea heralding the end of the drought that ravaged Israel (1 Kgs 18:44). In the cloud, according to a Carmelite tradition, Elijah saw the figure of the Immaculate Virgin Mary, Mother of God incarnate. The fiery rays shooting out from the oval-shaped shield, the moon beneath the Virgin's feet, and the crown of stars on her head recall our Lady's Assumption and Coronation in heaven and the vision of John of Patmos: "A great sign appeared in the sky, a woman clothed with the sun, with the moon under her feet, and on her head a crown of twelve stars" (Rv 12:1).

To complete the coat of arms there are two banners (ribbon-like scrolls) placed above the shield *Ego sum mater et decor Carmeli,* I am the mother and splendor of Carmel, and *Helias et Helisæus duces Carmelitarum,* Elijah and Elisha, the Leaders of Carmelites. The two texts express the spiritual traditions of Carmel: Elijah and Elisha are the spiritual guides of Carmel, who lead us to the Virgin Mary, the model and ideal of all Carmelites. Mary, the Virgin Most Pure, is the pattern of perfection, who draws us to walk in her footsteps. The purity of Mary—the woman without stain of sin—is further accented by the crescent of the moon beneath her feet.

This remarkable coat of arms with slight modifications continued to appear in various publications of the Order for the greater part of the sixteenth century.[3] A radical change, however, took place when a new coat of arms appeared in the publication of Decrees for the Carmelites of Spain and Portugal edited by John Stephen Chizzola, Prior General of the Order, at Seville in 1595.[4]

The new coat of arms or emblem of the Order, like the former, is oval, but with this striking and radical change: the images of the Virgin Mother and Child have disappeared. The Spanish engraving

VEXILLVM CARMELITARVM

ZELO ZELATVS SVM PRO DOMINO DE

1595 Coat of Arms from the Decrees of
Prior General Stefano Chizzola

in black and white is topped with the words *Vexillum Carmelitarum,* the Standard of Carmelites. Under these words there is a "cloaked shield"—called *incappato* because its field is divided into three parts by two lines, which run from a point in the center of the top of the shield and spread out to the middle of its sides. The two upper parts form a single white field with a dark star in the middle of each part. The shield is contained within a border, and it is surmounted by a crown with five flowered points and four pearls between the points. There are no stars above the crown. Rather, we see an arm emerging from the crown holding a flaming sword in its hand. To complete the emblem we have a banner or ribbon-like streamer that surrounds the shield with the words *Zelo zelatus sum pro Domino Deo,* I am most zealous for the Lord God.

This new design with minor modifications has not only survived to this day, but remains the approved coat of arms in the Order. It is, however, the subject of many interpretations.

Some see in the dark and white shield symbols of the brown and white habit of Carmel, and in the flaming sword and the words *Zelo zelatus sum,* etc., a symbol of the prophet Elijah.

Another interpretation, however, one that pleases this writer, is that the Spanish coat of arms is a symbolic representation of the shield of 1499. For example, Mount Carmel is presented in the lower field and the star in the middle signifies Elijah on the mountain. The field above is white and divided into two parts and represents the white cloud over Carmel seen by Elijah in which he saw the figure of the Immaculate Virgin Mother with Child. The black stars, one on the right and the other on the left in the white field, are symbols of the two natures of Christ, one divine and the other human. The crown over the shield is a symbol of the coronation of Mary, Queen of Heaven. The flaming sword over the crown recalls Elijah the fiery prophet whose words burned like a torch. Finally, the response of Elijah to Yahweh, *Zelo zelatus sum*, has replaced the two texts over the shield of 1499.

How does one explain this substantial change in the escutcheon of the Order: on the one hand the disappearance of the image of the Virgin and Child and of the motto "I am the Mother and Splendor of Carmel;" and on the other the introduction of the stars on the black and white fields and of both the sword of Elijah and his response to the Lord? In other words, how does one explain the sudden prominence of Elijah in the shield?

Various opinions can be given. This writer offers his own for the following probable reasons. First, toward the end of the sixteenth century, the church was caught up in the Counter-Reformation and fought to stave off the inroads of Protestantism. Carmel, along with other religious orders, entered into the renewal of the church's life. In its efforts to share in the church's fight for survival and renewal, it found in Elijah's response to God on Horeb an inspirational battle cry to arouse its members to a renewal of their spiritual life and to a more vigorous apostolate in preaching the Word of God. What better way to incite its members to action than to recall the burning zeal that motivated Elijah in his campaign against paganism in Israel!

Another reason for the change may be that in the sixteenth century the missionary spirit began to stir among the religious orders when Pope Adrian II authorized mendicant orders to evangelize the Indies. The Carmelites may have been slow in accepting the challenge, but in the post-Tridentine age the development of the missionary apostolate began in the order, especially in the provinces of the

Iberian Peninsula. And it was precisely in Spain that we find the coat of arms of 1595 with its Elijan motif published for the first time. What better way to motivate Carmelites to enter into the evangelization of the Indies than to call their attention to the burning zeal of their spiritual father?

Whatever the reasons that motivated the change in Carmel's coat of arms at the end of the sixteenth century, one thing is certain: the new Elijan emphasis has remained constant in the Order's shield down to the present time.

Still, a puzzling question remains. In accepting the new coat of arms has the Order lost something precious, something of its Marian identity? In other words, has the disappearance of Mary's image from the coat of arms diminished the importance of her role in Carmel? We hope not, but surely the prevailing coat of arms does not clearly elucidate Mary as the ideal of the contemplative life. Only those who know the history of the coat of arms would see in the present emblem Mary as the ideal contemplative. On the other hand, the crown of the coat of arms does recall the Assumption and Coronation of Mary in heaven, and so presents her as the pattern of all goodness and beauty, who reminds us that she is what we should be, and that where she is we will one day be. Moreover, the contemplative and active spirit of Carmel is represented in the flaming sword of Elijah and in the motto that recalls his zeal. For the prophet of Carmel was a contemplative, standing in God's presence as a servant should, always prepared to do his master's will. And his confrontation with King Ahab, his subsequent contest with the prophets of Baal on Carmel, and his conversation with the Lord on Horeb, all attest to his burning love for God that overflowed into action.

In summary, we have focused our observations on Carmel's coat of arms in order to show that

Elijah's *cri de coeur* on Horeb, *Zelo zelatus sum,* has exercised an immeasurable influence on Carmel, so much so that every Carmelite knows that he or she is called, like Elijah, to abhor mediocrity and to serve the Lord with his whole heart and strength.

II. Zeal in Carmel Today?

If Elijah were to return today, would he find any zeal in Carmel? This question was proposed recently to a small group during a community recreation. One of the younger members, with a smile on his face, responded that he was not sure that the prophet would find zeal in Carmel, but he would certainly find his words: "I am most zealous for the Lord God of hosts" not only remembered in the Order but indeed highly publicized. For, as he went on to say, Carmel has adopted these words for its motto and they can be found emblazoned on the walls of its monasteries, on the letterheads of its stationery, and on its banners that hang in its chapels, refectories and classrooms.

Another member of the group, a seasoned Carmelite, offered a more profound observation. If Elijah returned he would find genuine zeal, but expressed in a new, unique way. Not many Carmelites today, he went on to say, can be found living in caves, huts or hermitages as in the past, nor will many be found in large monasteries that once housed hundreds of Carmelites. But there are contemporary Carmelites living out the Elijan charism in small communities, serving in schools, hospitals and parishes. Some labor in Third World countries. These men and women serve the poor, the sick, the elderly, the oppressed. Some have suffered and still suffer persecution. All try to live as Elijah did in the presence of the Lord, and they find the face of the suffering Jesus in the anxious, tired and suffering faces of their people. Zeal surely exists in Carmel, he concluded, and we should recognize it and make it known to the skeptical.

We fully agree with this statement, and would like to offer concrete examples to substantiate it. But before we do, it would be helpful to determine more accurately what we mean by zeal, since not all zeal is praiseworthy.

According to Webster's Dictionary zeal is "intense enthusiasm as in working for a cause." Every cause, as we know, is not good and laudable, and consequently not all zeal is virtuous. As someone once said: "Zeal dropped in charity is good; without it, good for nothing; for it devours all it comes near." How true this is when we think of terrorists who with fanatical zeal drive trucks loaded with explosives into buildings housing people, destroying not only the inhabitants but themselves as well.

However zeal rooted in charity is commendable, and it is this enthusiasm that motivated Elijah and that is the ideal Carmelites try to emulate. With this distinction in mind we offer four models of Carmelite zeal, four people who have lived close to our times and who have left an indelible impression on this writer and perhaps on many others.

1. St Therese

The greatest inspiration of Carmelite zeal for this writer has been St Therese of the Child Jesus (1873-1897). She is a saint who lived toward the end of the nineteenth century but her spirit has overflowed into the twentieth. And it is in this century that her inspirational influence has been felt.

In St Therese one finds a Carmelite whose heart, like that of Elijah, burned with love.

Her zeal began early in life, increased steadily and matured when she was still a very young religious. We see the beginning of her 'heart of fire' in the following incident from her childhood that she describes with great charm.

> One day, Leonie, thinking she was too big to be playing any longer with dolls, came to us with a basket filled with dresses and pretty pieces for making others; her doll was resting on top. "Here, my little sisters, *choose*; I'm giving you all this." Celine stretched out her hand and took a little ball of wool which pleased her. After a moment's reflection, I stretched out mine saying, "I choose all!" and I took the basket without further ceremony. Those who witnessed the scene saw nothing wrong and even Celine herself didn't dream of complaining (besides, she had all sorts of toys, and her godfather gave her lots of presents, and Louise found ways of getting her everything she desired.)
>
> The little incident of my childhood is a summary of my whole life; later on when perfection was set before me, I understood that to become a *saint* one had to suffer much, seek out always the most perfect thing to do, and forget self. I understood, too, there were many degrees of perfection and each soul was free to respond to the advances of Our Lord, to do little or much for Him, in a word, to *choose* among the sacrifices He was asking. Then, as in the days of my childhood, I cried out: "My God, *I choose all!*" I don't want to be a *saint by halves*, I'm not afraid to suffer for You, I fear only one thing: to keep my *own will*; so take it, for *I choose all* that You will![5]

It was necessary to quote the whole of the above passage to understand the depth of meaning. Indeed, this writer has been for some time fascinated by it and especially by the words: "This little incident is the summary of my whole life." Her cry of the heart, "I choose all that you will," seems incredible. And in a way it is. Her self-forgetfull-ness, her unbounded generosity, her extraordinary courage in embracing suffering of every kind for the love of God, is superhuman. Only by the power of the Holy Spirit that filled her youthful heart could she say: "I choose all that you will," and then go on fulfilling this promise throughout every moment of her life.

Elijah said: "I am most zealous for the Lord God." Therese exclaimed: "I choose all that you will." Both the father and the child are consumed with the same love. Only the mode of expression is different.

What Therese promised as a child she actually fulfilled in her life. What determination, what courageous perseverance she demonstrated! It is all brought out in the words she penned to her sister Marie:

> Considering the mystical body of the Church I had not recognized myself in any of the members described by St Paul, or rather I desired to see myself in them *all*. *Charity* gave me the key to my *vocation*. I understood that if the Church had a body composed of different members, the most necessary and most noble of all could not be lacking to it, and so I understood that the Church *had a Heart and that this Heart was BURNING WITH LOVE. I understood it was Love alone* that made the Church's members act, that if *Love* ever became extinct, apostles would not preach the Gospel and martyrs would not shed their blood. I understood that LOVE COMPRISED ALL VOCATIONS, THAT LOVE WAS EVERYTHING, THAT IT EMBRACED ALL TIMES AND PLACES ... IN A WORD, THAT IT WAS ETERNAL!
>
> Then, in the excess of my delirious joy, I cried out: O Jesus, my Love ... my *vocation*, at last I have found it ... MY VOCATION IS LOVE![6]

Someone perhaps will say that Therese was exceptional, that there is no one like her in Carmel today. Only God knows this, but one thing we can verify is that there are others in Carmel even closer to our own time whose lives were consumed with love and who also incarnate the spirit of Elijah.

2. Bl Titus Brandsma

We think instinctively of Father Titus Brandsma (1881-1942) of the Dutch Province who was put to death most cruelly in the concentration camp of Dachau on July 26, 1942, and beatified on November 3, 1985. Books and articles in many languages have told the story of this exemplary religious, so there is no need to repeat it here.

Our intention here is solely to recall his jealous zeal for the Lord which marks him as one who lived in the power and the spirit of Elijah. Those who lived with him have time and again stated that if ever there was a Dutch Carmelite who knew and lived the life of a Carmelite it was Father Titus. His whole life was oriented toward seeking God.

> Just as Elijah had often to leave the solitude of Carmel in Palestine to convert his people to Yahweh, so Father Titus had often to leave Carmel in Nijmegen to bring God to man. As he poignantly expressed it, "to leave God for God."[7]

Indeed his whole life of multiple activities was in keeping with the fiery spirit of Elijah. In his lifetime he visited many countries, among them France, Germany, Spain, Italy, Canada and the United States of America. Always he was on some mission for the Order or the church. But whether he went as Chancellor of the Catholic University of Nijmegen or simply as a lecturer, scholar or minister of religion, he was the "new" Elijah living alway in God's presence and ready to serve.

This truth was brought out at a Eucharistic celebration in Rome on October 24, 1982, to mark the fortieth anniversary of Father Titus' death.

Cardinal Bernard Alfrink, the former Archbishop of Utrecht, presided at the celebration and preached the homily. In his tribute to Father Titus he recalled that the Man of God had been appointed representative of the Dutch bishops for all Catholic journalists assigned to work in The Netherlands. His task was to visit all the editors of the Catholic Press in Holland with directives to help them in their defence against Nazi infiltration. Always a faithful servant of the church, Bl Titus set out on his mission and visited fourteen editors before being apprehended by two members of the German Security Police and incarcerated at Scheveningen.

His imprisonment there recalls the forced stay of Elijah at Cherith, where he communed alone with the Lord. From Scheveningen Titus wrote: "Though I am here by myself, my Lord has never been closer to me. I even sing, although softly."

His detainment at this prison was brief. In less than two months he was shunted from prison to prison until he finally landed in Dachau. It was here that he met a cruel and horrifying death in the prison hospital where he had been sent for medical experimentation and treated like an animal. In the words of Cardinal Alfrink Father Titus could be compared with the hundreds of Christians who in the time of Emperor Nero were tortured and put to death for their faith. For Bl Titus, like the early Christians, was martyred because of a hatred for Christianity, and because of his courageous living out of the ideals of the gospel of Christ. The Cardinal concluded his tribute by saying: "'I think we can call Titus Brandsma a 'victim of the Nazi terror,' and 'a martyr of the anti-Christian Nazi ideology.'"[8]

Bl Titus, the Elijah of our times, is indeed a model and inspiration for all who embrace the Carmelite way of life, especially for those who labor daily in the midst of injustice and persecution.

3. *Hilarion Januszewski*

Another Carmelite, a companion of my school days, whose story should be told because he was a true son of the zealous prophet of Carmel, comes to mind. Who is this man? His name is Father Hilarion Januszewski (1907-1945), of the Polish Province. While prior of the Carmelite convent in Krakow he was taken prisoner by the Nazis who had overrun Poland in September, 1939. Condemned for his outspoken protest against this outrage, he was sent to the concentration camp at Dachau, where he died. He was only thirty-eight years of age.

I first met Father Hilarion in Rome in 1934, a few months after his ordination to the priesthood. I had come to Rome in the autumn of that year to begin studies of Theology at St Albert's International College. He was in his final year of studies and I was beginning, so we never met in the classroom. In fact I had little contact with him, and yet his presence in the community has left a lasting impression. This is difficult to explain since there was nothing extraordinary about him; on the contrary, he was quiet, soft-spoken, retiring, almost invisible.

Although he was part of our large community of some eighty persons and shared our daily liturgical prayers, he seemed to be a solitary, absorbed in his own personal relationship with the Lord. In our recreations he had little to say. In fact, I cannot recall anything he ever said. Among the students he was known to be industrious and intelligent. He left Rome quietly in 1935 to return to Poland to begin his ministry, and I never saw him again. Yet his studious, contemplative presence is etched in my memory. Why? I do not know. Perhaps it was the aura of aloofness and mystery that surrounded him which intrigued me.

However, when his name cropped up some thirty years later I was eager to learn more about him. The occasion was the Millenium celebration of Poland in 1966. I was fortunate to visit the country during this anniversary of its Christian birth, and to meet once again Father Albert Urbanski, Provincial of the Polish Province, who also had been a companion during our student days in Rome. Father Albert had known Father Hilarion very well. They had been members of the same community when the Nazis invaded Poland, and later were fellow prisoners in the infamous camp at Dachau. When he mentioned Father Hilarion's name to me I was keenly interested to hear more.

Our conversation took place on a train from Krakow to Gdansk, and during this long trip I plied Father Albert with questions about his harrowring experience in the concentration camp. The story of his suffering is worth telling, particularly since he was also a companion of Bl Titus Brandsma in the camp, but here I would rather relate what he told me about Father Hilarion.

One day during their internment Father Hilarion came to Father Albert and told him that typhoid fever had broken out in the camp and that many of their Polish compatriots were suffering in an isolation ward. The camp authorities had sent out an appeal for volunteers to assist the afflicted. Father Hilarion had quietly responded to the call and urged Father Albert to do the same. But the latter was reluctant, for the moment, and so Father Hilarion entered the sick bay alone.

Some weeks passed and there was no word from his friend, so Father Albert, touched by a twinge of conscience, volunteered to serve the sick. On entering the ward his first concern was to look for his confrere, but to his dismay he learned that Father Hilarion had succumbed to the dreaded disease and, like so many of the victims, had been cremated in the ovens of the camp. Father Albert was in a state of mild shock but, inspired by the example of his friend, continued to serve the sick until he himself was struck down by typhoid. For five weeks he lay unconscious, but somehow survived the ordeal. Slowly he regained his strength and lived to welcome the day of liberation. He was one of the more fortunate, for eight hundred and fifty Polish priests died at Dachau before the war ended.

As Father Albert recounted this story while the train rolled along the beautiful Polish countryside, it was evident that association with Father Hilarion had left its mark. Obviously he was filled with profound admiration for his companion. They had lived and worked together in the apostolate at Krakow; together they had opposed the Nazi invasion of their country, and for their outspoken protest had been sent into exile. While in Dachau Father Hilarion was not only a companion, but a source of comfort and spiritual inspiration to Father Albert. In this gloomy, bleak atmosphere their friendship blossomed. It was during these days that Father Albert came to appreciate the deep, interior life of his companion. Hence he had not been surprised when the latter had offered his services to assist the typhoid patients, even though he knew full well that he was exposing himself to the disease, and thereby choosing the lonely road to Calvary with Christ. For Father Albert there was no

171

doubt that his companion had freely chosen to lay down his life for his brothers.

When he finished the story Father Albert remarked: "We should never forget the heroic life of Father Hilarion. His story should be made known."

Has anyone recounted the story of Father Hilarion? I do not know. Here I wish only to relate what I had seen and heard lest his inspirational life be forgotten, for there can be no doubt that this so ordinary a man had an extraordinary mission in life. Put to the test he proclaimed his faith, surrendered to the cost of discipleship, and unselfishly gave his life for others.

Today when my thoughts reach back to that quiet, contemplative student of many years ago and the sacrifice the Lord demanded of him, I compare him with the prophet Elijah. In his unassuming way he could say with Elijah, "I have been most zealous for the LORD, the God of hosts."

4. Bartholomew Maria Xiberta

Finally, I would like to share a more personal encounter with a man of outstanding zeal. More than any other Carmelite of my acquaintance Father Bartholomew Xiberta (1897-1967) reminded me of Elijah. Small of stature but with a big heart, he was like a ball of fire. Filled with enthusiasm, he seemed to be always in a hurry. He never walked, but rather scurried along. Engaged in conversation, his face would light up, and if an argument ensued, especially on a theological issue, his whole body came into action. It was a delight just to watch him make his point. Some say that he had the same fiery zeal for the freedom of his beloved Catalonia. And for this he paid dearly. During the Spanish

Dear Irene,

This book was brought into the sacristy. I'm going to assume it's yours, as there is a card in it with the name Mariamonte

Yours in Christ

Colleen Fuentes

Colleen F. Fuentes

Civil War (1936-1940) he was expelled from Italy for his outspoken opposition to Fascism. It is said that the Spanish government had asked the Italian government to expel him. My own recollection is that one day he did not appear for class, and we were informed that he had left Italy for Holland since he was no longer welcome in Italy. This is not the place to speak of his love for Catalonia, but it does help to understand his fiery temperament that was irrepressible when truth and justice were at stake.

This same sense of truth and justice filled his heart for the things of God and of the church. He was gifted with a keen intellect, a quick and probing mind, and unusual energy. These gifts helped him to become an outstanding theologian of the twentieth century, and surely the most influential of Carmelite theologians. His doctoral dissertation, *Clavis Ecclesiæ*, written when he was still a young man, was a real contribution to the theology of the Sacrament of Penance. Years later during the Second Vatican Council Karl Rahner wrote him a letter expressing his pleasure at being a member of the same Theological Commission of the Council with the man who had given the church a better understanding of the Sacrament of Penance.[9]

Once again our interest is only to bring out the shining zeal of this man. In the classroom he was an enthusiastic teacher with a perpetual smile that manifested his pleasure in what he taught. He was not the most gifted teacher. His lectures were delivered in Latin, and with a rather weak voice, which made it even more difficult for students to follow his train of deep speculative thought. The most talented students did profit enormously, but all benefited from his enthusiasm and remained deeply moved by his love of God and truth. What he failed to teach by word he conveyed by example.

When Pope John XXIII announced the opening of the Second Vatican Council in 1960 Fr Xiberta received the news with joy. His appointment to the Theological Commission of the Council gave him added pleasure. It was his great desire that the Council would give to the church a clear, unequivocal answer to the question: Who is Jesus Christ? For even at that time it was his conviction that some contemporary theologians of great repute were undermining the divinity of Jesus, the unity of one person in two natures. However the preparatory commissions and the Council Fathers were of a different mind. They did not see any peril at this point and began their work with studies on the nature and constitution of the church. This was a great disappointment to Father Xiberta, and to those who were close to him he did not hesitate to voice his feelings. In his own heart the nature of the church could never be understood unless there was complete understanding of Jesus as true God as well as true man.

Today there are some who feel Father Xiberta was right, and that the Council should have opened with a document on Christology. This writer who lived very close to Father Xiberta during the Council years has often felt that his failing health during the first session of the Council was accelerated by his deep anxiety over the proceedings of the Council. This anxiety together with other work led to a stroke from which he never recovered, although he lingered on for a few years. We regret that his illness prevented him from sharing in the happy ending of the Council.

In retrospect what are our thoughts about this good and holy man? Those of us who were taught by him, who lived with him, prayed with him, listened to his deep theological insights, were deeply affected by his intense enthusiasm, his zeal for the Lord and the church. In him we saw Elijah reborn.

His words, like those of his spiritual father, burned like a torch. This was true in the classroom, the confessional, the conference room, and in theological meetings and congresses. Indeed, so great was his fiery zeal that if anyone even in a public meeting seemed to stray from the truth, he would not restrain himself but openly ruffled his adversary on the spot. This won him some enemies, but when the truth was at stake, he refused to compromise.

We cannot close without a reference to his love for the Order and the Virgin Mother of Carmel. His great joy was to see the remarkable increase of young men to the Order in the first half of the twentieth century. And this joy was doubly increased when he witnessed young women enter the cloistered convents of Carmel. He showed his appreciation of the contemplative vocation by spending his summer holidays giving conferences and retreats to cloistered nuns in Italy and Spain. Fortunately, the nuns understood the wisdom and holiness of the man and have preserved many of his conferences for us.

While he was certainly an intellectual giant, he enjoyed the faith and piety of a humble child. He loved the Virgin Mother of Carmel with an open and often reckless piety. How often we stood beside him in choir reciting the divine office only to see him, whenever there was a pause, kiss the image of Mary on the holy card placed in his breviary. However, he was never ostentatious, and his childlike devotion was never offensive; on the contrary, it was edifying.

During recreation he would often ask, sometimes playfully: What is the greatest problem in the Order? After listening to the many opinions, he would give his own in the form of another question: "Is the Blessed Virgin Mary pleased with Carmelites?" Whatever the truth may be, one thing is certain: throughout his life he made every effort to please her.

III. Conclusion

At the beginning of this inquiry we asked: If Elijah returned would he find zeal in Carmel? After what we have related, who can doubt it? We feel our reflections on the words of St Therese bring out clearly and convincingly that the power and spirit of Elijah were alive in this great saint. Zeal was her life, and her zeal was infectious: it has influenced countless souls down to this very day. Inspired by her example they follow her "little way."

Moreover, in the brief sketches of Fathers Titus, Hilarion and Xiberta it is obvious that Elijah's zeal, his consuming love, was expressed vividly in their lives. Finally, who of us has not witnessed time and again outstanding models of intense enthusiasm rooted in love among the hidden men and women, both lay and religious, who belong to the family of Carmel? May we carry on their spirit, always open, as they were, to the gentle whispering of the Lord.

VII

(handwritten marginalia:) love of yourself leads to neighbors

ordinate
inordinate

in perfect agreement — if presented to the
o the will senses o Art Glory to God
o of God Then give it up & Mortify
your senses

Elijah set out, and came upon Elisha, son of
Shaphat, as he was plowing with twelve yoke of
oxen; he was following the twelfth. Elijah went over
to him and threw his cloak over him. Elisha left the
oxen, ran after Elijah, and said, "Please, let me kiss
my father and mother goodbye, and I will follow
you." "Go back!" Elijah answered. "Have I done
anything to you?" Elisha left him and, taking the
yoke of oxen, slaughtered them; he used the plowing
equipment for fuel to boil their flesh, and gave it to
his people to eat. Then he left and followed Elijah as
his attendant.

1 Kings 19:19-21

The call of Elisha

I T was at God's command that Elijah left Horeb and took the long road to Damascus. On the way, at a time unknown and perhaps much later, he arrived at Abel-meholah at the northern end of the Jordan Valley where he encountered Elisha,[1] the son of Shaphat. He was plowing in the field when he was called by the man of God to follow him. The young farmer immediately responded to the invitation of Elijah, who threw his cloak over Elisha, no doubt the "hairy garment" that was his usual garb (2 Kgs 1:8).

This gesture, scholars tell us, was a symbol of the divine call to leave all and accept the prophetic vocation. Elisha, who understood the message, ran after the prophet saying: "Please, let me kiss my father and mother goodbye, and I will follow you" (1 Kgs 19:20). This request was a very human one that attests his reverence for his parents. At the same time to witness to the sincerity of his desire to leave all and follow the prophet he destroyed his oxen and plough, a sure sign of his total obedience to the divine call. Having broken with the past he then followed Elijah as his attendant.

In the beginning their relationship was more that of master and servant, confirmed by the statement that "he poured water on the hands of Elijah" (2 Kgs 3:11). There is no further comment on the relationship until Elijah at the end of his earthly sojourn is taken up to heaven in a whirlwind. At the time he was in the company of Elisha who had come with him from Gilgal. What, we may ask, had been their relationship during the few years they were together? Scripture is silent. But it seems that a bond of friendship had blossomed between the two men as they shared each other's company and mission. The affection of Elisha for his master is manifest in the anguish he displayed when Elijah was being taken up from him: he cried out, "My father! My father!" As a further sign of his grief he grasped his garment and tore it in two (2 Kgs 2:12).

But let us return to the first meeting of the two prophets. One cannot help but notice the dissimilarity of their vocations. Both are called by God, but how different their background! Elijah is the "mystery man" who appears suddenly and dramatically in the public life of King Ahab. We hear nothing about his parents, his youth, his education, his work. He is a solitary, a loner, without fixed abode. Elisha, on the other hand, is the son of Shaphat, a well-to-do farmer who owns among other things twelve pair of oxen. Moreover, he is a devoted son: before leaving to follow Elijah he asked to return to bid farewell to his parents. To this Elijah answered: "Go back, have I done anything to you?" This reply is enigmatic. Perhaps he meant to say: "Go back. Am I stopping you?" In other words, he seems to be informing Elisha that it would be better to reflect well on what he was about to do, and to weigh the cost he must pay before making a definite decision. This meaning seems acceptable, especially since Elisha returned to his mother and father, slaughtered the animals and fed the people. It was only then that he followed Elijah.

Some commentators consider the final meal of Elisha as a sacrifical banquet in which he asked his family to join him as he consecrated himself to a prophetic career that in the end would last over sixty years.[2]

One final comment: Elisha was answering a divine call. He did not choose Yahweh; rather Yahweh chose him. For it was Yahweh who said to Elijah on Mount Horeb: "Go, take the road back to the desert near Damascus ... When you arrive, you shall anoint ... Elisha, son of Shaphat of Abel-meholah, as prophet to succeed you" (1 Kgs 19:15-16). In the life of the prophets it is God who calls, man who responds. And usually, as in the case of Elisha, the cost was great. It meant not only the giving up of a comfortable world, the breaking away from home and natural ties; it also involved a great risk. It meant casting his lot with Elijah, a man who was far from being a popular hero. Indeed he had enemies, powerful enemies, in high places.

I. Carmelite Tradition

Avid Bible readers are familiar with the call and the response of Elisha to the prophetic life, his filial relationship with Elijah, and their common mission to preserve the pure faith of Israel, witnessed by their proclamation, "God lives, whose servant I am."

But what is not so well known is that these two prophets are inseparable companions in Carmel's tradition, not so much because they were prophets but because they were considered the fathers and originators of monastic life. Evidence for this statement is easily discovered by consulting the oldest Constitutions of the Order, the Carmelite coat of arms, and the papal documents that approved the Order. If more tangible proof were required all one need do is visit older Carmelite churches that invariably display in prominent places the statues of these founding fathers.

However it is not our intention to look into the long tradition of Elisha as a founding father. Our concern is the Carmelite interpretation of the vocation of Elisha. And so we ask: does our tradition attach any importance to the call and response of Elisha? And if so, how did the early Carmelites present the vocation of this remarkable prophet to its members?

An examination of the literature, art and liturgy of the Order that flourished especially in the 17th and 18th centuries indicates that members of Carmel were trained to believe that a vocation was a divine call, and that those who received the invitation were called to respond, after the example of Elisha, with a ready and generous heart. A few examples will illustrate the point.[3]

1. Literature

One of the earliest Carmelite writers was John of Chemineto, a doctor of theology from Paris, author of the *Speculum*,[4] who clearly enunciates for the first time that Elijah was the founder of the Order and that one of his first disciples was the prophet Elisha.[5]

However the importance of the vocation of Elisha in Carmel's tradition is brought out clearly in *The Institution of the First Monks,* the celebrated 14th century work of Philip Ribot so often quoted in these pages. This book, as we know, remained for centuries the ultimate authority for things Carmelite.

The author clearly states: The greatest disciple of Elijah was Elisha, who was plowing his field when Elijah called him to leave all and follow the monastic life.[6] It should be noticed that the *Institution* refers to Elisha's vocation as a call to the monastic life; and from that time on subsequent writers on Carmel's origin were to be influenced by this assertion.

Two of the more influential writers who carried on this tradition were the Spaniard, John Baptist Lezana (d. 1659), who spent many years in Rome, and the Belgian, Daniel of the Blessed Virgin Mary (d. 1678), whose works contain interesting materials although he was not a professional historian and, according to Smet, lacked a critical sense.

Lezana, in his defense of Elijah as founder of Carmelite monastic life, asks the question: Who was the first disciple of Elijah? By reason of dignity and importance it is Elisha, he asserts. His prompt response to the call to follow Elijah, his outstanding miracles, and his inheritance of the double spirit of Elijah as the latter was taken up to heaven, all manifest his primacy as successor and leader of the monks of Carmel.[7]

Referring to the vocation of Elisha, Lezana states it was a call to be not a servant, but the son of the father, the disciple of the master, in the monastic prophetic life. For this defender of the tradition, Elisha's call was to religious life on Mount Carmel.

Echoing the same teaching and influenced by both the *Institution* and Lezana, Daniel of the Virgin Mary declares that when Elijah anointed Elisha by throwing his mantle over him, he made him not only a prophet but a monk, indeed his companion and designated successor to the institute of monks. By this anointing, he says, the heart of Elisha was turned to good: from a lay person he became a religious, from a farmer a prophet. He goes on to relate that Elisha left everything—family, home, property—to embrace a life of poverty, a life that the apostles were to embrace when called by Christ. One day, he writes, Peter and Andrew would leave their nets and follow Christ, much as Elisha left his farm to follow Elijah. Long before Christ called his disciples, Elisha heard the call from Elijah and, in due time, lived on Mount Carmel with other prophets following the solitary life of monks according to the example of their master, who sought always to walk in the presence of the living God.

These three sources, the *Institution*, the *Annales* of Lezana, and the *Speculum* of Daniel of the Virgin Mary, exercised great influence on subsequent Carmelite writers and helped to foster the belief that Elijah and Elisha were founders of the Carmelite Order. Today we do not consider these two prophets juridical organizers of our religious life, but rather our spiritual founders, models who inspired our ancestors and who continue to inspire us to live in the presence of the living and true God and to be faithful witnesses to his presence and operation in a secularized world.

2. Art

Since art has always had a significant place in the education of people in the church, we are not surprised to see the vocation of Elisha depicted by artists. Among the more notable works are the following: the fresco in the monastery of St Elijah in

Romania (16th century); the painting of Jan Metsys in the Museum of Beaux Arts in Antwerp; and the painting of John Baptist Despax. The latter is just one of a series of paintings of the life of Elijah and Elisha that was done by the artist between the years 1747-1751 in the former chapel of the Discalced Carmelite nuns of Toulouse. Among works dear to Carmelites is the fresco of Gaspare Dughet, one of a series in the church of San Martino ai Monti, Rome, and the drawing of the Dutch artist Abraham van Diepenbeke (17th century) that is found in the *Speculum Carmelitanum* of Daniel of the Virgin Mary. Diepenbeke had close ties with the Carmelites and did other remarkable works for them in the churches of Antwerp and Boxmeer.

3. Liturgy

One of the more important sources that reveal the Carmelite charism is the cult of its saints. Early in its history Carmel venerated Elisha in its liturgy. However it should be observed that long before Carmelites came into existence both the Greek and the Latin churches commemorated the great prophet in their martyrologies on June 14. In the eighth and ninth centuries the Church of the Twelve Apostles in Constantinople celebrated a common feast in honor of Elijah and Elisha.

In the West, however, it is the Carmelites who celebrated the feast of Elisha. The Constitutions of 1369 contain the first official decree approving the feast. Later the General Chapter held in Florence in 1399 introduced the feast into the Order. This was before any liturgical honor was given to Elijah. Later still the General Chapter of Paris, in 1456, ordered the prayer: "St Elisha pray for us" added to the litany. By the beginning of the 15th century all liturgical manuscripts contain the feast of Elisha, prophet and leader of Carmel; his cult by this time is well established in the Order.

But since our concern here is restricted to the vocation itself of Elisha and not to his public or prophetic life we ask: Does the liturgy refer specifically to the call of Elisha? Indeed it does; it should be acknowledged that it gives more attention to his many miracles, however, and to the scene of his reception of the cloak of Elijah as the latter was taken up into heaven. Nevertheless, his vocation is clearly emphasized in the celebration of the Eucharist in the Missal of 1478, in which we find the following offertory antiphon:

> Elijah found Elisha plowing with twelve yoke of oxen and placed his mantle over his shoulders. And Elisha immediately left his oxen and ran after Elijah crying: "I pray you, let me kiss my father and mother farewell and then I will follow you."

The communion antiphon alludes to the response of Elisha when it recalls the words of Jesus: "Everyone who leaves father or mother, home or fields, for my sake will receive a hundredfold and possess eternal life." There is also a further reference to the call of Elisha in the postcommunion prayer in which we ask God through the intercession of Elisha to help us use temporal goods in order to attain spiritual goods: "O God, who has so wonderfully satisfied us with spiritual food, grant we beseech you, that through the intercession and merits of your prophet St Elisha, we may use temporal goods so that we may attain eternal ones."[8]

This emphasis on the vocation of Elisha, unfortunately, was not repeated in subsequent missals. The reformed Missal of 1587 for example, refers more to the double spirit of Elijah that descended on Elisha, and the Missal of 1703 makes no mention of the call of Elisha. Even in this century the Missal of 1935 omits the call in the feast day mass of June 14, as well as in the votive mass of Elijah and Elisha.

The revision of the liturgy after the Second Vatican Council, approved in 1979, omits the feast of St Elisha entirely; he is commemorated only in the votive mass of Elijah and Elisha, and this latter makes no reference to the vocation of Elisha. However, the Mass for Religious Profession found in the Roman missal and reproduced in the Carmelite missal offers a variety of readings, and one of these is the vocation of Elisha (1 Kgs 19:16b,19-21). Evidently the Latin church as well as the Order still finds the vocation of Elisha a subject of inspiration for young religious.

If we turn our attention to the divine office we discover that Lezana, the faithful chronicler of Carmelite affairs, refers to a proper office honoring Elisha for the years 1462 and 1495.[9]

A 1480 breviary contains the office of Elisha and describes his call to leave the farm to follow Elijah in the Magnificat antiphon. Later the Breviary of 1504 recalls in the hymn of first vespers that Elisha left all things to follow Elijah, and offers this as an example for mendicant religious. Again the first antiphon of the first nocturn mentions his response to the call of Elijah.

From the late 17th to the latter part of the 20th century—until the revised liturgy that appeared in the 1970's—the same office for Elisha was celebrated in the universal Order. In these breviaries we find significant references to the call of Elisha: for example, the five antiphons of first vespers and the Magnificat antiphon tell the story of the call of Elisha as found in the Book of Kings; the first lesson of the first nocturn of matins is taken from 1 Kgs 19:15-17, 19-20. This prominent position given to the call of Elisha in the divine office that was recited annually by Carmelites over a period of four hundred years surely indicates the spiritual value the Order placed on this event, one that no doubt inspired many a Carmelite to give him or herself more generously to the service of God.

From this brief survey it is obvious that the vocation of Elisha has had a conspicuous place in the prayer life of the formation of younger religious. Therefore it should not come as a surprise if some older men and women in the Order lament that the revised liturgy has given so little attention to the vocation of the most important disciple of Elijah. Surely it would be helpful to be reminded today as in the past that it is God who calls us to Carmel, and that, like Elisha, we are called to surrender totally to his will.

In concluding these thoughts on our tradition we believe it can be truthfully said that the Order in its literature, art and liturgy, to name only some of the more important sources, continued down through the centuries to present the vocation of Elisha as a model to be followed. Is it not true today as in the past that our response should emulate that of the foremost disciple of Elijah in its promptness and generosity? "Please, let me kiss my father and mother goodbye, and I will follow you" (1 Kgs 19:20). God wants an undivided heart.

II. Carmel's call today

The literature, liturgy and iconography of Carmel bear witness to the fact that the vocation of Elisha which led him to abandon parents, home and

188

property to follow Elijah has been a model for Carmelites, a subject of their meditations, a reminder that it is God who gives the invitation to embrace the prophetic life. In other words, our ancestors in Carmel learned from Elisha to accept willingly, without delay, the mantle of Elijah as a call from God, and to offer themselves generously in the spirit of Elijah to be prophetic witnesses in the church.

In the light of this tradition we ask: how do we interpret our Carmelite vocation today? Do we live in the spirit of Elijah and Elisha, our spiritual fathers?

1. The family of Carmel

Before answering this question let us preface our remarks by stating what we mean by a Carmelite vocation. It is a divine invitation to share in the life of the Carmelite family, a family that includes lay people as well as those living religious life in community. This family is well described in the Constitutions of the Order.

> The group of people, who receive inspiration from our Rule and who spiritually make up the Carmelite family in the Church today, are striving, each in his own way, to share Carmelite life. Although independent of one another as regards jurisdiction perhaps, they are still bound together by a special bond of love, of spirit, and of sharing spiritual benefits. Such is the case with us and our brothers of the Teresian Reform, the nuns of both Second Orders, the Third Orders Regular and Secular, the Secular Institutes and the people united to the Order by means of the Brown Scapular or enjoying affiliation in some other way.[10]

Returning to the question concerning our understanding of the Carmelite vocation today, and the way we live it, it seems that rather than offer a theological exposition of Carmel's vocation, it would be more practical to present the testimony of Carmelites of our time who have lived the life for a number of years. Let them tell us how they understand and experience their life in Carmel.

Our thoughts turn first to Blessed Titus Brandsma, a Carmelite of the twentieth century, who was beatified on November 3, 1985. He was martyred in Dachau on July 25, 1942, at 62 years of age. In a series of lectures delivered at the Catholic University of America in Washington, D.C., during the month of July, 1935, he stated:

> While the schools of St. Bernard and St. Francis are schools of love, seraphic love, and the Dominican, intellectual, the school of Carmel achieves a happy mean, a harmony of both. Surely those who dwell in Carmel would have caught from the flame a spark of the love and zeal which burned in the great Prophet. Fire is the most expressive symbol of love. "I am come to cast fire on the earth." It is this fire which enveloped Elias when, according to the witness of Scripture, he was taken up to heaven in a fiery chariot. Wrapped in that seraphic flame he was taken from the earth. Carmel must ever feel that glow of its founder's zeal. It is the mark of the true follower of Elias. It burns in all the Carmelite saints. Especially too we see it in the soul of seraphic St. Teresa of Avila. The smouldering fires that burned in the soul of "this undaunted daughter of desires" is Carmel's greatest witness to the spirit of Elias. In these great souls have been fulfilled the Prophet's words which encircle the Order's escutcheon, "With zeal I have been zealous for the Lord God of Hosts."[11]

Closer to our own time we have the witness of Father Bartholomew Xiberta, outstanding Carmelite theologian of this century, who spent his summer months for many years giving retreats and conferences to Carmelite cloistered nuns in Italy and Spain. "Let us live each day in the presence of God, singing his praises, mindful that in this way we share in some way in the life to come when we shall live always in the loving presence of God." In expressing these thoughts Father Xiberta had no intention of giving a complete description of the Carmelite vocation, but he does bring out the soul, the spirit of Carmelite life.

It is remarkable how similar his thought is to that of Blessed Elizabeth of the Trinity, beatified in November, 1984. Writing to a friend in 1903 she exclaimed: "The life of Carmel is a communion with God from morning to night and from night to morning ... We perceive him in everything, because we bear him within us, and our life is an anticipated heaven." We find in her a prophet of the presence of God reminiscent of her spiritual father, Elijah, and his disciple, Elisha.

More recently Father Falco Thuis, former General of the Order, at the close of his twelve years of leadership, penned these words:

> The course of action for the Order today is: to pledge ourselves seriously and authentically to individual contemplative prayer and to promote it in community;
>
> to accord a central place to the bible in the community plan; this is expressed in specific forms, proved by the experience of the last years, such as "meditation in common on the gospel," the practice introduced into various communities of listening to, confronting, and living the word of God read together with the people in the liturgy and in the meetings of the community itself;
>
> to live the presence of God in human history in a practical way which involves sharing of faith, community discernment, and revision of life;
>
> to offer the people what is most specifically expected of a Carmelite: experiencing God in one's life, rediscovering what this means together with the humblest classes of society and thus bringing out the transcendental dimension of one's own existence.[12]

If we look among the rank and file of the Carmelite family with whom we have lived we find them faithful to Carmel's tradition. For example, Father Ernest Larkin, a member of the Order for over forty years, a former professor at the Catholic University of America, a recognized authority on the writings of St Teresa and St John of the Cross, relates own experience:

> To be a Carmelite has meant the challenge to be prayerful, the gift of friendship, and the privilege of proclaiming God's word. All my life the Carmelite charism has meant these three things, and in that order. But in my latter years I have come to accept a different sequence. I see my life as sourced in community, and by that I mean friendship and authentic human relationships. If I don't live the Christian message with my brothers and sisters whom I see, how can I love God or serve him among people who are unknown to me?

A friend and school companion of Father Ernest, Father Eamon Carroll, a professor of theology at Loyola University Chicago, an eminent, internationally known Mariologist, offers this understanding of Carmelite life:

> Commitment to prayer, community prayer, above all the Mass and divine office, but also private prayer, especially mental prayer, and the service of God and the Christian people in imitation of Mary, the gospel woman of faith, loving patroness of the Order from its origins on Mount Carmel.

Another witness who offers his experience in Carmel is Father Redemptus Valabek, who has spent most of his twenty-five years in the priesthood in Rome, engaged in the formation of young religious, teaching theology and writing. He writes that Carmel for him means: "to share with all those whose lives we touch, and who touch our lives, the familiarity and intimacy of life in Mary's family of

Carmel, our communion in the divine milieu being vivified by a great variety of prayer experiences."

At this point one may ask how do the cloistered nuns understand their call to Carmel? The nuns of the Carmel of Hudson, Wisconsin, perceive their vocation as living with Christ. They write: "Carmel is centeredness in Jesus, being called to live as Mary, in attentive openness to God's Word. It is rooted and nourished in a community of prayer, interceding for his people, in freedom, joy and faithful love."

The Carmelite family includes many Congregations of Third Order Sisters. Each Congregation follows the spirit of Carmel with its own specific work. Mother Angeline Teresa, foundress of the Carmelite Sisters for the Aged and Infirm, who died on January 21, 1984, and who still inspires her sisters, often invited the latter to contemplate the great gift of their vocation. For the feast of the Immaculate Conception, 1952, she sent this message to all her communities:

> Yes, let our hearts be inflamed with zeal for our Carmelite vocation, and let us look back on the past year. From the time of the morning meditation until the end of the evening office—be faithful.

She goes on to point out the specific vocation of a sister called to the service of the aged and infirm. How she understood this call and wished to impart its spirit to all the sisters can be gleaned from the following prayer found among her personal papers:

> Dearest Lord, may I see Thee today and every day in the person of the aged and sick, and while caring for them, minister unto Thee. Though Thou hidest Thyself behind the unattractive disguise of the irritable, the exacting, the unreasonable, may I still recognize Thee and say: Jesus, my Patient, how sweet it is to serve Thee. Lord, give me this seeing faith. Then my work will never be monotonous. I will ever find a new joy in humoring and gratifying the fancies

and wishes of all the aged. O beloved sick, how doubly dear you are to me when you personify Christ, and what a privilege is mine to be allowed to nurse you. Sweetest Lord, make me appreciate my noble vocation and its many responsibilities. Never permit me to disgrace it by giving way to coldness, unkindness, or impatience; and my God, whilst Thou art Jesus, my Patient, deign also to be my Patient Jesus, bearing my with my many faults, looking only to my intention, which is always to love and serve Thee in the person of each and every one of the aged. Lord, increase my faith, bless my efforts and sanctify my work for the aged and infirm.[13]

The Sisters of Mount Carmel, another Congregation of the Order dedicated to the current needs of the church, especially in Louisiana and the Philippine Islands, is also faithful to the contemplative-Marian spirit of Carmel as we see in the words of Mother Dorothy Guilbault:

> Our vocation, like that of Elijah, is to be a prophetic witness. "God lives, whose servant I am!" Our task, like his, is to sow the seed and to leave the fruit to God's good time—we strive to cultivate the presence of the Living God and bask in His goodness and love.[14]

If we are wondering how Lay Carmelites perceive their vocation, we have the statement of Father Aloysius Sieracki, provincial director of the Lay Carmelites in Aylesford, Illinois: "When asked by many what does it mean to be a Lay Carmelite, I answer that it is an attempt to live a prayerful presence in a busy world. We have beautiful exemplars given to us in Mary, Mother of Carmel, and in Elijah, our spiritual Father. Let us follow their examples and rise to the challenge."

And this declaration is beautifully witnessed by Mrs Jude Langsam, a secular Discalced Carmelite for over ten years. She writes: "To live as a secular Carmelite is, with Mary, to hear the Word of God and treasure him in our hearts, giving witness with our lives, as did Elijah, that the Lord God lives, before whom we stand."[15]

However, we do not think you can find a more concise and complete statement of the Carmelite charism than the following:

> To follow Jesus Christ as brothers and sisters of the Blessed Virgin Mary, called together by the Holy Spirit to live as Elijah in the presence of God. To serve the needs of the Church and each other in love.

This statement was first drawn up by Father Paul Hoban, former Provincial of the Province of the Mose Pure Heart of Mary. During his term of office he canvassed the province of some three hundred men to determine their understanding of the Carmelite vocation, and he then composed the above formula which he believes is an accurate presentation of their responses. He then designed a very attractive plaque with the words of the formula enclosed within the shield of the Order; copies of this plaque can be found adorning the walls of many of the houses of the province.

We have presented a number of statements from members of the Carmelite family that represent different ways of life in Carmel. What conclusion can we draw from them? It is evident that all of them stress prayerfulness as one element that is characteristic of the Carmelite vocation—indeed the special characteristic of the Order. In this they are faithful to the Carmelite Rule that declares: "Let each one remain in his cell, or near it, meditating day and night on the law of the Lord and keeping vigil in prayer unless occupied with other lawful duties."[16]

Some did not mention Elijah. But all, we may be sure, if questioned would say that living in God's presence finds its exemplar in the life of Elijah who exclaimed: "That God lives, in whose presence I stand." Furthermore, they would agree that when Elisha asked Elijah for a double portion of his spirit as he was taken up to heaven, surely that spirit included living in God's presence and serving him well. And it is this "living in God's presence" of our spiritual fathers that we seek and hope to imitate in our Carmelite life.

To avoid any misunderstanding we would like to stress that the prayerful dimension, although essential and foundational, is only one element of the Carmelite charism. There are also the Marian element and the active apostolate that cannot and should not be overlooked. And it will be noticed that both these elements were mentioned by some members of the different groups. What we wish to stress is this: Carmel is essentially prayerful, contemplative by design. In the beginning on Mount Carmel the hermits worshiped God in love, guided by the example of Elijah and under the motherly protection of the Virgin Mary, the "mother of the place." This way of life overflowed in the course of time into apostolic activity and still does for many Carmelites. Carmel has always emphasized its contemplative dimension because Carmel without prayer is meaningless, a body without a soul.

2. The Body of Christ

These reflections lead us to a few final thoughts. Is there a place for Carmelite life in the church today? Are we relevant to the times? Are we necessary? In the final years of the twentieth century it would seem that the world and the church need men and women who choose the way of Carmel, the way of living constantly in the presence of the living God after the example of Elijah and Elisha, our spiritual fathers. We say this because in the Western world the danger persists of eliminating God from every sphere of daily life. The church needs witnesses to proclaim in their lives that God lives, that he is incarnate in Jesus Christ, and that he dwells in us through the power of the Holy Spirit. We are called to prepare the people of our time to meet the Lord. In this mission Carmelites surely share.

But how great is the danger of forgetting God? Listen to men who are in a position to know and to evaluate the times in which we live. When Pope John XXIII convoked the Second Vatican Council he did it to bring the modern world into contact with God whom it had excluded. He saw that to a great extent the world had lost sight of God. It had embarked on a search for earthly pleasure: "And hence there is," he said, "a completely new and disconcerting fact: the existence of a militant atheism which is active on a world level."[17]

Almost thirty years have passed since the pope made this startling statement. And so we may ask: has the world turned back to God? Has the church really entered into serious dialogue with secularism? Is the world less atheistic since the Vatican Council? Limiting his judgment to Europe Cardinal George Basil Hume, O.S.B., in an address to the European Laity Forum in Dublin on July 12, 1984, spoke of the spiritual impoverishment of Europe. Disturbed by the arms race, the disparity in wealth between rich and poor nations, and man's inhumanity to man—three manifestations of human wickedness—the Cardinal called for more active participation by the laity:

Europe is divided; Europe is faithless ... This is the continent ... which ... we are called to evangelize.

No longer is our continent united in the Christian faith ... Europe needs apostles. Europe needs

Christians who will live their faith and be witnesses to its truth ... Europe needs you to live the vocation Christ has given you ...

And now, in our own time in the latter half of the twentieth century, there is no doubt that to face the irreligion and unbelief of our time, to face sheer materialism and the cult of consumerism, the new apostles of our age must be Christian lay men and women ...

You are sent then by Christ to share in ... the sanctification of your immediate environment. That must surely begin in the family.[18]

Does the Cardinal sound too pessimistic? Anyone inclined to think so should ponder the story of the London jeweller who advertized gold and silver crosses for sale. The notice read: "With the little man on it, three pounds; without the little man, two pounds." Perhaps it is incidents like this that prompted Pope John Paul II to invite representatives of Europe to a symposium in October, 1982, on the evangelization of Europe.

But one might ask, does Christianity fare better in other regions? Some look to North America, and specifically to the United States, with hope. They point out that a large proportion of the people attend church regularly, believe in miracles, in scripture as the Word of God, and in life after death. This may be true, but secularization is also a fact in America. It is estimated that 90,000,000 Americans have no church family that they can call their own, and there approximately 15,000,000 Catholics who are inactive.

Father Alvin Illig, director of the Paulist National Catholic Evangelization Association, lamented a few years ago that "we Catholic evangelizers have failed over the past 10 years to raise public awareness among the 52,000,000 active American Catholics that the laity are to be the evangelizers." He wondered whether we are becoming an elitist church, with no room for fringe people who often make up the unchurched and inactive. "Are we," he asked, "forgetting that Christ founded his church for sinners?"

However, he was not daunted and called on Catholics to meet the challenge. Recalling that on December 8, 1975, Pope Paul VI had published his Exhortation *Evangelization in the Modern World,* in which he laid out a 25 year vision for Catholic evangelization, Illig added: "With God's grace, through prayer and work, Catholic evangelizers are committed in the next 15 years to finding more effective ways to carry out Christ's call to offer the good news of salvation to all people."

One such group of lay evangelizers who promise hope is the American Catholic Lay Network that is primarily a communications network among small faith communities, for mutual support, learning and action. Leaders in this group feel that Justice and Peace Centers, often under the guidance of religious orders, are not strong enough to change patterns of society. They believe the laity must share the action, take the major role in being a leaven to society to give it new purpose and spiritual life.

Does this say something to Lay Carmelites? Are they ready to meet the challenge?

Our reflections up to this point have concentrated primarily on the problems of Europe and North America. What is to be said of the state of the church in South America and countries of the East? And what place does Carmel have in the life of the church in these areas? Does the church in the non-Western countries face a bleak or a promising future?

Fortunately, the reports coming from Africa, Asia, India and South America—where there is a continuous growth of the church—are encouraging. Vocations to the priesthood and religious life are increasing, and new missionary congregations and institutes are rising.

One is pleasantly surprised to learn that whereas in 1900 about 80 percent of all Christians were in the West, by 1980 over 58 percent were living in non-Western or Third World areas. Consequently, Christianity is no longer the religion of the white race, and for the first time we have a world-wide Church. Some go so far as to predict that in the year 2000 we can expect 70 percent of Christians to be non-Western.

We could offer any number of specific examples to back up these statements, but for the sake of brevity we limit ourselves to a few related by the eminent historian, Monsignor John Tracy Ellis, who writes that

> South Korea is experiencing an almost startling growth in Catholicism, as a bishop friend told me after a visit there two years ago, where in the capital city of Seoul he found 4,000 under instruction in the cathedral parish. A year ago a priest friend made a trip to South Korea which included stops at all the seminaries in that country, all of which, he said, were filled to capacity.

Referring to Africa the Monsignor added this anecdote:

> A year ago ... I fell in line with a black priest from Africa at the university's [Catholic University in Washington, D.C.] opening Mass of the Holy Spirit, and as the procession moved into the National Shrine of the Immaculate Conception he informed me that he was from the largest seminary in the Catholic world, an institution that had over 400 students.[19]

III. Conclusion

If we compare the religious indifference and partial decline of Christianity in Europe—as described especially by Cardinal Hume—with the continous growth of the church in non-Western countries we are startled by the comparison. The diversity of the problems that face evangelizers in these different areas is surely enormous. Europeans, and to some extent North Americans, must find ways to give a positive turn to the process of religious decline in their areas, while the non-Europeans must find ways of inculturating Christianity in their regions.

It is not our place here to enter into these problems, but rather to ask the question: How do Carmelites, who belong to an international religious order, fit into the present problems of the church and its missionary spirit of evangelization with which it is now faced? Down through the centuries the Carmelites have carried out their apostolate in the church mainly in Europe and in South and North America. But today we are moving with the church and find ourselves engaged actively in Africa, Asia, India and with renewed commitment to South America. We find, too, that the Order is being enriched with many more religious vocations in these non-Western countries than in Europe and North America. We are becoming more and more an international or world-wide Order.

As we face the challenge of sharing in the building of the church in non-Christian countries do we as Carmelites have anything to offer? If it is true that in many of these countries, especially in Asia, the people have a natural inclination to a contemplative life of prayer, should not our Elijan charism "God lives, in whose presence I stand" find fertile ground in which to flourish? Should we not be encouraged to bring to new foundations the special characteristic prayer life of our Rule "meditating day and night on the law of the Lord and keeping vigil in prayer unless occupied with other lawful duties?"[20] Surely, the spirit of Elijah that was aflame in the heart of St Teresa of Avila, St John of the Cross, St Therese of Lisieux, Bl Elizabeth of the Trinity and Bl Titus Brandsma can burn brightly again in far off countries.

But first there must be those who can bring the spirit of Carmel to the people. This is our challenge today. Would that we could catch with Elisha a spark of the love and zeal that burned in the heart of Elijah, the prophet of Carmel. Would that we could share in the smoldering fire that burned in the heart of St Teresa, whom Bl Titus called the greatest witness of the spirit of Elijah.

VIII

Some time after this, as Naboth the Jezreelite had a vineyard in Jezreel next to the palace of Ahab, king of Samaria, Ahab said to Naboth, "Give me your vineyard to be my vegetable garden, since it is close by, next to my house. I will give you a better vineyard in exchange, or, if you prefer, I will give you its value in money." "The LORD forbid," Naboth answered him, "that I should give you my ancestral heritage." Ahab went home disturbed and angry at the answer Naboth the Jezreelite had made to him: "I will not give you my ancestral heritage." Lying down on his bed, he turned away from food and would not eat.

His wife Jezebel came to him and said to him: "Why are you so angry that you will not eat?" He answered her, "Because I spoke to Naboth the Jezreelite and said to him, 'Sell me your vineyard, or, if you prefer, I will give you a vineyard in exchange.' But he refused to let me have his vineyard." "A fine ruler over Israel you are indeed!" his wife Jezebel said to him. "Get up. Eat and be cheerful. I will obtain the vineyard of Naboth the Jezreelite for you."

So she wrote letters in Ahab's name and, having sealed them with his seal, sent them to the elders and to the nobles who lived in the same city with Naboth. This is what she wrote in the letters: "Proclaim a fast and set Naboth at the head of the people. Next, get two scoundrels to face him and accuse him of having cursed God and king. Then take him out and stone him to death." His fellow citizens—the elders and the nobles who dwelt in his city—did as Jezebel had ordered them in wrting, through the letters she had sent them. They proclaimed a fast and placed Naboth at the head of the people. Two scoundrels came in and confronted him with the accusation, "Naboth has cursed God and king." And they led him out of the city and stoned him to death. Then they sent the information to Jezebel that Naboth had been stoned to death.

When Jezebel learned that Naboth had been stoned to death, she said to Ahab, "Go on, take possession of the vineyard of Naboth the Jezreelite which he refused to sell you, because Naboth is not alive but dead." On hearing that Naboth was dead, Ahab started off on his way down to the vineyard of Naboth the Jezreelite, to take possession of it.

But the LORD said to Elijah the Tishbite. "Start down to meet Ahab, king of Israel, who rules in Samaria. He will be in the vineyard of Naboth, of which he has come to take possession. This is what you shall tell him, 'The LORD says: After murdering, do you also take possession? For this, the LORD says: In the place where the dogs licked up the blood of Naboth, the dogs shall lick up your blood, too.'" "Have you found me out, my enemy?" Ahab said to Elijah. "Yes," he answered, "Because you have given yourself up to doing evil in the LORD's sight, I am bringing evil upon you: I will destroy you and will cut off every male in Ahab's line, whether slave or freeman, in Israel. I will make your house like that of Jeroboam, son of Nebat, and like that of Baasha, son of Ahijah, because of how you have provoked me by *leading Israel into sin." (Against Jezebel, too, the LORD declared, "The dogs shall devour Jezebel in the district of Jezreel.") "When one of Ahab's line dies in the city, dogs will devour him; when one of them dies in the field, the birds of the sky will devour him." Indeed, no one gave himself up to the doing of evil in the sight of the LORD as did Ahab, urged on by his wife Jezebel. He became completely abominable by following idols, just as the Amorites had done, whom the LORD drove out before the Israelites.*

When Ahab heard these words, he tore his garments and put on sackcloth over his bare flesh. He fasted, slept in the sackcloth, and went about subdued. Then the LORD said to Elijah the Tishbite, "Have you seen that Ahab has humbled himself before me? Since he has humbled himself before me, I will not bring the evil in his time. I will bring the evil upon his house during the reign of his son."

1 Kings 21

Naboth's Vineyard

T HE confrontation of Elijah and Ahab in the garden of Naboth is the third episode in the Elijah cycle in which the prophet met the king. It is difficult to determine the time of the event. It could have taken place sometime after the vision on Horeb when Elijah returned to Israel. In the Bible the episode is placed between two wars: Ahab's victories over Ben-hadad of Damascus (1 Kgs 20), and his final battle in which he succumbed at Ramoth-gilead (1 Kgs 22).

In his attempt to expand his property near his second home in Jezreel, modern Zerin near Mount Gelboa, Ahab offered his neighbor, Naboth, a good price. He had no intention of stealing the property. However, Naboth in no way could sell the land which, according to the custom of the time, was ancestral family property and inalienable. In other words, it was not just 'private property.' It belonged to the family or clan; it was a sacred inheritance that was to be handed down from generation to generation. This was a unique custom among Israelites, for whom God was the true owner of the land. He had brought the people out of bondage and decreed that the land be divided among the tribes. Consequently, Israel considered the land God's property, and the dwellers only stewards. Naboth spoke the truth when he said: "The LORD forbid that I should give you my ancestral heritage" (l Kgs 21: 3).

Ahab, of course, was well aware of this; it made him sullen and inspired Jezebel to concoct her wicked plan. She had come from a commercial civilization in Phoenicia and had little respect for Israelite customs or religion. She had no scruples about taking Naboth's vineyard. For her there were no limits to royal power. So she planned her strategy to get the property even if it meant lying. She had Naboth falsely accused of blasphemy and had him and his sons put to death. The property then went over to the king.

It was then that Yahweh called on Elijah to protest this gross act of injustice. Elijah confronted the king, told him of God's anger and foretold the terrible punishment. Ahab still seems to have had some faith in Yahweh and recognized his wrong-doing. He repented and did penance, and God, moved by his penance, commuted the punishment. The kingdom would not be taken from him during his lifetime, but it would be taken from his children. Elijah's meeting with Ahab calls to mind the confrontation of Nathan with King David after the latter had committed adultery with Bathsheba.

Elijah's denunciation of the king demonstrates that the role of the prophet is not only to defend the honor of Yahweh, but to defend the rights of the people. Latter prophets, Amos for example, time and again speak out against sins of injustice.

The injustice inflicted on poor Naboth is a classical example of the contrast between Baalism and Yahwism in the field of social justice. On Carmel the contest between the priests of Baal and Elijah had been between false and true religion; the

Naboth incident is a confrontation between social right and wrong.

From the time of Moses the solidarity of the people was encouraged and refined: all, the rich and the poor, were equal before God and the law. And whenever injustice entered the land, Yahweh intervened to defend and restore brotherly solidarity in the community.

Baalism, on the other hand, did not defend the downtrodden but upheld the power of the royalty. Jezebel lived by this law: no one said "no" to the king. But the law of Israel was different, so the Lord predicted a bloody death for Ahab and Jezebel (1 Kgs 21:19-24).[1]

One final remark: The prophet's intervention shows that he came to reestablish and to reconfirm the Mosaic covenant, to protest against the evils of a commercial civilization, and to restore the dignity of the human person. All people, the rich and the poor, the mighty and the lowly, are equal in God's eyes.

> If one of your kinsmen in any community is in need in the land which the LORD, your God, is giving you, you shall not harden your heart nor close your hand to him in his need. Instead, you shall open your hand to him and freely lend him enough to meet his need .... The needy will never be lacking in the land; that is why I command you to open your hand to your poor and needy kinsman in your country (Dt 15: 7-8,11).

Yahweh is a God of justice.

I. Carmelite tradition

The condemnation of king Ahab by Elijah for his brutal treatment of Naboth is not given a prominent place in Carmel's tradition. However this does not come as a surprise because the seizure of the Naboth vineyard is not primarily an Elijan story. The main characters are Naboth, Ahab and Jezebel. Elijah comes in only at the end of the tragedy, after Naboth had been stoned to death and Ahab taken over his property. The prophet can do nothing to undo the crime; he can only announce God's wrath and foretell the punishment that will be inflicted on Ahab and Jezebel. Elijah's role here is in sharp contrast to other Elijan stories where the prophet is the chief protagonist. Here his only task is to be the messenger of the Lord sent to reveal that it is Yahweh, and not the king, who rules in Israel.

1. Literature

But when we perceive Elijah as a messenger of the Lord sent to denounce oppression, does not this say something to Carmelites? Are we not called along with others to denounce injustice? We certainly are. But in our tradition Carmelites were not among the out-spoken critics of the rich, which is not surprising since they were hermits withdrawn from the mainstream of worldly activity. And even after they entered into the mendicant way of life they were guided more by their eremitical spirit. In fact Nicholas of Gaul, the Prior General who resigned his office to return to a purely eremitical life, claimed that in his day (1270) few Carmelites were prepared for apostolic activity such as preaching, hearing confessions, giving counsel.

> I who have made the round of the Provinces and become acquainted with their members must sadly admit how very few there are who have knowledge enough or aptitude for these offices.[2]

Shortly after this acid comment Carmelites began to frequent the universities and to prepare themselves for the apostolic life among the faithful. Yet, when we examine *The Institution of the First Monks*, although it acknowledges an active dimension to Carmelite life, it explains only the contemplative spirit. There is no reference to the pastoral care of the people, of the poor and the oppressed; there is no mention of the Naboth story.

Naboth's tragedy, however, does not go unnoticed in later Carmelite tradition. Father John Baptist Lezana in his legendary life of Elijah presents a lengthy account of the story for his 17th century readers.[3] He describes Elijah dwelling on Carmel with Elisha and the sons of the prophets. It was while he was living in solitude on the mountain that God called the prophet of fire to go down and confront Ahab. The latter immediately senses that the coming of the prophet means trouble and greets his adversary with the words: "Have you found me out, my enemy?" (1 Kgs 21: 20).

Lezana recounts the prophecy of Elijah and the punishment to be imposed. He recalls that Elijah then returned to Mount Carmel and told his disciples about the unjust act of Ahab and the punishment decreed by God. The disciples for their part gave themselves with greater fervor to the worship of Yahweh in song accompanied by musical instruments. Apparently, for Lezana, the Naboth tragedy confirmed these disciples of Carmel in their belief that Yahweh alone rules in Israel. There is no outcry against injustice to the oppressed.

Daniel of the Virgin Mary, the Belgian historian also writing in the 17th century, often relies on Lezana for information. He comments on the Naboth episode in his " life " of Elijah.[4] For him the Naboth incident also took place during the sojourn of Elijah on Carmel in the company of Elisha and their disciples. He recalls that the *Institution* affirms that it was on Carmel that Elijah established monastic life on his return from Horeb. Consequently, when Elijah was called by God to confront Ahab he came from Carmel.

In his comment on Ahab's crime Daniel often quotes the fathers, for example, St John Chrysostom and St Gregory the Great, who bring out the fact that the really poor and miserable in this world are the greedy rich, who sell their souls to the devil, as did Ahab and Jezebel, in order to satisfy their avarice. Thus, the root of all evil is greed. With colorful words, Daniel describes the fall of the proud, vain, ambitious, evil Jezebel, whose crime is worse than that of the weak Ahab. In this he follows the fathers of the church and scriptural commentators. He offers reflections on the punishment of Ahab who, moved by the words of Elijah, did penance in sackcloth and ashes, fasting and walking with bowed head in sorrow before the Lord. He recalls the words of Gregory the Great that describe the penance of Ahab as an example of humility and of God's mercy.

Other Carmelite writers closer to our own time have included the Naboth story in their biographies of Elijah. We mention the Italian Giuseppe Fanuchi of Lucca,[5] the Irish Carmelite A. E. Farrington, also of the late 19th century,[6] and Elias Magennis, former Prior General of the Order, whose book on Elijah was published in 1925.[7] They retell the Elijan story in their own words, emphasizing man's iniquity and God's punishment.

It is interesting that none of these writers apply the lesson of the Naboth story to the oppressors of their own time. They might easily have made a comparison between the unjust, high-handed action of Ahab and that of some of the ruling powers in their own day. This is particularly true in the case of Father Magennis, who often spoke out against injustice. He was deeply involved in the social, political and religious problems that plagued his beloved Ireland in the 1920's. Perhaps his reticence can be explained in that he did not wish to go beyond the bounds of the scriptural story of Elijah.

2. Preaching

One source where we might hope to find Carmelites concerned with the Naboth theme would be among the writings of preachers. Sacred oratory entered a period of unparalleled eloquence in the second half of the 17th century:

> Preaching was one of the most important apostolic concerns of the Order and absorbed much of its effort and talent. It was an alternative to an academic career, open to those who had not the ability or did not wish to pursue graduate studies. Preaching, however, was also assiduously engaged in by doctors of theology.[8]

Many outstanding preachers in Italy, Spain, France and the Low Countries graced the pulpits in this baroque period. While many were remarkable for their Marian, Advent and Lenten sermons, none seems to be remembered as a great proponent of Elijan themes. In this context one thinks of sermons preached by Monsignor Ronald Knox when he was still an Anglican, and his tract "Naboth's Vineyard in Pawn" levelled against the seizure of monasteries and other church properties by King Henry VIII, an action that he compared with Ahab's seizure of Naboth's vineyard.[9] Would that we could refer to similar sermons by Carmelites.

3. Liturgy and art

If we turn our attention to Carmelite liturgy we find that for centuries the Naboth narrative was only briefly recorded in the divine office. There is no mention of it in the missal. In the first breviary of the 17th century (1683) the fifth antiphon of the first vespers for the feast of St Elijah recalls the crime and punishment of Ahab: "You have killed and you have taken possession. Behold, I will inflict evil on you and destroy your family." This antiphon is found in subsequent breviaries until that of 1938, the last to be published before the revision mandated by the Second Vatican Council.

As far as iconography is concerned we find few paintings, frescoes or carvings depicting the scene of Naboth's vineyard. The few we have seen are highly valuable; we refer to the work of Abraham Diepenbeke, the Dutch artist, who together with other drawings of the Elijan cycle has left us three scenes: Elijah confronting Ahab with his crime, the prediction of Ahab's punishment, and Ahab with bowed head doing penance.

It would be wrong to conclude from this brief summary that, since Carmelite literature, art, and liturgy were not greatly influenced by the Naboth tragedy, individual Carmelites showed little or no interest in the plight of the poor and the needy. On the contrary, they shared the sufferings of the poor, the sick and the dying, especially in time of plagues and wars. In the last century two Carmelites who were directly associated with the social problems of their day were Archbishop Joachim Luch y Garriga, a native of Spain, and Father John Spratt of the Irish Province.

Joachim Luch y Garriga (1816-1882) was a talented young Carmelite who attracted the attention of the Holy See. He became Bishop of the Canary Islands, and then moved on to Salamanca and Barcelona, and finally to the Archbishopric of Seville. Pope Leo XIII made him a Cardinal in 1882, but death intervened before he received the red hat. Father Joachim Smet summarizes his long and distinguished career in these words:

> Joachim Luch was an active and zealous bishop. His tenure in each of his sees was marked by concern for the poor and the workers, promotion of Catholic schools and hospitals and the sisterhoods needed to staff them, care of seminaries and restoration of church buildings. His attitude to emerging social problems was that of a 19th century bourgeois.[10]

In Ireland a contemporary of Bishop Luch, Father John Spratt (1796-1871), born in Dublin, spent most of his Carmelite life working among the poor of that city. Smet describes his charitable works in these edifying terms:

> From 1834 until his death he acted as honorary secretary of the Sick and Indigent Roomkeepers Society, devoting much time to this activity. Charitable institutions due to him were a Magdalen Asylum and St. Joseph's Night Refuge. In 1856 he founded the Catholic Young Men's Society which offered instructive lectures by qualified speakers. Perhaps he is best remembered as a temperance crusader. He converted the chapel in Cuffe Lane into a temperance hall. He was signing a deed for the purchase of a refuge for poor women and children, when he died, Whitsunday, May 27, 1871.[11]

II. More recent tradition

In the last quarter of the 20th century the tragedy of Naboth has taken on new significance in Carmelite life. Carmelites in many provinces are engaged in confronting injustice and poverty. This concentrated effort received a great impetus from the decrees of the Second Vatican Council. "Thus we are witnesses of the birth of a new humanism, one in which man is defined first of all by his responsibility toward his brothers and toward history."[12] Again in the Synod of Bishops of 1971 we read:

> Action on behalf of justice and participation in the transformation of the world fully appear to us as a constitutive dimension of the preaching of the Gospel, or, in other words, of the Church's mission for the redemption of the human race and its liberation from every oppressive situation.[13]

The challenge of the Second Vatican Council and the Synod of Bishops has been met by the Order. For example, the General Congregation of the Carmelites that convened in Rio de Janeiro in 1980, sought to develop the recommendations of the General Chapter of 1977. The theme of the Congregation was *Called to Account by the Poor*.[14] It presented as model the Carmelite community which shares the world of the poor and of exploited workers. It made an explicit appeal to brotherhood outside our communities that would embrace the "little ones."

In 1983 the General Chapter of the Order continued the theme of justice and peace, and the prophetic figure of Elijah emerged as a model for our times. The tragedy of Naboth was time and again brought to the attention of the members, especially by Carlos Mesters in an address in which he emphasized Elijah, the prophet who walked with God not just in prayer but in solidarity with the oppressed and in the cause of justice. Without a doubt the General Chapter aroused the consciousness of the Order to reexamine its responsibility to the cry of the poor and the oppressed.

And now that the Congregation for the Doctrine of the Faith has issued its document on liberation theology entitled *Instruction on Christian Freedom and Liberation,* Carmelites will have greater reason to take part in the Order's role, small though it may be, to help people seek liberation from every kind of evil in order to enjoy freedom. Once again Carmelites are being called to relive the spirit of Elijah, the messenger of God.

1. The cry of Naboth today

Looking at the world through the window of mass media we are overwhelmed by the vision that confronts us. It is a world of painful divisions, a "shattered world" to use an expression of Pope John Paul II. We look around and see

— the trampling upon the basic rights of the human person, the first of these being the right to life and to a worthy quality of life, which is all the more scandalous in that it coexists with a rhetoric never before known on these same rights;

— hidden attacks and pressures against the freedom of individuals and groups, not excluding the freedom which is most offended against and threatened: the freedom to have, profess and practise one's own faith;

— the various forms of discrimination: racial, cultural, religious, etc.;

— violence and terrorism;

— the use of torture and unjust and unlawful methods of repression;

— the stockpiling of conventional or atomic weapons, the arms race with the spending on military purposes the sums which could be used to alleviate the undeserved misery of peoples that are socially and economically depressed;

— an unfair distribution of the world's resources and of the assets of civilization, which reaches its highest point in a type of social organization whereby the distance between the human condition of the rich and the poor becomes ever greater.[15]

Listening to the Holy Father we think of the starving people in some countries of Africa, the oppression of the blacks in South Africa, the poverty and oppression in some Latin American countries, the suffering and persecution in the Middle East, the growing evil of terrorism, and the suffering of so many behind the Iron Curtain. Who cannot see that we live in a world of painful division, a "shattered world?"

But who hears the cry of the poor? No doubt there are sympathizers everywhere who respond to their cry. Scientists, politicians, church leaders, theologians, philosophers, economists, entertainers and others, all offer suggestions for a better world, but seem powerless. Meanwhile, the afflicted hope that among them will be true prophets who will lead them out of darkness.

And speaking of prophets, some will say we need a new Elijah with a message from God, or a new Moses to lead the people out of slavery. But should we just stand around waiting for the prophet? This is unrealistic. We need to look inside ourselves and respond to the personal responsibility we have to our brothers and sisters. We are all prophets called by Christ to make this a better world. One person, we are told, can make a difference. And surely, if many gather together and work together, their efforts and their gifts can make a difference.

But where do we start? What is the fundamental need for the solution of the personal and social problems that confront the world? We believe any solution must begin with the individual. There must be a turning away from sin; there must be a conversion of heart.

2. Conversion of the heart

The greek word for conversion is *metanoia*, a word that has found its way into Webster's Dictionary and means "a fundamental transformation of mind and character." It entails a single goal from the moment it is embraced, a purpose and plan that is affirmed or confessed repeatedly, unreservedly, throughout one's life.

In the biblical and spiritual sense, conversion is a radical turning away from evil to the Lord, from sin to the acceptance of God and his will. It is sometimes called repentance or regeneration. Christ began his public ministry with a call to conversion: The Kingdom of God is at hand; repent and believe in the gospel (cf. Mk 1:15). And his final words to his disciples were a commission to convert the world: "Go, therefore, and make disciples of all the nations" (Mt 28: 19).

If we look for a classic conversion in the New Testament, we find it in the life of St Paul (Acts 9: 1-19). Paul's religious experience on the road to Damascus was the beginning of a complete change of lifestyle that was decisive and total: Saul of Tarsus became Paul of Christ.

Not all conversions are the same. We have the gentle conversion of Zaccheus (Lk 19:1-10), and the countless conversions of "born again" people in the Acts of the Apostles and the Pauline letters. Recall the story of Paul and Barnabas as they passed through both Phoenicia and Samaria reporting the conversion of the Gentiles, and they gave great joy to all the brethren (cf. Acts 15: 3).

Among well-known conversions is that of St Augustine, who tells us that during a period of great anxiety and stress he was prompted to pick up the scriptures. He then relates what happened:

> I snatched up the book, opened it, and read in silence the passage upon which my eyes first fell: *Not in rioting and drunkenness, not in chambering and wantonness, not in strife and envying: but put ye on the Lord Jesus Christ, and make not provision for the flesh in concupiscence.* I had no wish to read further; there was no need to. For immediately I had reached the end of this sentence it was as though my heart was filled with a light of confidence and all the shadows of my doubt were swept away.[16]

Closer to our own time is the conversion of Bl Edith Stein, who as a teenager had abandoned Judaism for atheism. Her way back to belief developed gradually. She tells us that one evening, when she was about thirty years of age, while reading the life of St Teresa of Avila in the home of a friend, she became a believer. She read throughout the night and then towards dawn closed the book and said: "This is the truth." Once converted to Christ, her life underwent a continual transformation that led to baptism and finally, after eleven years of growth, to the door of the Carmel of Cologne. Before entering she was reminded by the superior of the convent that it would be better for her to stay in the world, since she would not be able to continue her intellectual work in the convent. Her answer was: "It is no human activity that can help us but the passion of Christ. It is a share in that that I desire." Her request was fulfilled. Taken from the convent of Echt in Holland, where she had fled the Nazi persecution of the Jews, she was arrested and sent to Auschwitz. Here she was put to death in the gas chamber in July, 1942. Before leav-

ing for the dreaded concentration camp she wrote
to her superior:

> One can only gain a *Scientia Crucis* [science of the
> cross] if one is made to feel the Cross oneself to the
> depth of one's being. Of this I have been convinced
> from the first moment and have said with all my
> heart: *Ave Crux, spes unica* [Hail Cross, our only
> hope]![17]

3. Prophetic voices

The scriptures and the lives of the saints speak
eloquently of the power of conversion, of how it can
transform the life of an individual and leave a lasting effect on society. It is this conversion of heart
that is needed on a wide scale in the world today.
Without it there can be no peace, no justice, no
union among peoples. And this is the common conviction of many leaders in the church. Like prophets
they cry out to us.

In 1965 Pope Paul VI, in his address to the
United Nations in New York, stated:

> the time has come for "conversion," for personal
> transformation, for interior renewal. We have to get
> used to a new way of thinking about man, a new way
> of thinking about man's community life, and last of all
> a new way of thinking about the pathways of history
> and the destinies of the world. As St. Paul says, we
> must "put on the new man, which has been created
> according to God in justice and holiness of truth"
> (Eph 4, 23). [18]

Some twenty years later Pope John Paul II continued this thought when he addressed all the
members of the church and people of good will:

> To evoke conversion and penance in man's heart
> and to offer him the gift of reconciliation is the

specific mission of the Church as she continues the redemptive work of her divine founder.[19]

On numerous occasions the same Pontiff has returned to this theme, and frequently to young people, as he did when speaking to the youth of Sardinia:

> To you, then, young friends, falls the responsibility of corresponding to the concerns of your pastors. They call you to *conversion of heart* as the primary condition for nourishing faith 'from within.' I, too, remind you of this fundamental path towards Christian growth, recalling that conversion also means reconciliation and prayer.[20]

Of singular importance is this statement from the Final Report of the Extraordinary Synod of Bishops in December, 1985:

> Because the Church in Christ is a mystery, she must be considered a sign and instrument of holiness. For this reason the Council proclaimed the vocation of all the faithful to holiness (cf. *LG*, cap. 5). The call to holiness is an invitation to an intimate conversion of the heart and to participation in the life of God, One and Three; and this signifies and surpasses the realization of man's every desire. In our day above all, when so many people feel an interior void and spiritual crisis, the Church must preserve and energetically promote the sense of penance, prayer, adoration, sacrifice, selfgiving, charity and justice.[21]

This intimate conversion of the heart so necessary for all the faithful has been addressed to religious men and women. Cardinal Jean Jerome Hamer, O. P., Prefect of the Congregation for Religious and Secular Institutes, in a conference to religious superiors made this bold statement:

> The religious life, as all Christian life, is a movement of conversion. 'I have come not to call the just but sinners so that they may be converted' (Lk 5: 32). ...

Every Christian, and *a fortiori* every religious, has need for true conversion, true repentance, a true setting aright, which is not only a changing of outlook or mentality, but a change of direction both in thought and in action. It is necessary ever again clearly to recognize our purpose and to reorient ourselves decisively toward it. This movement of conversion involves our entire being.[22]

From the above statements it is clear that leaders in the church are calling all of us and all people of good will to a radical conversion of the heart, to a renewed and on-going conversion. They see a solution to world problems only when individuals turn themselves away from evil in all its forms, and give themselves to Christ.

It is interesting that one spiritual writer has applied this need for conversion to a particular problem. Father William Johnston, S. J., in his book *Christian Mysticism Today*, argues that only a profound conversion of many people in Ireland can bring about a solution to the Northern Ireland conflict. Having lived for some years through the turmoil, and having also observed it from afar, he states:

> Only through a radical commitment to the gospel on the part of a significant number of people on both sides of the border and on both sides of the Irish Sea will peace and justice be born.[23]

His belief is that the conversion of the heart is the outcome of prayer; and it is the duty of pastors to teach people how to pray, to contemplate. He writes:

> Let us learn to sit in God's presence until the gospel comes to life at those archetypal levels where mysticism reigns. If I have stressed one thing in this book it is that intellectual understanding of the gospels is not enough. *Mysticism means loving the gospel, living the gospel, and allowing ourselves to be transformed by the gospel.*[24]

We are compelled to ask: should not his words be applied to conflicts in other parts of the world? Are we not all being called to walk in God's presence in order to be transformed into workers of peace?

4. Constant on-going conversion

In the preceding reflections our concern has been primarily with initial, fundamental conversion of the heart, the turning from evil, from deadly sin, to God. This kind of radical conversion is a real necessity in our century that has forgotten God, denied sin, and encourages rampant individualism. Sin is the fundamental evil that can only be eradicated by turning back to God.

But there is another phase of conversion, already hinted at in some of the above statements, that is needed today. There is a need to reawaken and renew baptismal grace among Christians: to come to grips with a total commitment that embraces the whole person. It is this kind of conversion of heart that we would like to address now, keeping in mind that this was the call that the Second Vatican Council made to all people of good will. How have we members of the Carmelite family responded to this call? How generous are we? Are we totally dedicated to a life of poverty, chastity, humility, and love of Christ, or are we victims of mediocrity? Could it be that we are bogged down in a state of spiritual flabbiness that makes us ripe for the condemnation of the Laodiceans? "I know your deeds; I know you are neither hot nor cold. How I wish you were one or the other—hot or cold! But because you are lukewarm, neither hot nor cold, I will spew you out of my mouth!" (Rev 3:15-16).

How does one go about achieving renewal of the spirit, ongoing conversion? Every conversion begins with the Holy Spirit, who moves the soul away from selfish concerns to seek the presence of the Lord. It is God who first loves us. He offers the help we need to turn more generously to him. The simple truth is that we are loved first, and because we are loved we are able to love. Without the Holy Spirit there can be no initial or ongoing conversion. That is why the Psalmist prays: "A clean heart create for me, O God, and a steadfast spirit renew within me" (Ps 51:12).

Just as in initial conversion, so also in ongoing conversion, it is often a crisis in our life that brings about a change in life-style. A serious illness, the death of a loved one, an important decision to be made, can turn our minds and hearts to seek the Lord's help.

I know a religious who never doubted his vocation but flirted with worldly friendships and worldly pleasures, although careful not to fall into serious sin. But the moment came when he had to face his final profession. He then began to ask serious questions: after final vows would he continue to lead a superficial religious life, or would he give up his worldly pursuits? He examined his conscience and found to his dismay that he was living a dishonest, hypocritical life. The thought of living a dishonest life filled him with horror and gnawed at him. He knew he had to make a choice. He could not serve two masters. He entered into a long period of stress goaded on by an inner feeling to let go of his selfishness. He had no peace until he committed himself totally to the Lord. To this day he is convinced that it was the Holy Spirit that he felt within him that gave him light to see himself as he really was, and the courage to make the change. Once he had made the choice, peace returned, and with it joy. My friend had gone through a deep, emotional experience, not of tender love and gratitude as that enjoyed by St Francis of Assisi and other saints who had undergone a conversion, but none the less a true spiritual upheaval that changed his world and the world around him. His conversion was not an instant change of heart; it was not dramatic. But it was a process that went on for months and culminated in a decision of total love for Christ. Once made, however, he knew that it would be a decision that he would have to renew time and again; it would be a demanding task for the rest of his life.

5. St Teresa's experience

Whenever I recall this story. I find myself thinking of the conversion of St Teresa. There is a similarity in the stories, although St Teresa was a far more gifted person and chosen by the Lord for an exceptional place in his church that few would ever attain. Yet her life for many years was ambivalent. She was always a good religious but, as she tells us, not totally committed to Christ. It was not until she was 39 years of age that she gave herself completely to the Lord. Let us listen as she tells her story: "So save for the year I mentioned, for more than eighteen of the twenty-eight years since I began prayer, I suffered this battle and conflict between friendship with God and friendship with the world."[25]

It was at this time that her total conversion took place.

It happened to me that one day entering the oratory I saw a statue they had borrowed for a certain feast to be celebrated in the house. It represented the wounded Christ, and was very devotional so that beholding it I was utterly distressed in seeing Him that way, for it well represented what He had suffered for us. I felt so keenly aware of how poorly I thanked Him for these wounds that, it seems to me, my heart broke. Beseeching him to strengthen me once and for all that I might not offend Him, I threw myself down before Him with the greatest outpouring of tears.[26]

I think I then said that I would not rise from there until He granted what I was begging Him for. I believe certainly that this was beneficial to me, because from that time I went on improving.[27]

This singular event in the life of St Teresa was only the beginning of the radical transformation that went on throughout life, bringing her to the summit of the mystical life, the bridal union of the soul with God. And it should be observed that her conversion helped to bring about a social change not only in Carmel but in the church. Even to this day she guides and inspires countless people to give themselves more totally to the service of Christ and his church.

What message does the conversion of St Teresa send us ? It invites us to shake up our own lives, to embrace the cross more generously. It tells us very clearly that we need to open our hearts and give ourselves completely to the Lord. It also tells us that her reform of Carmel, the foundations she made, her spiritual writings that are classics, and her tremendous influence on people, all have their source in the generous commitment she made of herself to the Lord.

6. Renewal today

Today I think her conversion also has a special message for us who are inclined to better our lives through adapting to the times and are forgetful of spiritual renewal. She is telling us that working together with enthusiasm, changing the structures of our personal and community life, defining goals, updating our liturgies, commiting ourselves to peace and justice meetings, to new and basic communities, are good and need to be fostered, but that *they are not enough*. Without personal renewal of our lives, without ongoing conversion, we will fail. Good Christians, good religious are not the answer; our times demand personal ongoing conversion. We need men and women who return to the source of living water—to the Holy Spirit—and responding to his call, give themselves generously to the following of Christ, sharing his poverty, humility and love. Without such generous souls we will not only fail to move mountains, blaze new trails, and ford rivers; we will hardly survive the temptations of the secular society that surrounds us.

This prompts us to ask: Are there any signs of renewal, of upheaval, of a reawakening of spiritual life in Carmel? Are there signs of a more generous conversion of heart? Personally I have been edified and inspired, especially by Carmelite missionaries who, forgetful of self, have given themselves generously to the service of the poor and needy. May their number increase. For the hope of Carmel is in a new Pentecost, in men and women who accept the challenge to live in an intense, personal relationship with Christ. We need courageous messengers, like Elijah, who confronted the unjust Ahab in Naboth's garden; we need the zeal and courage of the new Elijah, Bl Titus Brandsma, who sets the example. Our Holy Father, Pope John Paul II, indicates this to us in his address to journalists in Rome:

> Titus Brandsma could not have been the teacher, the journalist, the writer he was in the stormy center of that cruel drama had he not drunk at the fountain of an intense personal spirituality.[28]

He is a model for our times.

What program would we suggest to develop an intense, personal, spiritual life?

1) *Daily prayer to the Holy Spirit.* It is the Holy Spirit who begins the transformation in us. This is what our Lord taught Nicodemus: "Do not be surprised that I tell you you must all be begotten from above. The wind blows where it will. You hear the sound it makes but you do not know where it comes from, or where it goes" (Jn 3: 7-8).

2) *Fidelity to daily Mass*: "the great joy and comfort of daily life."

3) *Prayerful recitation of liturgical prayers of the church.*

4) *Daily mental prayer,* and the *reading and study of Sacred Scripture.*

5) *A life-style of genuine poverty,* sharing the lot of the poor.

6) *A tender devotion to the Blessed Virgin Mary,* Mother of Carmel, expressed by wearing the brown scapular and praying the rosary.

7) *Frequent reception of the Sacrament of Reconciliation,* and openness to a spiritual director from time to time.

These practices will help us sustain ongoing conversion and dispose us for whatever action the Lord may demand.

III. Conclusion

We began our reflections with the remark that the Naboths of this world, and their number is countless, are crying for liberation from every form of tyranny and oppression. They do not want charity; they want justice, and rightly so. Some may lament that we have offered no specific plan to answer the problems of "a shattered world." This is true. But there is no single, specific work to be undertaken, since problems vary in every country and in every locality. We must confront local problems and respond courageously and decisively. But it has been our contention here that any specific apostolate for the poor and the needy will succeed only if we have undergone a true conversion of heart, a renewal of spirit. In a word, we need to follow Christ unreservedly, clothed in the new self. We need to have the courage and the zeal of Elijah, who went wherever the Lord commanded, even to the palace of a king, to denounce his injustice and to show that God will not be mocked. The person who has undergone a conversion of heart, a complete commitment to the Lord, is the one best prepared to work for the political, social and economic liberation of the people. In the words of the Second Vatican Council: "An interior renewal must always be accorded the leading role even in the promotion of external works."[29]

This truth cannot be overemphasized.

IX

Ahaziah, son of Ahab, began to reign over Israel in Samaria in the seventeenth year of Jehoshaphat, king of Judah; he reigned two years over Israel. He did evil in the sight of the LORD, behaving like his father, his mother, and Jeroboam, son of Nebat, who caused Israel to sin. He served and worshiped Baal, thus provoking the LORD, the God of Israel, just as his father had done.

After Ahab's death, Moab rebelled against Israel. Ahaziah had fallen through the lattice of his roof terrace at Samaria and had been injured. So he sent out messengers with the instructions: "Go and inquire of Baalzebub, the god of Ekron, whether I shall recover from this injury."

Meanwhile the angel of the LORD said to Elijah the Tishbite: "Go, intercept the messengers of Samaria's king, and ask them, 'Is it because there is no God in Israel that you are going to inquire of Baalzebub, the god of Ekron?' For this, the LORD says: 'You shall not leave the bed upon which you lie; instead, you shall die.'" And with that, Elijah departed.

The messengers then returned to Ahaziah, who asked them, "Why have you returned?" "A man came up to us," they answered, "who said to us, 'Go back to the king who sent you and tell him: The LORD says, Is it because there is no God in Israel that you are sending to inquire of Baalzebub, the god of Ekron? For this you shall not leave the bed upon which you lie; instead, you shall die.'" The king asked them, "What was the man like who came up to you and said these things to you?" "Wearing a hairy garment," they replied, "with a leather girdle about his loins." "It is Elijah the Tishbite!" he exclaimed.

Then the king sent a captain with his company of fifty men after Elijah. The prophet was seated on a hilltop when he found him. "Man of God," he ordered, "the king commands you to come down." "If I am a man of God," Elijah answered the captain, "may fire come down from heaven and consume you and your fifty men." And fire came down from heaven and consumed him and his fifty men. Ahaziah sent another captain with his company of fifty men after Elijah. "Man of God," he called out to Elijah, "the king commands you to come down immediately." "If I am a man of God," Elijah answered him, "may fire come down from heaven and consume you and your fifty men." And divine fire came down from heaven, consuming him and his fifty men.

Again, for the third time, Ahaziah sent a captain with his company of fifty men. When the third captain arrived, he fell to his knees before Elijah, pleading with him. "Man of God," he implored him, "let my life and the lives of these fifty men, your servants, count for something in your sight! Already fire has come down from heaven, consuming two captains with their companies of fifty men. But now, let my life mean something to you!" Then the angel of the LORD said to Elijah, "Go down with him; you need not be afraid of him."

So Elijah left and went down with him and stated to the king: "Thus says the LORD: 'Because you sent messengers to inquire of Baalzebub, the god of Ekron, you shall not leave the bed upon which you lie; instead you shall die.'"

Ahaziah died in fulfillment of the prophecy of the LORD spoken by Elijah.

1 Kings 22:52-54 and 2 Kings 1:1-17

Elijah
and King Ahaziah

A FTER the bloody death of King Ahab his son
Ahaziah ruled over Israel for two years.[1]

The division of the history of the kings of Israel
into two books, with the dividing line in the middle
of Ahaziah's reign, is an artificial device of later
editors and not that of the original author. The unusual story of Elijah's confrontation with Ahaziah
represents a type of prophetic tradition different
from the Elijan narratives we have previously considered. In fact the whole episode is rather strange
and jolts Christian sensibilities.

What is the purpose of the narrative? It reveals
the evil reign of Ahaziah, who was no better than
his idolatrous father and mother, and consequently
incurred the anger and punishment of a just and
jealous God.

What actually brought on God's anger? Ahaziah
had fallen through the lattice work encircling the
palace balcony on the roof of his home in Samaria
and was severely injured. Being superstitious he
sent messengers to Baalzebub,[2] the god of Ekron,

to inquire whether he would recover his health. While the messengers were on the way to the Philistine city of some forty miles from Samaria, Yahweh called Elijah to intercept them and to warn them to go back and inform their king: "You shall not leave the bed upon which you lie; instead, you shall die" (2 Kgs 1: 4).

Angered by this prophecy Ahaziah sent out a company of soldiers to capture the prophet. What follows seems to be an inhuman destruction of innocent life. First, one captain and his fifty soldiers are destroyed when Elijah calls down fire from heaven. A second company suffers the same fate. Finally, the third contingent sent by the obstinate king came humbly to Elijah begging to be spared. At God's request Elijah spared them and then returned with them to the king, to whom he repeated the death prophecy.

How explain the severe punishment of the soldiers? There is no easy answer. Some say a king of Israel and his haughty soldiers who defied Yahweh deserved a stinging rebuke, a violent death. Moreover the oriental style demands great reverence and obedience to a prophet, something lacking in these soldiers. Other commentators find the whole episode bizarre and believe it is a composition of fact and legend, and more in the style of the wonder tales that fill the Elisha cycle. One highly respected commentator explains the strange affair by appealing to literary form and separates it from all the rest of the Elijah cycle: "In the preposterousness of the miraculous element, and in its inhumanity with the destruction of the innocent fifties, it is quite in humor with the Elisha cycle."[3]

This unusual story comes to an end with the words: "Ahaziah died in fulfillment of the prophecy of the LORD spoken by Elijah. Since he had no son, his brother Joram succeeded him as king" (2 Kgs 1:17).

236

Once the prophecy is fulfilled Elijah, as was his custom, disappeared. He had been brought suddenly to the scene and then vanished just as abruptly. Elijah is ever "the mystery man." At a sign from God he comes and goes. But he is more than a messenger; he possesses a word of power.

I. Carmelite tradition

Carmel has its own peculiar explanation of the Ahaziah story. In its early "history" filled with legends it draws attention away from Ahaziah and Elijah to Obadiah, the vizier of the royal palace during the reigns of Ahab and Ahaziah. He "was a zealous follower of the LORD. When Jezebel was murdering the prophets of the LORD, Obadiah took a hundred prophets, hid them away fifty each in two caves, and supplied them with food and drink" (1 Kgs 18:4). Once during the drought, while he was searching for grass for Ahab's horses and mules, Elijah came upon him and ordered him to go to the king to say that Elijah wished to speak with him. In scripture there is no other mention of this master of Ahab's palace. But Carmelite writers, not the first to be sure, identified Obadiah as one of the earliest and most distinguished disciples of Elijah.

1. Literature

Once again, it is *The Institution of the First Monks* that offers us a detailed story of Obadiah. It elaborates the brief accounts found in the *Speculum* of John of Chemineto and in the writings of other Carmelites. According to the *Institution* the hundred prophets spared by Obadiah were disciples of Elijah. Although Obadiah was a faithful servant of Ahab, he was a more faithful servant of Yahweh. Yet, after the death of Ahab, he continued to serve his son, King Ahaziah.

As the *Institution* relates, Obadiah was the captain of the third contingent of soldiers sent to apprehend Elijah. He pleaded to be spared and then brought the prophet to the bedridden king. Following the death of the king, Obadiah went to Mount Carmel and knelt before Elijah and begged for mercy. Struck by the humility of the man, and recalling his great charity to his one hundred disciples whom he had hidden in the caves, Elijah pardoned him and his soldiers. Grateful for the gift of life Obadiah left his royal post, his wife and children, and became a disciple of Elijah. In time he was filled with the prophetic spirit.

This legend, like so many others in the *Institution*, had great influence on Carmel's tradition. In the seventeenth century Lezana in his "life" of Elijah repeats the story.[4] Daniel of the Virgin Mary, guided by both the *Institution* and Lezana, embellishes it.[5] Subsequent writers in the Order would continue the legend and some would go so far as to identify Obadiah, a master of Ahab's palace, with the author of the inspired book in the Old Testament.

The editor of Daniel's *Speculum* found this story so intriguing that he published four engravings by the celebrated Diefenbeke, one before each of the four chapters on the relation of Ahaziah with Elijah: the prophecy of Elijah to Ahaziah; the fiery death of the first company of soldiers; the fiery death of the second company; and the presence of Elijah and Obadiah at the deathbed of Ahaziah.

However not all Carmelites have accepted this legend. For example, Father Elias Magennis, writing in the early years of the twentieth century, stated that identifying Obadiah with the captain of the fifty soldiers spared by Elijah "does not find favor with us."[6]

In fairness to Carmelite writers who claimed Obadiah as a disciple of Elijah, it should be said that long before Carmel's origin a few fathers of the church, St Epiphanius, for example, called Obadiah a disciple of Elijah, and St Isidore identified him with the captain of the soldiers spared by Elijah. It was on these writings, no doubt, that Carmelites based their early "history" of the Order.

2. Liturgy

Elijah's encounter with Ahaziah found its way into Carmel's liturgy. In the breviary of 1583 the third antiphon of first vespers for the feast of Elijah recalls that he called down fire on the captain and his fifty soldiers.

The response to lesson seven of the third nocturn of matins tells of Elijah's prediction of the death of the king. The response to lesson eight mentions Elijah calling down fire on the captain and his soldiers, and the hymn of lauds recalls the death of Ahaziah. This liturgical office continued down the centuries and is found in the breviary of 1938, the last published by the Order before the revision mandated by the Second Vatican Council.

It is also worthy of note that in the breviary of 1745 there is a votive office in honor of St Elijah to be recited once each month, rubrics permitting. This office was included in subsequent printings of the breviaries but omitted in the revised breviary of 1938. In this monthly office the response to lesson seven recalled Ahaziah's death, and the response to lesson eight tells of the fiery death of the captain and his soldiers. The hymn of lauds also recalls the death of the impious king and the slaughter of the soldiers.

The revised Liturgy of the Hours and of the Eucharist approved after the Second Vatican Council makes no mention of Elijah's confrontation with Ahaziah. Evidently the story did not find favor with the liturgists.

It is important to observe that down through the centuries the liturgy in its choice of antiphons and hymns followed carefully the accounts of the Elijah story as presented in the scriptures. Its purpose was surely to inspire Carmelites to follow the example of their father, a true defender of the faith. It was careful to avoid the legends that abounded in the writings of the Middle Ages and ballooned into prominence in the 17th century when some Carmelite writers, inspired by the renewal of the spirit of the Order, were not concerned with historical objectivity.

Reflecting on Carmelite historiography in the years 1600-1700, Smet observes:

> With learned display of references and abundance of imaginative detail, the Order is shown to derive historically from the prophet Elijah, counting among its members, if only of the Third Order, prominent figures of the Old Testament and just about any saint connected with Palestine and the beginnings of the eremitical life. That this baseless fabric, this insubstantial patent convinced some of the people all of the time and all of the people some of the time is not entirely surprising, for this style of historical writing was widespread.[7]

As we move into the declining years of the twentieth century Carmelites will find that its present writers and liturgists offer them little food for thought from the story of the prophet of fire and his encounter with Ahaziah and his soldiers. But can we not find here an example of the faith and courage we need as we come in conflict with the powers of darkness of our time?

II. Violence or love?

Elijah on the hilltop called down fire from heaven to consume the captains and their soldiers. Once again he proclaims the purpose of his life: he lives in the service of Yahweh; he is true to his name: "My God is Yahweh." Once again his weapon is fire, reminiscent of the fire from heaven that consumed the holocaust on Mount Carmel. Once again, and for the last time, he comes into conflict with evil.

No wonder that Sirach, in retelling the Elijah story, sums up his ministry as a judgment of fire in which he came to turn Israel's heart back to God: "Till like a fire there appeared the prophet whose words were as a flaming furnace" (Sir 48 :1).

But how foreign to our Christian sensibilities is the action of Elijah! His violence shocks us. Christ, as we shall see, would have none of it. It is true Jesus said he had come to bring fire on the earth, but how different from the fire of Elijah! The fire of Jesus is a fire of love that saves, not destroys. Like Elijah's his ministry would be to purify Israel from idolatry; he would go even further and offer the kingdom of God to all people. But he would not do it with violence against those who opposed him, but rather he would be the victim of violence. He would conquer with the fire of love.

However, let us not be too harsh with Elijah. He obeyed the divine command; he was the faithful servant. Christ too would be the faithful servant, but his mission of fire would be different. He would confront evil in a unique way.

That the fire of Jesus was meant to be different from that of Elijah is clear from the episode that relates the attempt of Jesus to pass through a Samaritan town on the way to Jerusalem. The people refused to let him pass because he was Jewish and on his way to the Holy City which they despised. John, one of the 'sons of thunder,' mindful that Elijah had once brought down fire from heaven to consume the captains and their soldiers—and perhaps wishing to be a new Elijah—said to Jesus: "Lord, would you not have us call down fire from heaven to destroy them?" But Jesus, and not the apostles, was the new Elijah, and his approach would be nonviolent. He simply left that place and set off to another town (cf. Lk 9: 51-56).

A little later along the road to Jerusalem Jesus declared: "I have come to light a fire on the earth. How I wish the blaze were ignited!" What fire? The fire of filial love ablaze in every heart. But to accomplish this he would first incite opposition. The fire he came to ignite, he tells us, would bring about division among families: "From now on, a household of five will be divided three against two and two against three" (Lk 12: 49-52). His coming among the people will bring conflict; he will be a sign of contradiction. His ministry will not be popular, the powers that rule will oppose him. The fire of discord will go on to the end of time.

How true this is, not only in the time of Jesus but in our own time! When Edith Stein became a Catholic and later a Carmelite nun, her staunch Jewish mother considered this an act of disloyalty, another sword that pierced the heart of this good woman during her long, sorrow-filled life. Edith was aware of this and tried to carry her mother's sorrow and her own as a sharing in the mystery of the cross. As Jesus, filled with the Holy Spirit—the Spirit of love—bore the cross with steadfast

242

courage, so Edith took up her cross. Will her suffering love help to purify the world of evil?

That Jesus should be a cause of conflict puzzles us. Did he not come to bring peace? In his farewell to his apostles at the Last Supper did he not proclaim: "My peace I give you, my peace I leave you?" Indeed, he did. He is the Prince of Peace; but a lasting and universal peace is to be the fruit of a long and sometimes bitter struggle. There will be conflict, even wars, to the end of time. A world at peace—all nations living together in harmony, worshipping the one true God—is to come, not in the course of human history, but only at the end of time. Until then there will be conflict between God and the sinful world. We can try to lessen the battle; indeed, it is our obligation to bring peace to the world, but we shall never succeed completely.

And so the lesson is clear. Those who wish to follow Elijah in his struggle with the powers of evil and to follow Christ in his zeal for his Father must be prepared to face up to the conflict with the powers of darkness. This struggle is of the very nature of the Christian vocation; it is therefore the lot of all Carmelites who, as sons and daughters of Elijah, wish to walk in the footsteps of Christ. Conflict is an integral part of our life.

How, someone may ask, are we to combat the powers of darkness? Shall we, like Elijah, cast down the fire of violence, or like Christ breathe the fire of love? Like Elijah we must be defiant and courageous on the hilltop: strike out for good over evil, for true worship over false worship, justice over injustice, but our weapon must be different. With Christ, the new Elijah, our weapon must be love.

As Carmelites we will face the battle with evil on many levels. We mention three: the evil we find in ourselves, in the church, and in society. A few words about each is in order.

1. Conflict in ourselves

Our faith teaches us that we human beings are a mystery, a puzzle; and the Second Vatican Council brought this out most clearly. Although men and women were created by God in a state of holiness, they abused their liberty at the urging of personified evil and set themselves up against God. Consequently all human life, whether individual or collective, is engaged in a constant struggle between good and evil. Wounded by sin we experience rebellious stirrings within ourselves. But with God's help we can strip ourselves of all that is sinful and offer God a pure and holy heart.

All of us experience this battle with our demons; but we should realize that it can be healthy and, if we cooperate with the grace of the Lord, it can lead to the holiness for which we were created.

In this interior conflict Carmelites need to take to heart Chapter 14 of the Rule of Carmel. There we are exhorted to put on our spiritual armor and face courageously the enemy:

> But because life on earth is a time of trial, and all who seek to live devoutly in Christ suffer persecution, and because your adversary, the devil, as a roaring lion prowls about seeking someone to devour, every care must be taken to put on the armor of God, that you may stand firm against the cunning devices of the enemy.

Carmelite writers down through the centuries have faced up to the challenge to fight the demons within us. *The Institution of the First Monks* proposed Elijah as the model to guide us in our

244

combat with the forces of evil. He fled the world, leaving behind his family and all his possessions. He embraced solitude in a cave at Cherith; choosing chastity he

> crucified the flesh with its passions and desires, mortifying his members of the sins which are on earth... Denying himself and renouncing his own will, he always promptly followed the will of a superior, namely, God.[8]

To God he offered a pure and holy heart, and was given the gift, at least from time to time, of experiencing the living presence of God.

Perhaps there is no better guide than St John of the Cross to lead us through dark nights of purification to a more perfect life. Who better than St John explains the mortification of the appetites, the journey in faith, and God's purifying action so necessary for union with God?

Finally, closer to our own time, we have *The Carmelite Directory of the Spiritual Life*[9] that brings together the wealth of Carmel's tradition. In the third part of this treatise, the compiler, Father John Brenninger, describes the struggle of the soul to acquire purity of heart as an emptying of the heart of all actual sins, of every inordinate affection for creatures, a clinging to God alone.

More modern writers would explain this spiritual combat by saying that every person has disordered inclinations. For example, we tend to rash judgment, cowardice, hypocrisy, inordinate sexual desire. Against such tendencies we must carry on a continual warfare, trusting in the grace of God. And the battle is not without its good results: we can attain a certain purity of heart, free from actual sins, that disposes us to enjoy even in this life the experience of the loving presence of God within us.

2. Conflict in the church

The continual struggles and misunderstandings that go on within the church should not surprise us. It has always been so, for the church is constantly in a state of renewal and growth. When Luke wrote his gospel for Theophilus he used all his talents to bolster confidence in the apostolic tradition. Evidently Theophilus was shaken by the problems that confronted the early church: persecutions, false teachers, the trials of missionary work, mediocre church leaders, and the inevitable clashes between the rich and the poor. Have not these same trials, persecutions and deficiencies faced the church down through the centuries? And have not we the faithful often been the cause of many of the problems, including separation from the church?

Writing about the rifts that have torn apart the seamless garment of the church, the Second Vatican Council in its Decree on Ecumenism declares:

> In this one and only Church of God from its beginnings there arose certain rifts, which the Apostle strongly censures as damnable. But in subsequent centuries much more serious dissensions appeared and large communities became separated from full communion with the Catholic Church—for which, often enough, men of both sides were to blame.[10]

Today as the Catholic Church renews its efforts for the unity of all Christians, it finds itself engaged also in a struggle with internal problems. We are asking ourselves: what is the true role of the laity? What of the equality of women and their role in society and the church? And how should we face the shortage of vocations to the priesthood and religious life in many countries of the world?

Finally, what is the proper role of authori
freedom?

Should these problems discourage us? On the contrary they should stimulate us to search for answers. A healthy confrontation can lead to a better church. We need to listen to Christ: "Be not afraid." Like Elijah we need to stand on the hilltop, confront the evil, but with the fire of love.

3. Conflict with society

Perhaps our greatest conflict is with society. Along with all Catholics, the members of the Carmelite family are called to be good Christians in the world. This role necessarily brings with it a conflict with evil that is unavoidable. Indeed, the first step in announcing the good news of the Gospel is denouncing the evil that is in the world.

This evil will not go away. It will be with us as long as time exists. A renowned theologian has this to say:

> The fight [against evil in the world] goes on within each individual one of her members, and will do so till the end of time. The Church is well aware of the fact; though she is never discouraged, she is also no utopian. The Reign of Christ which she continually promotes and prays for will, she knows, never be established on earth, where disturbance, error and perversity will always appear to compromise her work. The serene clarity of her faith does not stop her speaking of the apparent 'blind advance of things', and she is a perpetual witness of the defeat of the good. She sees all about her the resurgence of idolatries, and her own children at one another's throats.[11]

Sobered by these thoughts we turn to the problems of our day. They are many and varied;

they concern the dignity of the human person, marriage, the family, culture, social and economic life. Since we cannot respond, even briefly, to each of these we focus our attention on two: the devaluation of human life especially in its origin, and the severe poverty of so many millions that brings with it uncontrollable evils. First, let us consider the church's conflict with those who devalue human life.

a. IS EVERY HUMAN LIFE SACRED?

A distinctive mark of the church today is its pervasive concern for the dignity of every human life from the moment of conception to death. From this it follows that reverence and respect does not depend on the objective, lovable characteristics and qualities of an individual. Looks are deceiving. A broken, twisted body can contain a brilliant mind, a pure and saintly soul. On the other hand, even when there are few signs of life the person must be respected. We think of the sickly elderly, dirty and dying in the gutters of city streets. In spite of their wretched condition they are precious in God's eyes, temples of the Holy Spirit, destined for eternal life. They demand our total and unconditional love. And thanks to its clear teaching the church continually reminds us of this:

> Today there is an inescapable duty to make ourselves the neighbor of every man, no matter who he is, and if we meet him, to come to his aid in a positive way, whether he is an aged person abandoned by all, a foreign worker despised without reason, a refugee, an illegitimate child wrongly suffering for a sin he did not commit, or a starving human being who awakens our conscience by calling to mind the words of Christ: 'As you did it to one of the least of these my brethren, you did it to me.'[12]

But, we ask, does this reverence and respect extend to the unborn, even to the embryo? Many deny this and treat the unborn as commodities, mere tools for profit, unwanted property. The convenience of the woman is often given priority over the life of the unborn child. It is claimed that she has a right to her body and therefore is free to bring to term or to destroy the unborn human life within her. The church, faithful to her long tradition, has condemned this way of thinking and has clearly stated:

> God, the Lord of life, has entrusted to men the noble mission of safeguarding life, and men must carry it out in a manner worthy of themselves. Life must be protected with the utmost care from the moment of conception: abortion and infanticide are abominable crimes.[13]

Unfortunately, many governments refuse to accept that abortion is an evil and approve laws that permit abortion in certain circumstances. Consequently, millions of abortions are performed every year because the unborn child is not considered a human person, and the rights of a woman over her own body are given priority.

So numerous have abortions become that from 1973 to 1987 in the United States alone more than twenty million unborn children were destroyed—a number greater than that of the entire population of Australia. Contemplating these figures one recalls the words of Mother Teresa of Calcutta, awarded the Nobel Peace Prize in 1979: "To me the nations with legalized abortions are the poorest nations. The great destroyer of peace today is the crime against the innocent unborn child ... In destroying the child, we are destroying love, destroying the image of God in the world."

That God's image is slowly vanishing from the minds of people is believed by many who label abortion "the slippery slope." Once we have started down that hill—and we have—there will be no stopping. Nothing can halt us from taking "an unwanted life." God help the handicapped and the frail elderly! For in the mind of the ungodly the unborn are nothing but a collection of molecules, a complex of tissues, organs and functions without any unique value.

However, more recently the slide down "the slippery slope" has taken a strange turn. For, lo and behold, it has been discovered that unborn babies are not entirely worthless. Medical laboratories have discovered that their bodies have precious commodities. Especially their brain cells have wonderful medical properties that can be used to cure Alzheimer's disease and other neural disorders. In other words, the unborn should not be discarded in trash barrels: their organs have a special value in the market. This prompts us to ask: If we allow women to consider the unborn child to be their property, on what ground do we stand to tell women they cannot abort for profit, especially if medical laboratories are willing to buy the aborted fetus for tissues and organs to be used in transplants and medical research?

The church follows the new frontiers of scientific research and technological achievement, and it certainly does not wish to discourage it; but it is also keenly aware that scientific progress without a moral standard to guide it can be a disaster. Without a moral standard, is not the whole human race in danger of extinction?

Therefore, true to its mission to be a teacher of moral truth, she continues to speak out. In her "Instruction on Respect for Human Life in its Origin and on the Dignity of Procreation" she has stated once again: "God alone is the Lord of life from its beginning until its end: no one can, in any

circumstance, claim for himself the right to dest.._,
directly an innocent human being."[14]

The church has reconfirmed its traditional teaching. Human life is sacred; it is a gift of God; it is not a commodity, a property, a product of man's creative power; and therefore it is not in the total control of man. God alone is the arbiter of human life. The unborn child from the very first instant of his existence is precious in the eyes of God: a person, to be loved and respected, and destined for eternal communion with God.

In these waning years of the twentieth century as we witness the great surge of inhumanity, shall we be carried away by the apathy of so many or shall we stand strong with the church and many others of good will who defend and proclaim the sanctity of human life? Carmelites, who call themselves followers of the Prophet of Fire, where do they stand in this confrontation with evil?

b. WORLD POVERTY

While the church struggles to defend the dignity and rights of the unborn, it is also engaged in a battle against poverty that degrades the dignity of millions. By poverty we mean the lack of sufficient material resources required for a decent life. Eradicating poverty, to be sure, is not a peculiarly ecclesial problem. It concerns the whole world, and many governments, churches and societies are deeply engaged in searching for solutions. But the church, faithful to the teachings of Christ, has a special responsibility to the poor, and she has declared her preferential option for the poor. The challenge it presents to the people of God is to learn what it means to serve "the least of my brothers," to be neighbor to everyone.

In no uncertain terms we are called to serve others in their need and to work actively for social and economic justice. This is not a new task:

> It is as old as the Hebrew prophets, as compelling as the Sermon on the Mount and as current as the powerful voice of Pope John Paul II defending the dignity of the human person.[15]

Reflecting on these words we recall that the Second Vatican Council more than twenty years before the pronouncement of the American bishops, faced up to the evil of poverty in the world. It wanted to go on record as a council that gave preference to the poor.

A striking symbol of the Council's intent was dramatized in St Peter's Basilica on November 13, 1964. Following a beautiful liturgy of the Greek Byzantine Rite, Pope Paul VI came forward and placed his tiara on the altar. He offered it for the poor. It is said that it was worth $12,000 and had been a gift of the faithful of his former archdiocese of Milan. All of us who witnessed the event fully understood that the Pope of Poverty was calling all bishops, all Catholics, all people of good will to share their goods with the poor.

4. The church today

Almost twenty-five years have passed since the close of the Council. Has the world heard the cry of the poor? Not yet. Wherever we go we find people living in abject poverty: 450 million are malnourished or facing starvation.

These are statistics and do not necessarily move us to action. But we have all seen starving women and small children in certain parts of Africa on our television screens, and some of us have personally

witnessed people dying of starvation in Asia, beg-
gars living on the streets of India, and have walked
through the slums of Northern Brazil. And how
often have we met hungry people begging and
homeless in the cities of our own countries? Many
of the suffering in the world are victims of
economic, political and cultural domination, and
they cry for liberation. In the most industrialized
nations of Latin America 25% live as Europeans or
North Americans do; 75% live in extreme poverty in
subhuman conditions.[16] All these situations are intolerable. But what is being done about them?

When John Paul II visited Chile in April, 1987,
he went to a slum where he addressed the poor in
these words:

> The church is the mother of all. She extends her
> love to everyone without distinction and to everyone
> she extends her loving kindness. But it is right that, as
> a mother, she has a special space in her heart for
> those of her children who suffer, for those who are ill,
> for the needy, for the poor, for sinners.[17]

These words are encouraging, but what practical
steps is Mother Church taking to help the poor and
needy?

Poverty haunts not only people of countries in
development but even those of countries that are
wealthy with this world's goods. We recall the
words of the bishops of the United States of
America in their pastoral letter on "Economic
Justice for All":

> Harsh poverty plagues our country despite its
> great wealth .... Today children are the largest single
> group among the poor. This tragic fact seriously
> threatens the nation's future. That so many people are
> poor in a nation as rich as ours is a social and moral
> scandal that we cannot ignore.[18]

How answer the problem of poverty that haunts
the world? As Carmelites we are in the church and

the church and therefore look to church leaders for guidance. We are told that first we need to become aware of widespread poverty—really become conscious of it. For unless we are deeply aware and touched by the problem we will not be moved to action. Secondly, we need to become involved to alter the causes of unemployment, bad government and unbearable national debts that burden some countries.

All this sounds very good and wise, but how do we go about helping the poor in a practical way? How can we make Christian social thought a living, growing resource that can inspire hope and help shape the future as the American bishops propose?

There is no easy answer. But surely we can begin by listening to the leaders in the movement to eradicate poverty and working effectively with those already engaged in movements of justice and peace. If we take to heart "a preferential option for the poor" we must begin with an examination of our own personal and community economic behavior. All our talk about concern for the poor, for peace and justice, is "mere talk" and nothing else unless our life-style speaks of simplicity. How poor are we in our daily lives? We applaud the poverty of Dorothy Day. But how many of us are willing to adopt her program: "Poverty is my vocation; to live as simply and poorly as I can, and never cease seeking opportunities to talk and see ways to help the poor." Many do not feel called to follow her life of poverty, and she never expected that many would or should; but surely a simple life-style and sharing our goods with the poor is one part of our vocation.

III. Conclusion

In this chapter we have reflected on the final conflict of Elijah with the powers of darkness— Elijah on the hilltop casting down fire on the enemy to convince Israel that Yahweh alone is God. This fire was a symbol of the love ablaze in his heart. "I am zealous for the Lord God of hosts" was his act of faith on Mount Horeb, the cry that accompanied him in all his works. In his lifetime he did not succeed in exterminating Baalism from Israel, but he never ceased trying. To the end he was the faithful servant, walking humbly in the presence of the Lord, his heart on fire with love.

Like Elijah we need to face life's conflict with faith, courage and love. We may never eradicate all the demons that disturb our lives; we shall never see the church purified of all its internal dissensions, nor the world free of its evils, especially those that degrade the dignity of the human person and imprison us in abject poverty. But we must keep trying.

Where is the fire of love in Carmel today? Is it discernible in our prayer life? Where are the loyal troops engaged in the conflict against darkness? Could it be that we are lukewarm, bogged down in complacency and mediocrity? Are there many who heed the cry of Blessed Titus Brandsma: He who wants to win the world for Christ must have the courage to come into conflict with it?

Elijah's journeys

Giovanni Francesco Grimaldi, *Elijah's servant reports a little cloud rising from the sea* (1648; this is one of 18 frescoes executed between 1647 and 1651 under the direction of Gaspare Dughet, Basilica of San Martino ai Monti, Rome).

Photo: Riccardo Palazzi, O.Carm.

Elijah fed by a crow in the Wadi Cherith (Byzantine Museum, Athens; 17th century).

Photo: Riccardo Palazzi, O.Carm.

Francisco Salimena, *Elijah meets the widow of Zarephath and her son* (1696, Basilica of Carmine Maggiore, Naples).

Photo: Riccardo Palazzi, O.Carm.

Domenico Beccafumi (+1551), *Elijah's victory on Mount Carmel* (Pavement, Sienna cathedral)

Photo: Scala

Marc Chagall (+1986), *Elijah comforted by the angel* (Mainz, Stefanskirche).

Photo: Riccardo Palazzi, O.Carm.

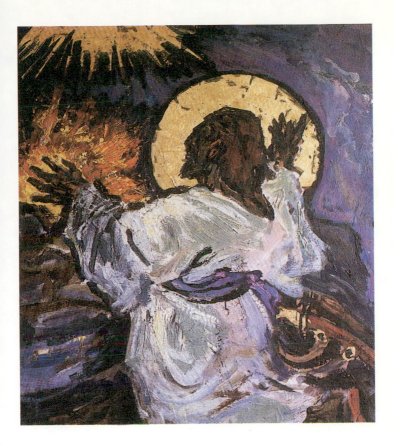

David Herskovitz, *Elijah calls fire from heaven* (c. 1965, Capilla, Casa parroquial N.S. del Carmen, Miraflores, Lima).

Photo: David Herskovitz

Francisco Salimena, *Elijah's farewell to Elisha* (1696, Basilica of Carmine Maggiore, Naples).

Photo: Riccardo Palazzi, O.Carm.

ТЫИ ПРОРОКЪ БЖИИ

ОГНЕННОЕ ВОСХОЖДЕНІЕ НА НЕБО ПРОРОКА ИЛІИ

XV

Elijah the Prophet (The Friars' Chapel, Carmelite Priory, Bamberg).

Photo: Riccardo Palazzi, O.Carm.

The Transfiguration of Jesus with Elijah and Moses
(Russian icon from the second half of the 16th century; A. Rubiev Museum, Moscow).
                              Photo: Russia Cristiana

The Assumption of Elijah, with scenes from his life (Russian icon from the 1700's).

Photo: Russia Cristiana

X

When the LORD was about to take Elijah up to heaven in a whirlwind, he and Elisha were on their way from Gilgal. "Stay here, please," Elijah said to Elisha. "The LORD has sent me on to Bethel." "As the LORD lives, and as you yourself live," Elisha replied, "I will not leave you." So they went down to Bethel, where the guild prophets went out to Elisha and asked him, "Do you know that the LORD will take your master from over you today?" "Yes, I know it," he replied. "Keep still."

Then Elijah said to him, "Stay here, please, Elisha, for the LORD has sent me on to Jericho." "As the LORD lives, and as you yourself live," Elisha replied, "I will not leave you." They went on to Jericho, where the guild prophets approached Elisha and asked him, "Do you know that the LORD will take your master from over you today?" "Yes, I know it," he replied. "Keep still."

Elijah said to Elisha, "Please stay here; the LORD has sent me on to the Jordan." "As the LORD lives, and as you yourself live," Elisha replied, "I will not leave you." And so the two went on together. Fifty of the guild prophets followed, and when the two stopped at the Jordan, stood facing them at a distance. Elijah took his mantle, rolled it up and struck the water, which divided and both crossed over on dry ground.

When they had crossed over, Elijah said to Elisha, "Ask for whatever I may do for you before I am taken from you." Elisha answered, "May I receive a double portion of your spirit." "You have asked something that is not easy," he replied. "Still, if you see me taken up from you, your wish will be granted; otherwise not." As they walked on conversing, a flaming chariot and flaming horses came between them, and Elijah went up to heaven in a whirlwind. When Elisha saw it happen he cried out, "My father! my father! Israel's chariots and drivers!" But when he could no longer see him, Elisha gripped his own garment and tore it in two.

Then he picked up Elijah's mantle which had fallen from him, and went back and stood at the bank of the Jordan. Wielding the mantle which had fallen from Elijah, he struck the water in his turn and said, "Where is the LORD, the God of Elijah?" When Elisha struck the water it divided and he crossed over.

The guild prophets in Jericho, who were on the other side, saw him and said, "The spirit of Elijah rests on Elisha." They went to meet him, bowing to the ground before him.

2 Kings 2:1-15

The assumption
of Elijah

THERE are two themes: the assumption of the prophet of fire that ends the Elijah cycle, and the bestowal on Elisha of his father's spirit which begins the Elisha cycle.

We begin with the assumption of Elijah which is preceded by a journey narrative in verses 1-8. The story of the actual "taking up" is in verses 7a-12. It is helpful to remember that we do not have a chronological development in these stories. Moreover there is little in them to show the growth of human and spiritual relationships between the two prophets; we can, however, infer the depth of their friendship from the account of their last journey and their emotional parting.

The final episode in the life of Elijah begins when the two prophets set out from Gilgal. "Stay here, please," Elijah tells his disciple. Evidently he wanted to be alone as he went to meet the Lord. But Elisha would have none of it. "'As the LORD lives, and you yourself live,' Elisha replied, 'I will not leave you.' So they went down to Bethel" (2 Kgs 2: 2).

Bethel was a famous sanctuary dear to the Israelites: it was there that Jacob and other patriarchs arc buried (Gen 50:12). It was also in the temple at Bethel that a golden calf was to be erected by King Jeroboam, which would lead Israel into sin (2 Kgs 10: 29).

Arriving at Bethel, Elisha is confronted by the guild prophets attached to the sanctuary. They know the secret of Elijah, that he is to be taken from them. (Guild prophets lived in community and are associated with Elisha; Elijah, on the other hand, always stood in solitary greatness.)

Just as at Gilgal so now in Bethel the conversation of the two prophets is repeated, and once again Elisha refuses to remain behind when Elijah reveals his intention to go on to the Jordan. So they continue their journey to the river accompanied by the guild prophets. There Elijah strikes the water with his mantle; the water parts and they cross over. The incident recalls the miracle of Moses at the Red Sea, and of Joshua when he crossed the Jordan.

The journey now finished, Elijah is about to leave this world. He turns to Elisha and says: "'Ask for whatever I might do for you before I am taken from you.' Elisha answered: 'May I receive a double portion of your spirit'" (2 Kgs 2:9). This request brings to mind that in Israel the eldest son generally received a double share of the paternal inheritance (Dt 21:17). What Elisha is asking for is the right to be the spiritual heir of Elijah, since he is his firstborn disciple.

But the charism of Elijah is not inherited: it is a gift of God. Elisha appears ambitious, but the gift will be given to him providing he sees Elijah as he is taken up. Elisha does see him as Elijah departs in a fiery chariot and he cries out: "My father, my father, Israel's chariots and drivers." This last statement is ambiguous: it may be a profession of faith in which Elisha proclaims Elijah to be his master and more powerful in the defense of Israel than a whole army with its horses and chariots.

After the assumption of the fiery prophet Elisha picked up the mantle dropped by Elijah as he went up, smote the river Jordan, parted the waters, and crossed over. The guild prophets in Jericho, who were waiting on the other side, saw his action and exclaimed: "The spirit of Elijah rests on Elisha" (2 Kgs 2:15). They went to meet him, bowing to the ground before him. Elisha had become the father of a family of prophets.

Elijah taken up in a whirlwind leaves an unanswered question: Did Elijah die? If not, will he return? and if so, when? The Book of Kings does not say Elijah died, nor does it say he did not die. Nevertheless, some have held that Elijah did not die and will return again at the end of time. They believe their opinion is strengthened by the interpretation of Malachi 3: 23-24: "Lo, I will send you Elijah, the prophet, before the day of the LORD comes, the great and terrible day." Consequently, among the pious traditions of the Jews (Haggada) Elijah still lives. He appears frequently in this world, much like an angel, to accompany Jewish people on their long and sorrowful pilgrimage. At the rite of circumcision a chair is left vacant: it is the Elijah chair. Who knows, the prophet might appear during the ceremony. And at the Passover meal an extra glass of wine is on the table: it is for Elijah should he come during the celebration.

In a charming essay, Elie Wiesel, renowned writer and survivor of the holocaust of Auschwitz, relying on Jewish traditions, writes:

> But one day he [Elijah] will come and stay. On that day he will accompany the Messiah with whose destiny he is linked. One cannot fulfill his

mission without the other. For the Messiah to come, he must be preceded—and announced—by Elijah.

In the meantime, he consoles, and occasionally cures, the sick. He encourages the helpless. He takes risks and defies enemies to safeguard Jewish survival: we have no better defender in heaven than Elijah.[1]

Not only Jews but also Christians have pious stories about Elijah. Fathers of the church and other Christian writers more often than not believed Elijah would return at the end of the world with Christ. One of the clearest statements of this patristic view is that of St Augustine:

Just as there are two comings of the judge, so there are two heralds ... He [the Lord] sent before him the first herald; he called him Elias because in the Second Coming Elias will be what John was in the First.[2]

What shall we say about these pious traditions among the Jews and Christians? Many Jews at the time of Christ expected the return of Elijah (Mk 6:15): he would prepare the way for the Messiah. Hence the question put to Jesus by his disciples: "Why do the scribes claim that Elijah must come first?" (Mt 17:10). This belief was based on the literal interpretation of Malachi 3:23-24 quoted above. However, Christ put an end to their hopes when he declared: "'Elijah is indeed coming, and he will restore everything. I assure you, though, that Elijah has already come, but they did not recognize him and they did as they pleased with him. The Son of Man will suffer at their hands in the same way.' The disciples then realized that he had been speaking to them about John the Baptizer" (Mt 17:11-13).

From this one may conclude that Jesus declared Elijah had already come in the person of John the Baptizer, who is Elijah in spirit. This then, is the meaning of the words of the angel Gabriel concerning John to his father Zechariah: "God himself will go before him, in the spirit and power of Elijah, to turn the hearts of fathers to their children and the rebellious to the wisdom of the just, and to prepare for the Lord a people well-disposed" (Lk 1:17). Hence, John the Baptizer is the new Elijah. At no time do the evangelists say that Elijah in person will return; there is no need to look for any further fulfillment of the prophecy of Malachi. Indeed, some exegetes today believe that the assumption of Elijah is simply a poetic way of saying that he died.

However when we come to the spirit of Elijah there is no doubt that it passed to Elisha. The same power, the same mission, the same presence of God was bestowed on the disciple.

I. Carmelite tradition

The final day of Elijah on earth did not go unnoticed in Carmelite circles. The assumption into heaven of the prophet and the giving of his spirit to Elisha have left an indelible mark on Carmel's identity; indeed the spirit of Elijah bestowed on his beloved disciple has received more attention than his assumption. Nevertheless first let us consider the fiery ascent of the prophet in Carmel's tradition, especially in its literature, liturgy and art.

1. Literature

When the Carmelites in the Middle Ages began to reflect on the assumption of Elijah they were greatly influenced by Hebrew and early Christian traditions which believed that although Elijah was taken up to heaven he was still alive and would one day return. For example the Constitutions of 1357 make reference to the return of Elijah at the second coming of Christ. In the same century *The Institution of the First Monks*, that storehouse of early Carmelite traditions and legends, informs us that Elijah still lives. He was not taken up into the heaven of the beatified, since the heaven of the blessed who see God face to face had not yet been opened, for Christ had not yet risen. Consequently Elijah ascended into an earthly paradise, a place of peace and joy. At the end of the world he will return. He will battle with the Antichrist, be martyred and after three days rise to be with Christ.

Faithful to their custom of following the lead of the *Institution*, Carmelite writers continued to retell the story that Elijah will one day return. Writing in the 17th century Lezana repeated the story of the *Institution*. We can, he adds,

> invoke Elijah and celebrate a feast in his honor even though he has not yet attained the heaven of the blessed, because living in an earthly paradise, he is separated from all people in this world and leads a sinless life that renders him civilly, morally and politically dead.[3]

Daniel of the Virgin Mary tells substantially the same story.[4] He asks the question: Why was Elijah taken up without dying? He suggests many reasons: his zeal for God's glory and the salvation of souls, his intimacy with God, his virginal chastity and his fasting.

Influenced by the common tradition of the Order, Carmelites down through the centuries would have been inclined to believe that Elijah still lives and will return before the second coming of Christ. Early in this century Father Elias Magennis, former Prior General of the Order, tells the story of the passing of Elijah.[5] Relying on the fathers of the church and the scripture commentators, and with no reference to Carmelite authors, he accepts the opinion that Elijah lives and will return. However he says it is only a pious thought that Elijah lives in a terrestrial paradise, and that he will return to challenge the Antichrist and then be put to death before entering into glory.

What is the Carmelite belief today? There is no common teaching. In fact the matter is not even discussed. Father Roland Murphy, a renowned Carmelite scholar of the Old Testament, says that scripture does not give an answer: it does not say that Elijah died, nor does it say he did not die.[6] Nevertheless one is inclined to believe with many exegetes that there is no clear revelation that Elijah in person will one day return. Jesus said that Elijah had already come in the person of John the Baptizer (Mt 17:11-13).

2. Liturgy

The Order's liturgy both in the Mass and the Divine Office abound in references to the assumption of Elijah. For example the breviaries of 1585 and 1683 refer to the assumption in the oration and in the response to the ninth lesson of Matins. The latter recalls the cry of Elisha: "My father, my father," etc. as Elijah is taken up in the whirlwind. Moreover the antiphons of Lauds and the hymn refer to the assumption. This office continued down through the centuries and was reprinted in the edition of 1938 that was used throughout the Order until the revision of 1979 mandated by the Second Vatican Council. The revised Liturgy of the Hours recalls the assumption of Elijah throughout, from Evening Prayer I to Evening Prayer II.

If we examine the liturgy of the Eucharist we find that there was no Mass in honor of St Elijah approved for the whole Order until the Missal of 1551. This is a late date when we consider that the Mass in honor of St Elisha was introduced as early as 1399. One reason for the delay would be the uncertainty of liturgical cult for Elijah, whom many considered to be still alive and who would one day return before the second coming of Christ.

The Mass in the Missal of 1551, and that in the Missal of 1574, recall the assumption of Elijah in the oration. The preface in the Missal of 1840 also mentions the assumption. After the Council of Trent, the revised Missal of 1787 continues to recall the assumption in the oration.

However the Missal of 1979 makes no mention of the assumption in the Mass in honor of St Elijah, celebrated in the Order as a Solemnity. The votive Mass of Elijah and Elisha, however, offers an alternative reading of the assumption of Elijah and the conferral of his mantle on Elisha (2 Kgs 2:6-15).

3. Iconography

Artists have for centuries found the assumption of Elijah an attractive subject. Two of the most famous portrayals of the fiery assumption are in Rome: the frescoes in the cemetery of Domitilla and the carved wooden doors of the church of St Sabina (c. 430). Carmelite churches are also well-known for their paintings of the assumption of Elijah. We mention the painting of Dughet in the church of San Martino in Rome; and in Spain churches in Cordoba, Valencia, Madrid and Toledo are graced with beautiful paintings. Other European countries—Germany and Holland, for example—also have valuable paintings. Finally, we recall the stained glass windows that portray the life and mission of Elijah in the Carmelite chapel at Niagara Falls, Ontario. Among them is a beautiful scene of Elijah being taken up to heaven in a fiery chariot.

To sum up: in literature, liturgy and art Carmel has constantly borne witness to the assumption of Elijah into heaven. Today we are led to believe that God has taken unto himself his faithful servant in Israel.

II. The spirit of Elijah

It is understandable that artists would be fascinated by the fiery ascent of Elijah into heaven, and that Carmelites would also find it an intriguing subject for contemplation. Yet is is the *spirit* of Elijah conferred on Elisha that has been of greater interest to Carmelites: Elijah is their spiritual father, their model. His spirit is their spirit. Carmel is Elijan.

To understand how this spirit was interpreted in Carmel we return to *The Book of the Institution of the First Monks*. We recall that it was written for a young man, Caprasius, who was inquiring about the beginning of the Carmelite Order. The writer informs him that to know "the spirit of the Order" one must first live it. However, one can still learn much about this spirit by studying the dignity of its authors and founders. He presents Elijah as the "Supreme Founder of the Order" and offers his life as a model for the young man:

> For it was he who, desirous of greater progress in the pursuit of divine contemplation, withdrew far from the cities and, despoiling himself of all earth-

ly and mundane things, was the first to adopt the holy and solitary life of a prophet which he had established at the inspiration and command of the Spirit.[7]

The *Institution* then goes on to describe the twofold goal of the solitary life of Elijah, now claimed by Carmel as its own. The first is to offer God a pure and holy heart free of all actual sin. This state disposes the soul for the second goal, namely, to receive, if God so wills, a taste of his divine presence, the sweetness of the glory of heaven, the gift of contemplative prayer. With the grace of God one can attain purity of heart, but contemplation is pure gift. The Carmelite vocation, then, is a call to contemplative prayer or, as some say, to the mystical life, a taste of heaven on earth.

It should be observed that the *Institution* describes an eremitical way of life that makes no reference to an active apostolate. It presents Elijah as the model of the solitary contemplative; it is a way of life suitable for hermits.

However the contemplative life can be adapted to include an active ministry. Carmelites who followed the eremitical way on Carmel left the mountain less than fifty years after receiving the Rule of St Albert and went to Europe. There they adopted a mendicant lifestyle with the approval of the Holy See. They began to engage in the spiritual care of the faithful, retaining, however, their deeply contemplative character. Some Carmelites continue to live out the eremitical way even to this day; but in the course of time the greater number of friars began to engage in apostolic work. Yet in spite of this change the *Institution* continued to remind them that the primary dimension of Carmel is the contemplative life.

Once the mendicant way of life was accepted, however, there was bound to be tension between the call to prayer and the call to ministry. As a result there were periods when the contemplative spirit of the Order was overshadowed by pastoral activity, and the spiritual life in Carmel declined. But reforms also took place and the Elijan spirit was revived. Among the reforms, for the sake of brevity, we mention only two. In these the *Institution* had a formidable place.

In the 16th century, when St Teresa of Avila began her most illustrious reform, there was a copy of the Spanish translation of the *Institution* where she lived. How familiar she was with it is difficult to say, but there is no doubt that she followed its spirit.

In the course of time the Teresian reform became a separate branch of the Order. Its contemplative spirit, however, had a salutary effect upon the older observance. For example, about twenty years after the death of St Teresa, a small group of Carmelites in France following the older observance sought to renew their spirit. They founded a movement that became known as the Reform of Touraine. The problems of these friars were greater than those of St Teresa and her contemplative nuns: they were engaged in active ministry and wanted to harmonize it with a contemplative life that would give primacy to prayer. The spirit of their reform was expressed in their *Directory of Novices*[8] which stated expressly that the principal obligation of their institute was to attend and stand with God in solitude, silence and continual prayer.

It was a blind lay brother, John of St Samson, who was the spiritual guide of the reform. He was gifted with a high degree of contemplation. Some say he ranks with St Teresa and St John of the Cross as a mystical writer, and his influence even during his lifetime extended beyond the Order. He tells us that all who enter the Carmelite Order are called to the mystical life, that is, to experience the presence of God even in this life. Therefore neither study, nor work, nor pastoral duties should ever put prayer into the background. The vocation to Carmel is a call to contemplative prayer.[9]

Michael of St Augustine, a Belgian (d. 1684), was one of the more influential Carmelite writers of the reform in the 17th century. He was a great defender of the mixed life, and found no difficulty in harmonizing the active apostolate with the contemplative spirit. For him the spirit of Elijah is both contemplation and action. He pointed out that Elijah on various occasions at God's command left his place of solitude to engage in protest against the infiltration of idolatry in Israel. Nowhere is this more clear than when the prophet went to Carmel to engage in conflict with the prophets of Baal, whom he defeated. This twofold spirit of Elijah, he said, can be found in Carmelite saints: e.g., St Peter Thomas and St Andrew Corsini were bishops and exemplary Carmelites, devoted pastors and men of prayer. However, true to the spirit of Carmel, Michael also taught that the principal and more important dimension of Carmel is the contemplative spirit which we should strive for in this world. His writings are a true witness of the Reform of Touraine in which he was an outstanding leader.[10]

The spirit of Touraine has left a lasting effect on the Order. The *Carmelite Directory*, written for the formation of novices, was steeped in the spirit of Touraine and of *The Institution of the First Monks*. To be faithful to the spirit of Carmel, the spirit of Elijah, the Carmelite must strive to offer God a pure and holy heart, and in this way dispose himself for the gift of contemplation.[11]

Finally, after the Second Vatican Council, the revised Constitutions of the Order (1971) again insisted on the twofold purpose of the Order: they first quoted verbatim the *Institution* on the contemplative dimension, and then added: "With this as their goal they were careful to fulfill the other dimension of their spirit, namely 'to produce and bring forth with the Church children in Christ through the Gospel.'"[12]

Consequently we speak today of the spirit of Elijah, bestowed on Elisha and sought by his followers, as a contemplative spirit that overflows into active ministry. Elijah sought the face of God in prayer and, on fire with love, went forth into the world: "his words were as a flaming furnace" (Sir 48:1).

However, the spirit of Elijah is lived fully by those who dedicate themselves to a purely contemplative life. A cloistered Carmelite nun is encouraged to serve the People of God

> through living in the presence of God, through ardent prayer and through apostolic zeal. In imitation of Elijah ... she follows the prophetic way as a characteristic of her life, which is oriented to listening interiorly to the Word of God and which is a special witness to the living God and to the supreme demands of his kingdom.[13]

We conclude: in its long tradition Carmel has always upheld Elijah as its model, and the spirit of Elijah has always been considered a contemplative spirit that may or may not overflow into apostolic activity. For this reason the purely contemplative as well as the active Carmelite finds the Elijan spirit in the words of the prophet himself: "I have been most zealous for the LORD, the God of hosts" (1 Kgs 19:14). And lest there be any doubt, it is clearly spelled out in the opening prayer of the revised liturgy of the solemnity in honor of St Elijah:

Almighty, ever living God,
Your prophet Elijah, our Father,
lived always in your presence

and was zealous for the honor
    due to your name.
May we, your servants,
    always seek your face
and bear witness to your love.

III. A new Elijah? Blessed Titus Brandsma

As we come to the closing years of the twentieth century and look forward to the third millenium, members of the Carmelite family along with all members of the church find themselves pilgrims in a foreign land, a shattered world that has forgotten God.

How should a religious family like the Carmelites face up to this crisis? Can its Elijan spirit—which has been its special charism for almost 800 years—still inspire new generations of Carmelites? And more importantly: does the church of the future need the charism of the Carmelite family? These questions are vital and need an answer.

We are convinced that the Elijan spirit of Carmel is timeless. It is as relevant today as in past ages. Carmelites, if faithful to their vocation, still have something to offer the life and holiness of the church. There will always be a place in the church for the spirit of Elijah, that is, for those who open themselves to the Holy Spirit and dedicate themselves to live constantly in the presence of the living God, on fire with zeal to do his will.

As we look to the future we should remember that Elijah was sent by God to Israel at a moment when, under King Ahab and Queen Jezebel, the chosen people were vacillating between worship of the one true God and that of false gods. "How long will you straddle the issue? If the LORD is God, follow him," (1 Kgs 18:21) cried the prophet. In his victory over the prophets of Baal on Carmel, Elijah did not succeed in exterminating Baalism from Israel, but he did cooperate in preserving the kingdom from going over completely to false worship. In this he played an important role in sustaining faith in the one true God of Israel.

The Carmelite family today certainly can fulfill a role in a world that often excludes God from daily life. It can do this if it renews its spirit. One great help would be the emergence of a new Elijah to lead us. Is there such a prophet ? We believe there is: Blessed Titus Brandsma. His life is an incarnation of the spirit of Elijah. He is a saint of our times.

Born in Bolsward, The Netherlands, in 1881, he joined the Dutch province of Carmel as a young man. Throughout his religious and priestly life he was devoted to the contemplative spirit of Carmel, talking to God or about God. On fire with the love of God he made himself available to everyone. No activity was foreign to him. He even became a professional journalist, and in 1935 he was appointed ecclesiastical adviser to Catholic journalists. It was while exercising this office that he incurred the wrath of the Nazi regime both before and during its occupation of The Netherlands. Eventually he was imprisoned; on July 26, 1942, he was put to death in the concentration camp of Dachau. Pope John Paul II beatified this priest and martyr on November 3, 1985, in St Peter's Basilica, Rome.

Just as Elijah stood before Ahab and cried out: "I have been most zealous for the LORD, the God of hosts," so Titus stood before the representatives of Nazism in the prison of Scheveningen and ended his defence with the words:

God bless The Netherlands.

God bless Germany.

God grant that both nations soon stand abreast in complete peace and freedom to acknowledge and honor Him, and for the salvation and prosperity of these two nations so closely allied.[14]

One day later, on January 23, 1942, he wrote in a letter: "God is by me and in me and with me. 'For it is in Him that we live, move and exist.' 'God is so close by and so far. God is ever present.'"[15]

Who cannot see here the Elijan spirit of Titus? It is this spirit that we wish to examine. In doing this it would be most helpful if we had a record of his religious experiences; unfortunately, he left no diary, no doctrine, no account of his spiritual journey. Nevertheless, from his writings and from the witness of those who either knew him personally or studied his life, we have two rich sources from which to judge the spirit that inspired him. We begin with his writings.

1. The writings of Bl Titus

Our reflections will rely to a great extent, but not exclusively, on two of his published works: *Carmelite Mysticism: Historical Sketches*,[16] and "Carmes." The former is a series of nine lectures he delivered in 1935 at the Catholic University of America, Washington, D.C. One year later, after the first edition of these lectures, his article "Carmes" appeared in the *Dictionaire de Spiritualitè*.[17]

Here I would like to add a personal note concerning the article "Carmes." Father John Brenninger, 0. Carm., the compiler of the *Carmelite Directory* (1940), told me that he had been invited by Father Joseph de Guibert, S.J., editor of the

Dictionnaire, to write the article on Carmelite spirituality. But he recommended Father Titus as being more competent. He was happy he made this choice, he told me, because the contribution of Titus far surpassed anything he might have done.

As for the lectures of Titus, I never heard them delivered; but having read them, I would agree with the observation of Father Adrian Staring, O. Carm., a most reliable student of the life and writings of Titus, that no one has offered a better synthesis of Carmelite spirituality.

Having made these observations let us examine the writings of Titus to see how he promoted the spirit of Elijah in Carmel. The first of his nine lectures in *Carmelite Mysticism* bears the title: "In the Spirit and Strength of Elias." Referring to the fiery prophet of Carmel and his influence on the prophetic life of early Jewish and Christian hermits, he stated:

> He was also the first in a long line of those who would worship God in spirit and truth. In his lifetime disciples gathered around him and learned from him the deep secrets of his prayer and communion with God. His double spirit passed to Eliseus, and from him to the school of the prophets, and down through the ages, the life of Elias has been continued in these hermits who ever sought inspiration in their great exemplar.[18]

He goes on to say that centuries later the lifestyle of these early hermits was continued by Carmelite hermits who gathered together on Mount Carmel to live an eremitical life according to the Rule of St Albert, given to them about 1209. "Is it not providential that the first monks of the Order of Carmel, symbolizing the imitation of Elias, drank the water from the fountain that bears his name?"[19]

How did Titus understand the spirit of Elijah? His thoughts and ideals were influenced greatly by

The Book of the Institution of the First Monks, which, as we have seen in the previous section, proposes a twofold goal: purity of heart and contemplation.

Titus often refers to this twofold goal as the twofold spirit of Elijah. What he meant was that we are called to be ascetics, living a life of penance and mortification, so as to acquire the purity of heart that frees us from all actual sin. This purity of heart, accompanied by a spirit of prayer, will then dispose us for the gift of contemplation. But since it is pure gift it may or may not be given to all. However we are called to it—to the mystical life—and we should dispose ourselves to receive it. Indeed Carmelites as spiritual children of the prophet should pray for this double spirit. For Titus "the life of Elijah is the shortest summary of the Order's life."[20] This conviction led him to state:

> Never in any Order, to my knowledge, has a book furnishing a norm of life and declaring the end toward which its members should strive, enunciated the vocation to the mystical life in so formal a manner.[21]

In his writings and lectures Titus was fond of speaking of the mystical life and mysticism, expressions that many may find confusing since they mean different things to different people. For Titus, who taught a course on the History of Mysticism at Nijmegen University, these terms were common. What did he mean by them?

> People have to see God again and live in contemplation of God. This is called mysticism. So be it. I can even applaud this usage if in it I can find the expression of the truth that in mysticism we have to see the progressive and highest development of what has potentially been posited in human nature. It is a great pity that this is no longer understood.[22]

Titus encouraged everyone to seek God, to live in his presence; but he saw this as the special call of the Carmelite, as he tells us in his lectures.

> This living in the presence of God, this placing himself before the face of God, is a characteristic which the children of Carmel have inherited from the great prophet. *Conversatio nostra in coelis est,* "Our conversation is in heaven." Elias was not taken up to heaven, but here on earth lived in heaven and stood with a pious heart before God's throne: "God lives, I am standing before his face."[23]

Continuing this train of thought, Titus remarks that the practice of living in the presence of God is an essential element in religious development, encouraged by all spiritual writers, "But in Carmel it takes a special place."[24] Consequently, prayer is the chief characteristic of the great prophet. We must strive to grow in prayer and to prepare for the highest forms of prayer by offering God a pure and holy heart. This is the vocation of all Carmelites; this is the spirit of Elijah.

2. Prayer marked with zeal

It is one thing to strive to live constantly in God's presence, and another to do this with zeal. Elijah, the man of God standing in God's presence, was filled with zeal. He sought to do God's will as a faithful servant. On Mount Horeb in God's presence he exclaimed: "I have been most zealous for the Lord, the God of hosts." Commenting on this event Titus wrote that no Carmelite should be without zeal. Carmel must ever feel that glow of its founder's zeal, the mark of the true follower of Elias. It burns in all Carmelite saints."[25]

Reflecting on the lives of these saints he saw St Teresa of Avila as the model of the spirit of Elijah.

She lived in the presence of God, on fire with zeal, prompt to do whatever he asked. From his earliest days in religious life Titus was inspired by the Spanish mystic, and he even made an anthology of her sayings. Later he joined a few of his confreres in translating into Dutch the works of St Teresa. However he did not live to see the completion of this project which he encouraged even while awaiting death in prison. During his confinement he attempted to write a biography of St Teresa, even though he had few sources to guide him. He never finished this venture, but the fact that he even attempted it shows the great love and admiration he had for her.

His testimony to the zeal of St Teresa, a model for the spirit of Elijah, is found in his lectures: "Especially do we see it [zeal] in the soul of seraphic St Teresa of Avila. The smouldering fires that burned in the soul of 'this undaunted daughter of desires ' is Carmel's greatest witness to the spirit of Elias."[26]

Too often when speaking of zeal we refer to external apostolic works and the labors of missionaries, and we fail to realize the apostolic value of the prayer of contemplatives. Titus never made this mistake.

> The mystical life is in the highest sense apostolic. Without activity it has the greatest influence. St Teresa of Avila, St Mary Magdalen de Pazzi, and especially the little St Therese of Lisieux, teach us the apostolate of prayer. Many Carmels are considered the real centres of missionary work, not because of their activity but because of their contemplative life.[27]

3. Zeal among active Carmelites

Many members of the Carmelite family are both contemplative and active. Their zeal overflows into their ministry. This, of course, is nothing new: Carmelite saints even back in the 14th century were renowned for their activity. For example, Saints Peter Thomas and Andrew Corsini were bishops. They were men of prayer and yet zealous pastors. Consequently, zeal is the mark of the spirit of Elijah, Titus tells us, whether we are living a purely contemplative life or engaged in apostolic ministry.

4. What others said about Bl Titus

From the writings of Titus it is clear that for him the spirit of Elijah is composed of two elements: living in the presence of God; on fire with zeal. Now we ask: did Titus practice what he preached? Yes. Even though we do not have any spiritual journal, his contemporaries bear witness to the depths of his union with God and his untiring zeal. The successor of Titus at the Nijmegen University, Smits van Waesbergan, testified in reference to his life and work:

> His solid naturalness, his balanced character, his theological schooling, the tradition of his Order, made him fully realize that mysticism is the freely bestowed development of the interior life, which is at once gradual and organic, and by no means rare. And may we speak in this context of his personal experience? We think so. Much, or rather everything justifies this conjecture. His person and life's work would otherwise remain inexplicable.[28]

Father James Melsen, former Procurator General of the Carmelite Order, who as a young religious lived in community with Titus, testifies:

> His was a very strong, all pervading passion to seek God in order to live united to him. Only God could fascinate him and only the highest forms of union with God could satisfy him.[29]

Another confrere of Titus, Aemelius Breij, echoes the same conviction:

> His prayer for example, was not restricted to the hour of daily meditation, holy Mass, or to the Divine Office, for he never considered prayer as a mere part of his daily duty. Rather for him prayer filled every moment of his life. We find among his notes these profound words: "Prayer is life, not an oasis in the desert of life!" ... The spiritual life of Father Titus could ... be summed up in two words: *seeking God.* Men and things, he saw them all in their proper relation to God; for all things reminded him of God.[30]

Many other witnesses to the spirit of Titus could be offered. But their testimony can be best summed up in the words of Father Redemptus Valabek, Postulator General of the Cause of Beatification of Father Titus. In his homily to commemorate the beatification, delivered in the Cathedral of St Matthew, Washington, D.C., February 23, 1986, he alludes to the spirit of Elijah in the life of Titus when he proclaimed:

> The secret of Father Titus' spirituality is *PRESENCE.* His indomitable faith was that God is with us and never abandons us. In his inaugural speech as Rector Magnificus he stated: "We must not separate God from the world, rather we must see him as the ground of our being, as the background of all—our neighbor first of all, the earth, the heavens, the universe." Father Titus was able to maintain a contemplative/mystic stance even in the multiplicity of activities because he KNEW he was not alone—the Carmelite practice of the presence of God had been solidly riveted in him during his formative years and he never forgot it. In prison he could exult: "O blessed solitude! My Lord, I never felt you closer. ... Now I am able to dedicate that time to you that formerly so often was interrupted by others. I have seldom been so happy. If it be God's will, I am willing to remain here forever." It was this sense of God's presence that made him aware of the real presence of other persons and which made them his highest priority.[31]

5. Witnesses to Bl Titus' zeal

Confreres of Titus and others not only testify to the prayerful life of Titus; they are eloquent when they speak of his zeal in ministry. His fiery love of God overflowed into many activities.

So great and varied were these that a Dutch humorist and former pupil, Godfried Bomans, jokingly remarked: "He was the mystic on the Continent of Europe who had a season's railroad ticket and who became holy in train compartments."[32]

How varied were these activities? We mention three specific areas: First, in his religious and priestly ministry he fulfilled ordinary roles in an extraordinary manner. He was known among his confreres for his zeal in offering Mass, hearing confessions, preaching, giving counsel and teaching. He employed all the means of communication current in his time: the press, the radio, the lecture hall. Secondly, his concern for social affairs was obvious to all. Father Melsen, whose observations we previously recorded, stated:

> Thus Titus ... for all his ideal of contemplation, had a deep sense of social responsibility, labored hard to establish new grammar schools for the cultural development of Catholics, Frisian in particular and Dutch in general, grudged neither time nor care in order to strengthen the position—and the financial position too—of journalists, and was tireless in helping the poor, the aged, the homeless, the needy and those in search of a job.[33]

Finally, his zeal for peace and the sanctity of every human life brought him national attention. On many occasions he denounced anti-Semitism, National Socialism rampant in Germany, and the Dutch Nationalist Socialist Movement.

The tireless zeal of Titus, his prominence in the Catholic community, and his public display of love for Christ and the church were not lost on the Dutch bishops. They appointed him their representative to all Catholic journalists. His mission was to visit them and offer direction, to guide them against attempts of National Socialism to infiltrate the Catholic press. It was while he was fulfilling this task that he was arrested and imprisoned.

But even imprisonment did not dampen the ardor of this remarkable man. He continued to preach the love of Christ, offering encouragment and hope to his fellow prisoners, praying for forgiveness for his enemies.

Throughout his life since childhood, suffering had been no stranger to him. Now in prison during the last months of his life he would walk to Calvary with Christ. On Good Friday in the camp of Amersfoort he gave a lecture to his fellow prisoners. It turned out to be a sermon on the passion of Christ that touched the hearts of his listeners. From his notes we read: "On this day, glad, thankful feeling with vivid imagination of the Passion of Christ, in union with *our* suffering. God for us, God with us, God in us, our strength."[34] Some months later in Dachau, where he was cruelly put to death, he had an opportunity to put into practice what he had often preached in retreats: "Consider life as a Way of the Cross, but take the cross on your shoulders with joy and courage, for Jesus with his example and grace made it light."[35]

III. Conclusion

Today people in every walk of life can look at the life of Titus and find something to admire and to imitate. Carmelites, lay and religious, for their part see Elijah come to life in him. He is a prophet of our times: the faithful servant of God, living always in his presence, burning with fiery zeal for all that concerns God and his people.

At the beginning of these reflections we mentioned that we live in a shattered world, a world that has forgotten God. What can we as a Carmelite family do to renew faith in God ? What can we do to help people live in the presence of the living God? One thing we can do is to renew the Elijan spirit that we inherited from our ancestors. In doing this we are fortunate to have as a model Blessed Titus Brandsma, the incarnation of the spirit of Elijah in our century. He shows us how to live. He is our inspiration. His way of life was that of Elijah: "God lives, in whose presence I stand. With zeal I have been most zealous for the LORD, the God of hosts." On fire with love, he was the faithful servant of the Lord. Elijah was his spiritual father; St Teresa his model. He can surely be ours. He is a "new Elijah."

In the final months of his life, confined to prison and often alone, he likened his confinement to the cell of his monastery—in both he could be alone with God. His contemplative spirit comes through clearly in "A Prayer before a Picture of Christ," a poem he composed during his imprisonment at Scheveningen before his transfer to Dachau. The intimate, personal relationship he enjoyed with our Lord during his life shines forth in his poem. We recall it once again. It has been translated into many languages, published frequently but never too often, for in it we find the spirit of Titus, the spirit of St Teresa, the spirit of Elijah, and the spirit that once again can renew the life of the Carmelite family.

O Jesus, when I look on you
My love for you starts up anew,
And tells me that your heart loves me
And you my special friend would be.

More courage I will need for sure,
but any pain I will endure,
Because it makes me like to you
And leads unto your kingdom too.

In sorrow do I find my bliss,
for Sorrow now no more is this;
Rather the path that must be trod,
That makes me one with you, my God.

Oh, leave me here alone and still,
And all around the cold and chill.
To enter here I will have none;
I weary not when I'm alone.

For, Jesus you are at my side;
Never so close did we abide.
Stay with me, Jesus, my delight,
Your presence near makes all things right.[36]

Notes

INTRODUCTION

1   Gerhard von Rad, *Old Testament Theology* (London: SCM Press, 1975), I:335, note 4.

CHAPTER I

1   Unless otherwise noted, all biblical texts are taken from the *New American Bible* (Nashville: Thomas Nelson Publishers, 1970). The Psalms are cited as found in *The Liturgy of the Hours* (New York: Catholic Book Publishing Co., 1976).

2   *Jerome Biblical Commentary* (Englewood Cliffs, New Jersey: Prerntice-Hall, 1968), 10:40.

3   *Constitutiones Ordinis Fratrum Beatissimæ Virginis Mariæ de Monte Carmelo a Capitulo Generali Romæ celebrato anno 1971 approbatæ* (Romæ, 1971), art. 7; preliminary translation from *Constitutions of the Order of Brothers of the Most Blessed Mother of Mount Carmel, Approved by the General Chapter of 1971* (Barrington, Illinois: Carmelite Provincial House, n.d.) Hereafter *Constitutions 1971.*

4   Joachim Smet, O.Carm., *The Carmelites: A History of the Brothers of Our Lady of Mount Carmel* (Darien, Illinois: Carmelite Spiritual Center, 1976-1988), I:15. Hereafter this work will be cited as *The Carmelites*, volume 1 from the revised edition (1988).

5   *Liber de institutione primorum monachorum,* chapter 9, in *Carmel in the World* 13 (1974), 257. Hereafter this work will be cited simply as *Institution*; it is Book I of the *Liber de institutione et peculiaribus gestis religiosorum carmelitarum* (c. 1370). The

translation of chapters 1-9 used throughout this book is that of Bryan Deschamp, O.Carm., published in *Carmel in the World* 13 (1974) 69-75, 152-161, 244-260. Another translation of these same chapters was prepared by Bede Edwards, O.C.D., *The Book of the Institution of the First Monks* (Oxford: Boars Hill, 1969). The earlier, but more complete translation by Norman Werling, O.Carm., will be used for chapters 10-41; see *The Sword* 4 (1940), 20-24, 152-160, 309-320; 5 (1941), 20-27, 131-139, 241-248; 6 (1942), 33-39; 147-155; 278-286; 7 (1943), 347-355. A critical edition of the text is being prepared by Paul Chandler, O.Carm., as a doctoral dissertation at the Centre for Medieval Studies, the University of Toronto.

6   Cited in Kilian J. Healy, O.Carm., *Methods of Prayer in the Directory of the Carmelite Reform of Touraine* (Rome: Institutum Carmelitanum, 1956), p. 18.

7   *Ibid.*, p. 19.

8   Blessed Titus Brandsma, O.Carm., *Carmelite Mysticism: Historical Sketches* (Darien Illinois: The Carmelite Press, 1986), p. 4. Hereafter cited as *Carmelite Mysticism*. This work was previously published as *The Beauty of Carmel* (Dublin: Clonmore & Reynolds, 1955).

9   *The Carmelite Directory of the Spiritual Life* (Chicago: The Carmelite Press, 1951), p. 481. Henceforth cited as *Carmelite Directory*. This work is the translation of *Directorium Carmelitanum vitæ spiritualis* (Typis Polyglottis Vaticanis, 1940).

10   *Constitutions 1971*, art. 14.

11   Saint Therese of Lisieux, O.C.D., *Story of a Soul: The Autobiography of St Therese of Lisieux*, translation by John Clarke, O.C.D. (Washington: ICS Publications, 1975), p. 188. Hereafter, *Autobiography*.

12   *Washington Post*, January 3, 1982, p. 3.

13   The Rule of St Albert, Chapter 14. The English translation is that published in *Albert's Way: The First North American Congress on the Carmelite Rule*, edited by Michael Mulhall, O.Carm. (Rome: Institutum Carmelitanum, 1989), pp. 2-21. Hereafter, cited simply as Rule.

14   Cf Rule, Chapter 7.

15   Decree on the Appropriate Renewal of the Religious Life *(Perfectæ caritatis)*, 7; English translation is taken from *The Documents of Vatican II*, Walter M. Abbott, S..J., General Editor (N. p.: Guild Press, [1967]).

16   *St Therese of Lisieux by Those Who Knew Her: Testimonies*

from the *Process of Beatification*, edited and translated by Christopher O'Mahoney, O.C.D. (Dublin: Veritas Publications, 1975), p. 140.

[17]   Therese of Lisieux, *Autobiography*, pp. 213-214.

CHAPTER II

[1]   *Élie le Prophète*: I - *Selon les écritures et les traditions chrétiennes*, in *Etudes Carmélitaines* 35 (1957), 55.

[2]   For a more complete treatment, cf. Louis Réau, "L'Iconographie du Prophète Élie," *Etudes Carmélitaines* 35 (1957), 233-267.

[3]   See chapter 1, note 5 on page 305.

[4]   *Institution*, chapter 2, in *Carmel in the World* 13 (1974), 72.

[5]   John Cassian, *Colatio Abbatis Moysi* I & II, in *Sources Chrétiennes* 42.

[6]   Brandsma, *Carmelite Mysticism*, p. 18.

[7]   *The Carmelites*, I:29.

[8]   *Ibid.*, I:90.

[9]   Blessed John Soreth, O.Carm., *Expositio paraenetica Regulæ Fratrum Beatissimæ Dei Genitricis et Virginis Mariæ de Monte Carmelo* (Parisiis: Josephum Cottereau, 1625), Praefatio.

[10]   *Ibid.*, Textus III, caput unicum.

[11]   *The Carmelites*, I:115.

[12]   *Ibid.*

[13]   Saint Teresa of Jesus, O.Carm., *The Interior Castle*, V, 1, n. 2, in *The Collected Works of St. Teresa of Avila*, translated by Kieran Kavanaugh, O.C.D., and Otilio Rodriguez, O.C.D. (Washington: ICS Publications, 1976-1985), II:335-336.

[14]   Gabriel of St Mary Magdalen, O.C.D., "Carmes Déchaussés," in *Dictionnaire de Spiritualité*, II:173.

[15]   Brandsma, *Carmelite Mysticism*, p. 64.

[16]   *Constitutions 1971*, arts. 10, 12.

[17]   The Contemplative Dimension of Religious Life (Letter of

the Sacred Congregation for Religious and for Secular Institutes, *La plenaria*, January, 1981), 30; translation from *Vatican Council II: More Postconciliar Documents*, Austin Flannery, O.P., General Editor (Collegeville, Minnesota: The Liturgical Press, 1982).

[18] Nicolaus Gallicus, *Ignea sagitta* (1270 or 1271); translation in *The Flaming Arrow (Ignea Sagitta) by Nicholas, Prior General of the Carmelite Order 1266-1271* (The complete text, translated and introduced by Bede Edwards, O.C.D., from the critical edition by Adrian Staring, O.Carm.), in *The Sword* 39:2 (1979), 3-52; p. 35. Hereafter cited as *Ignea sagitta*.

[19] Pastoral Constitution on the Church in the Modern World *(Gaudium et Spes)*, 43.

[20] Therese of Lisieux, *Autobiography*, p. 257.

[21] Saint Therese of Lisieux, O.C.D., *St. Therese of Lisieux: Her Last Conversations*, translated by John Clarke, O.C.D. (Washington: ICS Publications, 1977), p. 228.

[22] *Carmelite Directory*, p. 354.

[23] Venerable Maríe Petyt of St. Teresa, T.O.Carm. *Union with Our Lady: Marian Writings of Ven. Maríe Petyt of St. Teresa*, translated by Thomas E. McGinnis, O.Carm. (New York: The Scapular Press, 1954), pp. 60-61.

[24] Saint Teresa of Jesus, O.Carm., *The Way of Perfection*, 28, 12, in *Collected Works*, II:145.

[25] Guigo II, *The Ladder for Monks and Twelve Meditations* (Eng. trans. 1978). The text was once thought to have been the work of either St Augustine, *Scala paradisi* I, 1 *(PL* 40:997-1004), or St Bernard, *Scala Claustralium (PL* 184:475-484). Cf. R. du Moustier, "Guigo II," *New Catholic Encyclopedia* 6:843-844.

[26] Saint John of the Cross, O.Carm., *Maxims and Counsels*, n. 79, in *The Collected Works of St. John of the Cross*, translated by Kieran Kavanaugh, O.C.D., and Otilio Rodriguez, O.C.D. (Washington: ICS Publications, 1979), p. 680.

[27] *The Cloud of Unknowing and The Book of Privy Counseling*, translated by William Johnston (Garden City, New York: Image Books, 1973). See especially chapters 3, 4 and 7.

CHAPTER III

[1]   *Itineraria Iherosolymitana* in *Corpus scriptorum ecclesias-ticorum latinorum* (Vindobonae: C. Geroldi, 1866-1971), 39:160.

[2]   Elie Wiesel, *Five Biblical Portraits* (Notre Dame: University of Notre Dame Press, 1981), p. 139.

[3]   *Institution*, chapter 12, in *The Sword* V:25.

[4]   Soreth, *Expositio paraenetica*, Textus III, caput unicum.

[5]   In Healy, *op. cit.*, p. 18.

[6]   *Carmelite Directory*, p. 505.

[7]   *Constitutions 1971*, art. 10.

[8]   *L'Osservatore Romano*, May 31, 1982, p. 2.

[9]   *St. Therese of Lisieux by Those Who Knew Her*, p. 93.

[10]   Cf. R. Garrigou-Lagrange, O.P., *The Three Ages of the Spiritual Life: Prelude of Eternal Life*, translated by M. Timothea Doyle, O.P. (St. Louis: B. Herder Book Co., 1948), 2:507

[11]   Ronald W. Clarke, *Einstein: The Life and Times* (New York: Avon, 1971), p. 502; cf. also pp. 35-38, 516-517.

[12]   John Eccles, *The Brain and the Unity of Conscious Experience*, pp. 43-44.

[13]   Edgar Mitchel, *Psychic Exploration*, edited by John White, p. 29.

[14]   Therese of Lisieux, *Last Conversations*, p. 257.

[15]   Teresa of Jesus, *Way of Perfection*, 26, 9, in *Collected Works*, II:136.

[16]   Saint John of the Cross, O.Carm., *The Spiritual Canticle* 1, 6 in *Collected Works*, p. 418.

Chapter IV

1   *Institution*, chapters 32-36, in *The Sword* 6 (1942), 278-286.

2   Eamon R. Carroll, O.Carm., "The Marian Theology of Arnold Bostius, O.Carm. (l445-1499)," *Carmelus* 9 (1962), 231. Carroll mentions non-Carmelite authors who also offer this interpretation in notes 60 and 120.

3   Cf. Valerius Hoppenbrouwers, O.Carm., *Devotio mariana in ordine fratrum b.m.v. de monte carmelo a medio saeculo xvi usque ad finem saeculi xix* (Rome: Institutum Carmelitanum, 1960), pp. 88-89.

4   C. 1595.

5   For a study of iconography dealing with this, cf. the excellent, splendidly illustrated article by Bruno Borchert, O.Carm., "L'Immaculée dan l'iconographie du Carmel," *Carmelus* 2 (1955), 85-131.

6   *The Carmelites*, I:7-8.

7   *Ibid.*, I:16.

8   *Ibid.*, I:8.

9   *Institution*, chapter 9, in *Carmel in the World* 13 (1974), 255.

10   Wiesel, *Five Biblical Portraits*, p. 40.

11   St Ambrose, *De virginibus*, Lib. I, cap. 3, in *PL* 16:202c.

12   St Jerome, *Epistola xxii*, 21, in *PL* 22:408.

13   Pope Pius XII, Encyclical Letter on Holy Virginity *Sacra virginitas* (*AAS* 46:161-191), translation in *The Pope Speaks* I (1954), 102.

14   *Ibid.*, p. 115.

15   Teresa of Jesus, *Way of Perfection*, 4, 7; in *Collected Works*, II:55.

16   *The Letters of St Teresa of Jesus*, translated by E. Allison Peers (London: Sheed and Ward, 1980), Letter 385, November 8, 1581, to María de San José.

17   *Ibid.*, Letter 261, December, 1578, to Ana de Jesús.

18   *Perfectæ caritatis*, n. 12.

CHAPTER V

1   Von Rad, *Old Testament Theology*, II:19.

2   Cf Smet, *The Carmelites*, III: 618.

3   Daniel of the Virgin Mary, O.Carm., *Speculum Carmelitanum sive Historia Eliani Ordinis Fratrum Beatissimæ Virginis Mariæ de Monte Carmelo* ... (Antverpiae: Typis Michaelis Knobbari, 1680). Hereafter cited as *Speculum*.

4   P. E. Magennis, O.Carm., *The Life and Times of the Prophet of Carmel* (Dublin: M. H. Gill & Son, 1925). This is a popular presentation and lacks both bibliography and notes.

5   *Ibid.*, pp. 223-246.

6   *Ibid.*, p. 229.

7   *Ibid.*, p. 231.

8   Carlos Mesters, O.Carm., *The Road to Freedom*, translated by Michael McLaughlin (Dublin: Veritas Publications, 1974).

9   *Ibid.*, pp. 30-31.

10   *Ibid.*, p. 31.

11   Painted between 1647-1651, these works are described in Marie-Nicole Boisclair, "Gaspard Dughet à Saint-Martin-des-Monts," *Storia dell'Arte* N. 53 (1985), 87-102 with 22 plates; a brief description can also be found in Emanuele Boaga, O.Carm., *Il Titolo di Equizio e la Basilica di S. Martino ai Monti* (Roma: n.p., 1988), pp. 25-29.

12   *The Carmelites*, III: 561-611.

13   Réau, "L'iconographie du Prophète Élie," in *Etudes Carmélitaines*, 35 (1957), 255.

14   Concilium Tridentinum, Sessio XIII, October 11, 1551: *Decretum de ss. Eucharistia*, cap. 8, in *DS* 1649; the English translation is to be found in *The Church Teaches: Documents of the Church in English Translation* (Rockford, Illinois: Tan Books and Publishers, 1973), n. 727.

15   Approved in 1972.

16   *Proper of the Liturgy of the Hours of the Order of the Brothers of the Blessed Virgin Mary of Mount Carmel* (Rome: Institutum Carmelitanum, 1987), p. 171.

17   *The Carmelite Missal: Containing the Masses proper to the*

Carmelite Order and the Order of Discalced Carmelites, translated respectivly, with certain authorized additions, from the Proprium Missarum Una Cum Lectionario Ordinis Fratrum B.mæ Mariæ Virginis De Monte Carmelo, *Rome 1974, and the* Proprium Missarum Fratrum Discalceatorum Ordinis B.mæ Mariæ Virginis De Monte Carmelo, *Rome 1973* (N.p.: n p., 1979), pp,, 27, 28. Hereafter, *Carmelite Missal.*

[18]   Viktor E. Frankl, *Man's Search for Meaning: An Introduction to Logotherapy* (New York: Simon & Schuster, 1984), see pp. 123-125.

[19]   *Time*, June 6, 1983, p. 38.

[20]   *The Priest and Stress,* The Bishops' Committee on Priestly Life and Ministry, United States Catholic Conference, 1982, p. 1.

[21]   Excerpt from an address given in London, *The Tablet*, May 14, 1983, p. 462.

[22]   The blessing at the end of Mass on the Solemnity of St Elijah, *Carmelite Missal*; see note 17 above .

[23]   Therese of Lisieux, *Autobiography,* p. 208.

[24]   Saint Thérèse of Lisieux, O.C.D, *General Correspondence,* translated by John Clarke, O.C.D. (Washington: Institute of Carmelite Studies, 1982-1988), letter 58 to her father, July 31, 1888, I:452.

[25]   Vernon Johnson, *Spiritual Childhood: A Study of St. Teresa's Teaching* (London: Sheed and Ward, 1953), p. 4.

[26]   Therese of Lisieux, *Autobiography,* pp. 238-239.

[27]   Therese of Lisieux, *Last Conversations,* p. 257.

CHAPTER VI

[1]   See Charles Santa Maria, "Our Carmelite Coat of Arms," translated by Albert H. Dolan, O. Carm., in *The Sword* 1: 3 (1937), 29-38; Borchert, "L'Immaculée dan l'iconographie du Carmel," *Carmelus* 2 (1955), 122-126, and especially figure 19. See too the examples reproduced in *Proper of the Liturgy of the Hours of the Order of the Brothers of the Blessed Virgin Mary of Mount Carmel* (Rome: Institutum Carmelitanum, 1987), *passim.*

[2]   See Chapter 4 above, pp. 114-115.

3   See the examples reproduced in the articles cited in note 1 above, especially in Borchert, figures 19-25.

4   Borchert, *op cit.*, figure 26.

5   Therese of Lisieux, *Autobiography*, p. 27.

6   *Ibid.*, p. 194.

7   Aemelius Breij, O.Carm., "The Spiritual Life of Titus Brandsma," *The Sword* 22 (1962), 157. This work is also available in *Essays on Titus Brandsma: Carmelite, Educator, Journalist, Martyr*, edited by Redemptus Valabek, O.Carm. (Rome: Institutum Carmelitanum, 1985), p. 98; hereafter this book will be cited as *Essays*.

8   "40th Anniversary of the Death of Fr. Titus Brandsma, O.Carm.," *Carmel in the World* 22 (1983), 80.

9   A special number of *Carmel in the World* provides a deeper understanding of this remarkable Carmelite: 15:2 (1976), 81-159.

Chapter VII

1   The name means: "God is my salvation."

2   850-787 B.C.E.

3   For a critical appraisal of historical attitudes in the 17th and 18th centuries, see *The Carmelites*, III: 617-625.

4   *Speculum*, A.D. 1337; see chapter 5, note 3, above.

5   *The Carmelites*, I: 63.

6   *Institution*, chapter 13, in *The Sword* 5 (1941), 26-27.

7   Joannes Baptista de Lezana, O.Carm., *Annales Sacri, Prophetici, et Eliani Ordinis Beat. Virginis Mariæ de monte Carmelo* ... (Romæ: Typografia Mascardi, 1645-1656), I:174-175. Hereafter, *Annales*.

8   Norman G. Werling, O.Carm., "The Liturgical Cult of Saint Elias and Saint Eliseus in the Carmelite Rite," *The Sword* 6 (1942), 6.

9   *Annales* I:286-287.

10   *Constitutions 1971*, art. 16.

[11] Brandsma, *Carmelite Mysticism*, p. 10.

[12] Falco Thuis, O.Carm., *The Wonder at the Mystery of God. Contemplation: The Life-stream of Carmel* (Rome: n.p., 1983), pp. 43-44.

[13] M. Bernadette de Lourdes, O.Carm., *Woman of Faith, Foundress: Mother M. Angeline Teresa, O.Carm., Carmelite Sisters for the Aged and Infirm* (Germantown, New York: Carmelite Sisters for the Aged and Infirm, 1984), pp. 467-468.

[14] M. Dorothy Guilbault, O.Carm., "Lord: Teach Us to Pray," *Mary, Aylesford News* 45:5 (October, 1984), p. 6.

[15] Jude Langsam, "The Discalced Carmelite Secular Order—One Member's View," *Spirituality Today* 37 (1985), 130-139; this article should be read and pondered by all Carmelites.

[16] Rule, Chapter 7.

[17] *Humanæ salutis* (Apostolic Constitution of Pope John XXIII, December 25, 1961, to convoke Vatican Council II); English translation is taken from *The Documents of Vatican II*, p. 704.

[18] George Basil Hume, O.S.B., "New Apostles: The Role of the European Laity," *Origins: National Catholic Documentary Service* 14 (1984), p. 148.

[19] John Tracy Ellis, "The Priesthood: A View from History," *Origins: National Catholic Documentary Service* 15 (1985), p. 62.

[20] Rule, Chapter 7.

Chapter VIII

[1] Some commentators believe 1 Kgs 21:20-26 to be the work of a Judean editor who, in place of the message given Elijah in v.19, substituted a sweeping and definitive judgment against Ahab's entire family.

[2] *Ignea sagitta*, p. 24.

[3] *Annales*, I:194-196.

[4] Cf. *Speculum*, I: Tractatus III, cap. 19-21.

[5] Giuseppe Fanuchi of Lucca, O.Carm., *Della vita di S. Elia Profeta: Patriarca e istitutore dell'Ordine Carmelitano* (Lucca:

Tipografia Arciv. S. Paolino, 1888), pp. 106-111.

6   A. E. Farrington, O.Carm., *St. Elias and the Carmelites* (Dublin: James Duffy and Co., 1890), pp. 35-41.

7   Magennis, *The Life and Times of the Prophet of Carmel;* cf chapter 5, note 4.

8   *The Carmelites*, III:464.

9   Ronald A. Knox, *A Spiritual Aeneid* (London: Longmans, Green and Co., 1918), pp. 141-142.

10   *The Carmelites*, IV:133.

11   *Ibid.*, IV:103.

12   *Gaudium et spes*, no. 55.

13   Justice in the World (Synod of Bishops, *Convenientes ex universa*, November 30, 1971), Introduction. Translation from *Vatican Council II: More Postconciliar Documents.* Cf. also Tracy O'Sullivan, O.Carm., *A Call to Involvement: The Justice Perspective* (Darien, Illinois: Carmelite Press, 1982).

14   General Congregation of Rio de Janeiro, 1980, "Called to Account by the Poor;" English text in *Towards a Prophetic Brotherhood: Documents of the Carmelite Order 1972-1982* (Melbourne: The Carmelite Centre, 1984), pp. 85-96.

15   *Reconciliation and Penance* (Post-Synodal Apostolic Exhortation of Pope John Paul II to the Bishops, Clergy and Faithful on Reconciliation and Penance in the Mission of the Church Today), 2.

16   *The Confessions of St. Augustine*, translation by Rex Warner (New York: The New American Library, 1963), VIII, 12.

17   Cited in Hilda C. Graef, *The Scholar and the Cross: The Life and Work of Edith Stein* (Westminster, Maryland: The Newman Press, 1955), p. 223.

18   Address of Pope Paul VI to the United Nations General Assembly, October 4, 1965, n. 7; in *The Pope Speaks* 11 (1966), 56.

19   *Reconciliation and Penance*, 23.

20   *L'Osservatore Romano: Weekly Edition in English*, November 11, 1985, p. 10.

21   Extraordinary Synod of Bishops, Final Report, II:4, *L'Osservatore Romano*, December 10, 1985, p. 6.

22   Jean Jerome Hammer, O.P., "Is Religious Life Still

Possible?" *Origins: National Catholic Documentary Service* 15 (1985), p. 190.

23   William Johnston, S.J., *Christian Mysticism Today* (San Francisco: Harper & Row, 1984), p. 176.

24   *Ibid.*, p. 178.

25   Saint Teresa of Jesus, O.Carm., *The Book of Her Life* 8, 3 in *Collected Works*, I:66.

26   *Ibid.* 9, 1, in *Collected Works*, I:70-71.

27   *Ibid.* 9, 3; in *Collected Works*, I:71.

28   Pope John Paul II, Address to Journalists in Rome, February 28, 1986; in *L'Osservatore Romano*, March 1, 1986, p. 5.

29 *Perfectæ caritatis*, 2e.

CHAPTER IX

1   853-852 B.C.E.

2   Baalzebub: the 'Baal of flies,' a contemptuous name for Baalzebul, 'Prince of Baal.'

3   J. A. Montgomery, *A Critical and Exegetical Commentary on The Books of Kings*, edited by Henry Snyder Gehman (Edinburgh: T. & T. Clark, 1951), p. 348.

4   *Annales*, I:198-200.

5   *Speculum*, I: Tractatus III, capita 22-25.

6   Magennis, *The Life and Times of the Prophet of Carmel*, p. 139.

7   *The Carmelites*, III:617

8   *Institution*, chapter 9, in *Carmel in the World* 13 (1974), 255.

9   Cf chapter 1, note 9 above.

10   Decree on Ecumenism *(Unitatis redintegratio)*, no. 3; translation from *Vatican Council II: The Conciliar and Post Conciliar Documents*, Austin Flannery, O.P., General Editor (Collegeville, Minnesota: The Liturgical Press, 1975).

11   Henri de Lubac, S.J., *The Splendor of the Church* (London: Sheed and Ward, 1956), p. 145 .

12   *Gaudium et spes*, no. 27; translation from *Vatican Council II: The Conciliar and Post Conciliar Documents*, Austin Flannery, O.P., General Editor.

13   *Ibid.*, no. 51.

14   "Respect for Human Life in Origin and the Dignity of Procreation: Instruction on Bioethics;" translation in *The Pope Speaks* 32 (1987), 141.

15   "Economic .Justice for All: Catholic Social Teaching and the U.S. Economy," Pastoral Message of U.S. Bishops, n. 8, in *Origins* 16 (1986), p. 410.

16   Cf. Paolo Evaristo Arns, "People, Poverty and Progress," in *Origins* 16 (1987), 621. The Cardinal Archbishop of São Paulo gave the first Pope Paul VI Memorial Lecture, established to mark the silver jubilee of the Catholic Fund for Overseas Development, an angency of the English and Welsh bishops, on January 10, 1987, in London.

17   "L'incontro con gli abitanti delle borgate di Santiago," n. 6, in *L'Osservatore Romano*, April 4, 1987, p. 4.

18   "Economic Justice for All: Catholic Social Teaching and the U.S. Economy," Pastoral Letter of U.S. Bishops, n. 16, in *Origins* 16 (1986), p. 414.

Chapter X

1   Wiesel, *Five Biblical Portraits*, p. 63.

2   St. Augustine, *Tractates on the Gospel of John 1-10*, translated by John W. Rettig, in *The Fathers of the Church*, 78 (Washington: The Catholic University of America Press, 1988), 4:5,2

3   *Annales*, pp. 208-209.

4   *Speculum*, II:561.

5   Magennis, *The Life and Times of the Prophet of Carmel*, chapter 33.

6   Roland E. Murphy, O.Carm., "The Figure of Elias in the Old Testament," *Carmelus* 15 (1968), 237.

7   *Institution*, chapter 1, in *Carmel in the World* 13 (1974), 71.

8   See chapter 1, note 9.

9   Brandsma, *Carmelite Mysticism*, p. 64.

10   Michael of St Augustine, O.Carm., *Introductio ad vitam æternam et fruitiva praxis vitæ mysticæ*, curante P. Gabriele Wessels, O.Carm. (Romæ: Collegio S. Alberti, 1926), II:1-12, pp. 137-158.

11   *Carmelite Directory*, p. 177.

12   *Constitutions 1971*, art. 12.

13   *Constituzioni delle Monache dell'Ordine dei Fratelli della Beata Vergine Maria del Monte Carmelo* (1988), art. 22; unofficial English translation. The official text is found in *Le Carmelitane: Regola, Costituzioni, Direttorio* (Rome: n.p., 1990).

14   Cited by Hein Blommestijn, O.Carm., "Titus Brandsma—Prophet of Peace and Martyr of War," *Carmel in the World* 25 (1986), 25.

15   *Ibid.*, p. 33

16   See Chapter 1, note 8.

17   Titus Brandsma, O.Carm., "Carmes," *Dictionaire de Spiritualité* II:155-171; English translation in *Essays*, pp. 219-240.

18   Brandsma, *Carmelite Mysticism*, p. 1.

19   *Ibid.*, p. 2.

20   *Ibid.*, p. 3

21   Brandsma, "Carmes," in *Essays*, p. 224.

22   Blessed Titus Brandsma, O.Carm., "Godsbegrip," cited by Jacobus Melsen, O.Carm., "Mysticism: The Aim in Life of Fr. Titus Brandsma (1881-1942), *Essays*, p. 100.

23   Brandsma, *Carmelite Mysticism*, p. 4.

24   *Ibid.*, p. 5

25   *Ibid.*, p. 10.

26   *Ibid.*

27   *Ibid.*, p. 15.

28   Cited in Melsen, "Mysticism," pp. 100-101.

318

29   *Ibid.*, pp. 101-102 .

30   Breij, *op. cit.*, pp. 89-90, 93-94.

31   "Celebrations in Honor of Bl. Titus," *Carmel in the* (1986), 222-223.

32   Melsen, "Mysticism," p. 100.

33   Jacobus Melsen, O.Carm., "Catholic Spirituality," *Essays*, p. 7ℓ

34   Adrianus Staring, O.Carm., "The Mysticism of the Passion," *Essays*, p. 128.

35   *Ibid.*, p. 126.

36   Translation by Joachim Smet, O.Carm., in *The Carmelites* IV:237-238.